Sports Agent:

Up the Mountain and Down

Oscar L. Shoenfelt III

The
LISBURN
PRESS

The Lisburn Press
www.TheLisburnPress.com

THE LISBURN PRESS
3115 OLD FORGE DRIVE
BATON ROUGE, LOUISIANA 70808

SPORTS AGENT: UP AND DOWN THE MOUNTAIN

PUBLISHED IN THE UNITED STATES OF AMERICA

Visit our website at www.TheLisburnPress.com

First edition published in 2021

Cover layout by Compose Digital Design
Text design by Ashley Powell
Editing by Emily Cogburn

Library of Congress Cataloging-in-Publication Data is available.

IBSN: 978-0-578-23877-7

For more information regarding special discounts for bulk purchases, please contact The Lisburn Press Special Sales at info@TheLisburnPress.com.

Printed in Canada.

This book is printed on acid-free paper.

Elizabeth Currie Shoenfelt

Lightning Liz, Kenan Stadium, Chapel Hill, N.C. 1951.

This book is dedicated to my parents, Oscar and Elizabeth Shoenfelt Jr., for all the inspiration they gave me while living and continue to give me each day.

Brent "BJ" Johnson
1955-2020

I worked on this book for over three years with a lot of help from a lot of people including my dear friend B.J. As I finished reviewing the manuscript for the last time, the unthinkable happened: B.J. was killed in a tragic biking accident on October 15, 2020, in Houston, Texas. B.J. had just begun to cycle for exercise and was traveling over thirty miles a day to and from work at the Rockets facility. He always worked out and enjoyed his physical exercise.

B.J.'s death was not only a tragedy for his wife, son and two step-children but for all those that loved him and whom he touched over the years. He was one of my closest friends and it is impossible for me to put into words my feelings of loss and sadness. I can only reconcile the utter sadness and pain of his death by considering the incredible amount of joy and happiness he brought to so many throughout his life. He was truly a one-of-a-kind person who brought laughter and happiness wherever he went to whomever he met. When I think of B.J., I am reminded of a passage in the 23rd Psalm, "Surely, goodness and love will follow me all the days of my life."

He continued to work the job he loved, as a scout for the Rockets, until the time of his death. His death has brought not only mourning but appreciation throughout the NBA and all basketball for all he accomplished and all those he helped throughout his career. B.J. had for fifteen years volunteered to go to Africa each summer to work in the NBA's Basketball Without Borders Camp where he again touched the lives of thousands. His love for Africa and the thousands of children he mentored was the realization of a lifelong dream. On the Sunday following his death, I was honored to be on an NBA zoom conference of over 300 persons all over the world paying honor to and grieving over B.J.'s death. On the conference call were NBA employees, players, general managers, coaches, agents and others connected to basketball, all paying tribute and expressing love for my friend.

B.J. and I are brothers born of love and adversity. Not a day goes by I don't think about him. Rest well my brother, you will always live on in our hearts. I know you are dwelling in the "House of the Lord Forever."

I wish to recognize and thank the following for their help in the writing and compiling of this book. I must thank my lovely wife, Linfang, for all the support and encouragement she gave me while I wrote this book. Thanks to my kids Katie, Oscar, Mimi and Sally and my step-son Ruiqi for all their support.

My special assistant, Jeannie Brown, did a great job not only editing but organizing the book. The following were of great help in reading and giving me corrections and additions: Steve Thompson, Jim Childers, Paul Brown, John McLindon, Michael Shelton and my Uncle Hoke Currie. Additional editors were Emily Cogburn, Gloria Weaver, and Stewart McCullough whom I wish to thank loads. Thanks to my former clients for giving me the opportunity to represent them and particularly Stanley for all the information he gave me. I must also thank Jim Brown for his help in putting my book together. I must remember my former sports partner B.J. and thank him for making the business fun and his friendship throughout the years. I also wish to thank my former law partners Charles Moore, Ed Walters and Steve Thompson for allowing me to venture into the world of sports.

I would like to thank the physicians who have taken such good care of me while I have been fighting a heart problem and writing this book: Dr. Carl Luikart my cardiologist in Baton Rouge; the DeBakey Heart Group in Houston Texas; Dr. Chet Patel, Duke University and my internist Dr. Joe Albergamo , Baton Rouge.

Sports Agent:

Up the Mountain and Down

Oscar L. Shoenfelt III

Table of Contents

———·———

ONE
My Beginnings and Background

———————·•·———————

I must begin by thanking my parents for all they have given me. My father and mother were talented and interesting, and both were avid North Carolina fans, particularly in basketball. My father, Oscar L. Shoenfelt Jr., joined the Navy in 1944 during World War II at the age of seventeen and trained as a tail gunner. The war ended just as he finished his training. After his discharge from the Navy, he attended Wofford College where he ran track and played football as a 150-pound tackle. He wrote a sports column while at Wofford entitled "Sporting with Oscar." My father would watch almost any type of sports contest but focused on football, basketball, baseball, and tennis. My mother, Elizabeth Currie, grew up in North Carolina playing sports in high school. She continued her sports career at Randolph-Macon women's college from which she graduated in 1950. My mother was also an intense sports fan and enjoyed watching tennis, football, and basketball. She and my father met at the University of North Carolina in the English master's program. They were married in 1952 and I was born in Mt. Vernon, New York, in 1954.

My father Oscar L. Shoenfelt Jr., a 150 lb. tackle at Wofford College.

My family moved to Shreveport, Louisiana, when I was seven years old. Shreveport was not known for being one of the most racially tolerant places in the world. However, in my home I never heard a single derogatory term about a person based on the color of skin or religion. My parents had a diverse group of friends and would entertain all types of strangers, taking great interest in learning about their histories, languages, and backgrounds. As Christians, my parents taught me that all people were the same and that hard work was the status we all lived by, not race, religion, or sex. They taught not only with words, but by example in how they lived and treated other people. This tolerance for difference and interest in other people led me to become a history major in college. My parents' upbringing would serve me well, not only in life but also in my career as an agent.

I played football in high school at Captain Shreve High School from 1969 to 1972. During this time, the public schools were integrated, and I was hit with my first dose of the reality of race relations. I saw, sadly, for the first time that my parents' views were not those held by some of the white students and parents at my high school. Our school was integrated by shutting down an African American high school and moving the black students to Captain Shreve. This plan was met with wide resistance from both sides and led to numerous confrontations of all types, which resulted in several turbulent years. We experienced a student strike by the black students and police stationed in our halls during part of a school year.

Our football team was integrated with much less difficulty, thanks in part to our excellent coaching staff. Our head coach was Coach Lee Hedges, a great athlete who had played running back at LSU. Coach Hedges had a great football mind and was a true teacher, but he was laid back and not the disciplinarian for the team. He was loved by all the players. Coach "Billy Jack" Talton, our defensive coach and the strength and conditioning coach was the disciplinarian on the team, and a real leader. He had played defensive line at Louisiana Tech and was powerfully built, but not over six feet tall. Coach Talton was way ahead of his time with weight training and in 1968 we had a full-time off-season weight and conditioning program with at least eight sets of Olympic weights. Coach Talton was the type of coach who would get in your face if you did something wrong but also praised you for a job well done. Coach Talton had the ability to inspire fear of himself and of failure, but also loyalty and a desire to play your heart out for the team, Coach Hedges, and him. During the off season, every day near two o'clock my stomach would tighten just knowing I would soon be under the watchful eye of Coach Talton for either weights, running the stadium, or other types of conditioning, including wrestling my teammates.

When we merged our team with the team from the African American high school, Coach Talton and Coach Hedges let it be known that we would not be black or white football players but just football players and that we would be judged on how we played and nothing else. One example that stood out to me was when Coach Talton singled out one of the many talented players who had been transferred to our team during spring practice, a guy by the name of Roland Harper. He played running back, stood about six feet, one inch tall, and had tremendous strength and balance. We had been told he had a lot of talent, and this was confirmed during a spring scrimmage when he scored two touchdowns on our first defense. My good friend, starting cornerback Richard Hiller stated, "no one could tackle him." Coach Talton was really proud of his defense. The next time first offense was called Roland just stood there. Out of nowhere Coach Talton grabbed a ball and handed it to Roland, instructing him to get over with the first offense, adding that "anyone who could score twice on our first defense was on first offense." With that move, Coach Talton showed the team that performance and hard work was the key to playing, not race. Coach Talton left before my junior year but his and Coach Hedges' influence would remain with the players they coached forever.

Roland Harper was a senior and I was a junior for the 1970 season, and I had the pleasure to block for him often playing left offensive guard. Roland made numerous big plays not only running but also catching the ball. He went on to play college ball at Louisiana Tech and in the NFL with the Chicago Bears. We truly had a "Remember the Titans" situation and lost only two games during my junior and senior seasons 1970-1971.

(Left) 1970 blocking for Roland Harper at Captain Shreve on a halfback pass where I pulled from left guard.

(Right) 1970 blocking for Roland Harper at Captain Shreve on a sweep where I pulled from left guard.

My experience playing alongside African American athletes set me up well for my later agency career. In sports, race is important since a large percentage of football and basketball players are African American. You can't be in the business without relating to and caring for your clients. Almost all of my clients were African American, and this book will focus on a few of those clients who will always be like family to me.

Although I never considered myself a sports fanatic, sports nut, or a "jock sniffer" (as some in the business term those fans who worship at the feet of today's gladiators), in 1988, I decided to try becoming a sports agent. I had a love of sports, was a dedicated Louisiana State University football and basketball fan and enjoyed following the LSU teams, but had no experience as an agent or any contacts in the sports world. However, I had read some in-depth newspaper and magazine articles about local and national agents. The articles stirred my interest because they made the business seem exciting and glamorous. The fact that one of the articles centered on some local agents made me believe I might have a chance in the business.

Practicing law as a personal injury attorney and being married with three children left me quite busy; however, I had spent parts of the years 1986 and 1987 working on political campaigns and had still been able to fulfill my obligations to my law firm and family. I had enjoyed the ability to move from politics to work, and it had made my law practice seem less tedious in some ways.

The firm consisted of myself, Charles "Chick" Moore, and Ed Walters and was called, as you might guess, Moore, Walters, and Shoenfelt. Yes, we were (and I'm proud to say still are) trial lawyers who had been on a remarkable run since I joined the Baton Rouge firm in 1985. I told Chick and Ed about my desire to become an agent, and they wanted me to pursue my endeavor, so long as I was able to generate sufficient money from my plaintiffs' malpractice to pull my weight at the firm.

With my partners' blessings, I was inclined to test the waters. I've always believed that there are no limitations to what you can achieve if you have some underlying talent, a plan, and most of all the inward desire to succeed. Accordingly, becoming a sports agent did not seem outside of the realm of possibility. Failure held no dire consequences except the loss of some time and money, and these were consequences I could absorb because I already had a day job. I remembered a conversation with a high school friend who had become a producer of sorts. He told me that he had broken into the business just by doing one thing each day that would help him reach his goal of reinventing his career. This stuck with me and seemed like a good game plan in pursuing the elusive sports agent path. My adherence to this plan along with God's help and just plain luck allowed me to climb the mountain of sports agency.

Some underlying qualities and talents are necessary even to begin pursuing becoming a sports agent, qualities which I believed I was born with and developed along the way. Those qualities include the ability to sell yourself to others, a love for negotiating and making a great deal, a real thirst for a challenge, a love of all kinds of people (being a people person), and a knowledge and love of sports.

As an agent, you are constantly selling, not only yourself in pursuing the ever-elusive client, but also in marketing your clients' abilities to teams. I had gained some hardcore sales experience working part time in college from 1972 to 1976 as a door-to-door salesman for the Fuller Brush Company. Door-to-door sales had taught me that you cannot get discouraged by failure. One core principle in sales is that success is only a door away. You may not make a sale for ten houses, but there is always the possibility that door number eleven could be the big sale. To be successful in door-to-door sales, you also must be able to meet and deal with absolute strangers on a continual basis.

Through my law practice, I had become what I considered a good negotiator. In a personal injury practice, you are continually negotiating the value of your cases in order to bring them to a conclusion, either through negotiations or, if that fails, a trial. When I joined Moore and Walters in 1985, Chick and Ed were respected not only as brilliant and ethical trial attorneys on both sides of the bar, plaintiff and defense, but also as excellent negotiators. I learned through my years of law practice, both defense and plaintiff, that negotiations are a matter of preparation, power, and the ability to weigh risks and rewards.

I had the necessary qualities and the desire to become a sports agent, so I began to do research on how to break into the business. I focused first on football, as I had played football and understood the game. I also felt like it would be easier to break into football as opposed to any other sport. In Baton Rouge, football is a year-round obsession and easy to follow, so I felt like that was where to begin.

I had no idea about the legal process of becoming an agent. My research revealed that under labor law, all legitimate agents had to be certified by the Player's Union in order to represent individual players. Under Labor Law, the Player's Union is considered the exclusive bargaining agent for all members of the Union. The Union negotiates a collective bargaining agreement (CBA) on behalf of all the players with the owners of the League. The CBA allows for individuals to become agents for individual players if the individual is certified by the Union to do so. In law school I did not take labor law, but when I launched my career as an agent, understanding labor law developments became important. Accordingly, I studied some labor law and had an education along the way, particularly with the NFLPA (National Football League Players Association) and its litigation, which occurred in conjunction with my becoming an agent.

Initially, I contacted the NFLPA, which was very helpful in providing the information I needed to become officially "certified." At that time, the process simply involved filling out an application, paying a fee, and later attending a one-day seminar. Now, the process is purposefully much more arduous, difficult, and no sure thing. Applicants must not only fill out paperwork and usually possess educational degrees, but also pay fees, attend a two-day seminar, and then sit for an incredibly complex three-hour test with less than a fifty percent chance of passing. Initial fees, dues, expenses, and insurance run well over $6,000.

I should add that there is no requirement that an agent be an attorney at the time, but I felt that my legal education and the fact that I had been a trial attorney for nine years gave me the training and background to begin my career as a sports agent. This was true from an educational point of view but not from an agent "street smarts" point of view. I had no idea when I initially started that there would be fierce and underhanded competition to sign and maintain clients. I thought a plaintiffs' personal injury law practice was competitive, but it does not compare to the ethical boundaries that are continually tested in the sports agency business. Most of the competition will do almost anything to sign players and then steal clients whenever possible. This was especially true when I entered the business in 1988.

My career as an agent was filled with excitement. I got to do and see interesting things, make some money, and endure some stress, but my biggest takeaway was the relationships I built along the way. It was a crazy climb, a climb up a mountain and back down again, and a climb that I still love to think about to this day. At times, I am amazed at all that happened, did not happen, and could have happened.

Our law firm breaks ground for our new office in the summer of 1991. From left to right Ed Walters, Chandler Loupe, Grey Sexton (not in firm), Charles Moore, Me, Steve Thompson and former Governor John McKeithen (of counsel).

TWO

Labor, Anti-Trust, and Legal Regulations of Sports Agency

———— • • ————

Before finding a client and working as a bona fide sports agent, it is essential to become familiar with the overlapping regulations to which sports agents are subject. These regulations are both legal and institutional and come with varying degrees of enforceability and penalties. I will discuss those with which I am familiar and particularly those relating to football and basketball. If you are interested in a more casual read of the book, you can skip Chapters 2 and 3 and go straight to Chapter 4 where my stories begin.   Chapters 2 and 3 are for those who want to work in the sports field or want to get a more extensive background for the agent business.

Players Unions

The U.S. labor movement had an important relevancy to modern sports law and particularly the NFL and the NBA during the years that I was an active NFL Players Association (herein-after NFLPA) and NBAPA agent. Those years were 1988–2003 with the NFLPA and 1991–2006 with the NBAPA. (I also became recertified by the NFLPA [2014–2015] and the NBAPA [2013–2016].) An amazing amount of the sports information on the sports news outlets centers on issues with both labor law and antitrust law origins. These issues range from player discipline, the drafts, agent regulation, salary caps, negotiation and application of Collective Bargaining Agreements (CBA). In fact, the last three decades have seen more conflict between labor and management in sports than any other industry in America.

Beginning in the 1800s, the American economy saw the development of several giant businesses known as "trusts." These trusts controlled entire portions of the economy such as the railroads and oil. Standard Oil and John D. Rockefeller were the most iconic names involved. Rockefeller, as head of Standard Oil, controlled the price and the supply of the oil. In order to help control these monopolies and create a competitive business market, the U.S. Congress enacted the Sherman Anti-Trust Act in 1890. While aimed at big business, portions of the 1890 Sherman Act were used to fight unions, which were organizations formed by laborers to demand better working conditions, including increased wages and fewer hours.

Many battles raged between labor and management from the 1890s until 1935 when the disastrous conditions of the Great Depression allowed Franklin D. Roosevelt to push through passage of the Wagner Act of 1935, the foundation for modern labor law. The Wagner Act brought a new party, the federal government in the form of the National Labor Relations Board (hereinafter NLRB), into the labor equation along with labor and management. The Wagner Act granted employees (Section 7) the right to organize themselves into unions, engage in collective bargaining (the union on behalf of the whole), and to go on strike or take other actions for their mutual aid and protection. Employees were granted the right to bargain or refrain from bargaining (Sec 8) and several unfair labor practices were prohibited. The NLRB was given the primary responsibility for implementing, interpreting, and administering the Act, and was charged with protecting employee and employer rights with some judicial review by the federal appellate courts. The NLRB enforces federal labor laws by adjudicating claims of "unfair labor practices" alleged to have been committed by management or labor. The Wagner Act was revised in 1947 by the Taft-Hartley Act and in 1959 by the Landrum-Griffin Act.

In the 1950s, all four major sports formed player organizations; however, all of the organizations were deliberately named associations rather than unions because elite athletes (in my opinion correctly) did not consider themselves in the same category as the working men who had lived and died laying the foundation for the passage of the Wagner Act. The *NFLPA Playbook* gives a complete and interesting history of the development of the NFLPA. The story begins with the Green Bay Packers in 1956 organizing because the owners of the team refused to provide clean jocks, socks, and uniforms for twice a day workouts. The history states that it was not until the 1970s after the merger of the AFL and the NFLPA in 1970 that the NFLPA became a "real union." It was in 1970 that the players filed a petition with the NLRB and were granted certification for the first time as the professional football union. It was at this time that the NLRB took jurisdiction over football players as professional athletes for the first time. The NFLPA's timing was no accident because in *American League of Professional Baseball Clubs & Association of National Baseball League Umpires*, 180 N.L.R.B. 190 (1969), the NLRB ruled that professional baseball is an industry affecting interstate commerce; therefore, it was within the board's jurisdiction. This case actually involved the efforts of umpires to unionize, but set the stage for professional athletes to form unions and come under the protection of the federal labor law and the NLRB.

Once a union is duly certified by the NLRB, the union becomes the exclusive bargaining agent for all employees within the unit. This means that all active players in a United States professional sports league come under the power of the union that has been chosen to represent them, and the players are bound by the union's actions and the terms of any collective bargaining agreement (CBA) that is negotiated between the union and the league. The union and league are required to negotiate and bargain on all labor issues such as wages, hours, and terms and conditions of employment. The CBA lays out in detail the rights and obligations of the parties. The CBA covers items such as payrolls of players, which includes salary caps and luxury taxes; player movement such as drafts, trades, waivers, and free agency; and player working conditions such as fines, suspensions, grievances, and appeals.

The union is able to allow individual players to hire representatives (agents) to represent them in their individual contract negotiations with their teams, as long as the agents become certified by the unions. In effect, the union has done most of the heavy legal work in drafting and negotiating the standard player contract and the rules that players must adhere to while under contract. Agents generally are used to negotiate the amount of salary, the length of the contract, whether the contract is guaranteed, and many types of additional bonuses that may be added to the standard contract.

Once the NLRB certifies the union as the exclusive bargaining agent, the union and the owners are exempt from anti-trust laws, as they fall under the jurisdiction of the NLRB. This is why, in the sports labor litigation of the 1980s and 1990s, there were threats of and even times when the unions were decertified.

Sports agency began during the early 1960s when some

attorneys began to represent professional athletes. According to "The Football Lawyers" (ABA Journal, September 1985, Vol. 71), Bob Woolf became the pioneer of sports agents when, as a criminal attorney in 1962, he represented a baseball player in an automobile accident and then began to help him negotiate some endorsements. By 1985, Woolf had represented more than 2,000 athletes. The article also described Leigh Steinberg, who began representing players in 1975 after he met soon-to-be NFL number one draft pick, Cal quarterback Steve Bartkowski when Leigh was a college graduate counselor at Bartkowski's dorm. He was representing over 60 football players in 1985. This article piqued my interest in becoming an agent. By the end of my career, I had had dealings that connected me with both Bob and Leigh.

Under the terms of the 1982 NFL CBA, all agents had to be certified in order to represent veteran NFL players. The 1983 CBA between the NBA and the NBPA allowed for players or agents certified by the Players Association to bargain with clubs as to individual contracts that were within the rules of the CBA. During this time period, the football and basketball unions were just developing the rules of conduct for agents. The NFLPA adopted a set of rules and regulations for agents (contract advisors) in 1983, and the NBPA adopted agent regulations in 1986. Since my entrance on the sports scene in 1988, in my opinion, the NFLPA has been much more active in regulating its agents, and its regulations have been much more frequently amended to control and quantify the large number of people interested in becoming football agents. Meanwhile, the NBPA last amended its regulations in 2016 and 2018 but prior to that had not changed its regulations since 1991. The NBPA really just relied on self-regulation of a sort. Actually, becoming an NBA basketball agent was intensely competitive because of its minuscule market size of possible clientele and the close-knit group of agents, coaches, and businesses such as shoe companies that have controlled and continue to control basketball.

The NFLPA and NBPA regulations governing player agents impose a fiduciary duty on the agent to deal honestly with his client and act in his best interest without conflicts of interest, similar to the ethical rules for attorneys. The regulations set maximum agent fees (not more than 4% in the NBA and 3% for the NFL) and set rules for when the agent is to be paid, provide a standard player-agent contract that allows an agent to be discharged at will, and set up an arbitration procedure to handle any disputes that may arise between an agent and his client. Of course, fees are collected by the Union from the agents and the NFLPA now requires the agents to carry agent malpractice insurance.

Due to the large amount of client poaching—agents stealing other agents' clients—the NFLPA made an amendment to its regulations in 1996 to prohibit the following:

> Tortious interfering, either directly or indirectly, with the contractual relationship of another Contract Advisor and a player when those parties have entered into a Standard Representation Agreement and such Standard Representation Agreement is on file with the NFLPA.

The above regulation was amended the next year to eliminate the legal phrase "tortious interference" but prohibited an agent contacting a player under contract to another agent unless the player had less than sixty days on his NFL player contract and had not signed a new player-agent contract. The agent is allowed to send written advertising and can talk to a player if the player initiates the contact. The NFLPA sets up an arbitration procedure to resolve grievances between agents. The actual enforceability if another agent tampers with your player would be difficult, especially if the poached player were a willing participant and no longer wished to help his former agent. There is also a prohibition against directly or indirectly soliciting a rookie who has never signed an NFL contract if the rookie has signed a standard player-agent agreement and it is thirty days before the draft.

The NBPA stayed out of the issue of agent disputes by never promulgating any rules similar to the NFLPA. However, in its recent rules amendment in 2018, the NBPA did call for an arbitration under its rules for any dispute arising "between two or more Player Agents with respect to their individual entitlement to fees owed, whether paid or unpaid, by a Player who was jointly represented by such Player Agents" (Section 5, NBPA Regulations Governing Player Agents). It seems as if this requirement of mandatory arbitration will help streamline resolving any disputed fees when players change agents, which is regularly the case.

In 1988, in my opinion, neither the NFLPA nor the NBPA were really much concerned with regulating agents like they are today. Prior to and in 1988, when I became a certified agent, both unions were concerned with developing their own identities, consolidating their base support with their players, and fighting for the rights and revenue for their membership, based on antitrust law, from management (the NFL and NBA) and not the regulation and certification of agents. This would be especially true as to resolution of disputes between agents and even disputes between agents and players.

Despite regulation of agents beginning in the 1980s, the player-agent landscape in football and basketball remained a "wild west" even into the 2000s. Even today, the wars continue. Before agent regulation, the early agents set their own fees, ignored NCAA rules, and if there were union rules, found ways to circumvent them if necessary. They also were known to ignore obvious conflicts of interest involving negotiation of their clients' contracts and handling their clients' money. Some of these agent violations continued while I was an active agent, and some continue to this day.

One of the prime examples of early agent misconduct was the case of Norby Walters and Lloyd Bloom. Walters and Bloom teamed up in 1985 to move into the sports agency business. Walters had been a booking agent for some big entertainment acts, including Janet Jackson. Bloom played football in college and acted as a bouncer at some nightclubs. It was reported that the two had ties to the Mafia. In fact, an FBI investigation of Walters and Bloom began after a rival agent's associate was beaten up by a masked man in a parking lot in Chicago in 1987. The rival agent had lured several of the Walters and Bloom players into his stable. The assaulted associate was the wife of a well-known baseball pitcher, and this drew the attention of the U.S. Attorney and the FBI.

Walters and Bloom came up with a plan to sign players to player-agent contracts by offering the players money, cars, trips to entertainment venues, and other things of value. Their plan was to sign the players to the player-agent contract, date the contracts to the end of the players' college eligibility and place the contracts in a safe. This wasn't necessarily a novel plan; however, Walters and Bloom took it over the top with the number of players involved, the amount of money spent during the players' college eligibility, and the use of threats of physical violence against players and their families and player agents when the players reneged on the deals.

Walters' and Bloom's actions were in clear violation of NCAA rules and would render the players ineligible if the scheme was discovered. The agents knew this and even consulted a sports law firm that told them it would violate NCAA rules. However, at the time there were no legal statutes in effect backing up the NCAA rules. Walters and Bloom simply did not recognize the authority of the NCAA to legislate as to their actions.

Walters and Bloom were surprisingly successful in handing out the money and other inducements to the players, who almost universally came from poor economic backgrounds. They signed fifty-eight players to falsely dated player-agent contracts that were to take effect after the player finished playing. The players included football and basketball future first-round picks. Only two players eventually stuck to their word and let Walters and Bloom later represent them as their agents, which led to the alleged threats and acts of violence. The fact that only two players stayed with the duo despite having taken the incentives does speak to the attitude of some players when dealing with player agents. Athletes, many times, are not innocent victims but willing accomplices without any loyalty in receiving payments that they know are in violation of NCAA rules.

Walters and Bloom were eventually indicted for various federal crimes after an extensive FBI investigation. The charges included conspiracy and mail fraud. The two were convicted by a jury, but the conviction was subsequently overturned. (See United States v. Walters, 997 F.2d 1219 [7th Cir 1993])

Walters and Bloom even brought a lawsuit against one player, Brent Fullwood, to enforce the contract he signed with them in 1986, and recover $4,000 that Fullwood had accepted at the time of signing the contract and another $4,000 accepted later in the season. The judge held the agreement was unenforceable under state law and the grievance procedures of the NFLPA. He basically reasoned that since the contract violated NCAA regulations, which promote the academic integrity of the NCAA member institutions, it was against public policy and he would not reward such fraudulent behavior. (See Norby Walters and Lloyd Bloom v. Brent Fullwood, U.S. District Court, Southern District of New York, 1987 [675 F.Supp. 155])

Bloom and Walters did not last long in the sports business, but the case illustrates the lengths to which prospective agents will go to sign clients. Walters is alive today and working in Hollywood as a promoter. I met his son, Gary, several years ago. Gary is a producer and at one time worked with my good friend, David Lancaster. Bloom died at age thirty-four in Los Angeles when he was gunned down in his rented home in Malibu, California. Whether Bloom was killed as a result of his sports dealings remains an unsolved mystery.

Another illustrative case of early agent mismanagement is found in Collins v. National Basketball Players Association, 850 F.Supp. 1468 (D. Colo.1991), aff'd, 976 F.2d 740 (10th Cir1992). Collins was an agent for several NBA players from 1974 to 1986 before he became certified by the NBPA in 1986. However, he voluntarily quit functioning as a player agent because of a lawsuit involving himself and Kareem Abdul-Jabbar, one of the greatest basketball players of all time. Abdul-Jabbar's lawsuit primarily concerned improper handling of his finances that ultimately cost him millions of dollars. Abdul-Jabbar's claims involved mishandling of his state and federal taxes, which resulted in approximately $300,000 of financial loss; improper investment of his money; mismanaging of assets; and improper transfer of money out of his account. Other charges include a phantom $20,000 withdrawal from Abdul-Jabbar's account, $13,000 for a car, and $60,000 in credit from a California bank in the NBA player's name. According to "When Agents Pull the Strings" by Albert Gross (*Trial Magazine*, June 1990), in his lawsuit Abdul-Jabbar alleged that he was left liable for $7.4 million, which was borrowed by Collins and others.

In 1998, Collins's certification was revoked because he failed to pay his agent fees and didn't attend a required seminar. Abdul-Jabbar and Collins eventually settled out of court on November 7, 1989, and on February 15, 1990, Collins applied to be reinstated by the NBPA. The NBPA certification committee launched its own investigation into whether to recertify Collins and obtain materials relating to the case regarding Abdul-Jabbar and another lawsuit filed by Lucius Allen. By this time, word was out on Collins, and he lost several other clients including Alex English, Rickey Sobers, Terry Cummings, Ralph Sampson, Rudy Hackett, and Brad Davis. Collins was granted "interim certification," which allowed him to continue to represent Terry Cummings, an NBA player, until he fired Collins. In 1990, the NBPA decided to not allow Collins to regain his status as an agent in the NBPA. It was determined, through the evidence of the lawsuit with Abdul-Jabbar and other evidence from separate cases, that Collins was unfit to serve in a fiduciary capacity on behalf of the NBA players and that he had lied to the Committee concerning the investigation.

The NBPA allowed Collins to appeal his decision; however, Collins instead decided to sue the NBPA, claiming that the NBPA's exclusive right to represent players and certify agents was an anti-trust violation. Collins alleged that the NBPA interfered with his contract and intentionally interfered with his prospective business advantage. The court ruled that the lawsuit lacked merit and pointed out that Collins could have appealed but did not; furthermore, that the NBPA was exempt from antitrust laws and that recertification of Collins would have been a breach of fiduciary duty the association owed to its athletes. This case meant that the unions do have the power to say who is and who is not fit to be an agent.

Of course, there could always be a new test case if the unions become too restrictive in the use of their power or abuse their power. The certification process has gone from very relaxed in the NFLPA to rigorous and expensive. The NBPA has recently raised their dues and begun to require testing. One area of concern for the NBPA is some of its top members becoming actively involved in the agent process even though its new regulations explicitly prohibit players from acting as agents. The Introduction of the player-agent rules read as follows:

The NBPA's Authority to Regulate Player Agents, Section 3, Prohibition of Players as Agents:

> For purposes of negotiating the terms of a Uniform Player Contract or otherwise dealing with a Team over any matter, players are prohibited from (a) representing other current or prospective NBA players as an agent certified under the Player's Association Regulations Governing Player Agents, or (b) holding an equity interest or position in a business entity that represents other current or prospective NBA players as an agent certified under the Players Association's Regulations Governing Player Agents.

We will have to see to what degree players in the future become more or less involved in the agent process and what apparent conflicts may arise in that regard.

State Law Agent Regulations

Lloyd Bloom's brief but well-documented sports agent career led to the passage of numerous state laws regulating agents and stricter player union agent rules. State law agent regulations are the statutory legal requirements agents must abide by. There are state regulations in approximately forty states regulating player agents. The state law requirements center on registration in states where agents are recruiting players and requirements on contact with players. These laws are generally laxly enforced except for registration, and in many instances are so cumbersome that it would be difficult to comply with all the provisions and actually recruit and sign players. I have not reviewed more than a handful of specific state regulations, but it seems to me that some provisions could be contested on various legal and constitutional grounds.

I helped draft some of Louisiana's regulations concerning requirements that agents in Louisiana must be certified by the respective Union Player Associations with the help of then State Representative William Daniel. Nick Saban even got into the act after he felt there had been some unwanted agent activity during his tenure at LSU. He went to the state legislature along with LSU's athletic director and was successful in enhancing some of Louisiana's agent statutes. To date, I know of no agent who has been successfully prosecuted under any state agent law. In reality, the state laws really only add to the burden of agents trying to follow all the rules. Generally, if an agent is going to cheat, he will cheat with the help of the player, so it is nearly impossible to gather evidence to successfully prosecute a criminal case against the agent.

The numerous state laws can be problematic and expensive for the sports agent. An agent based in one state and recruiting in several different states is legally obligated to register in the state in which they are located and each state where they recruit. Based on my experience, fees can run from $100 to $1,000 and it creates an administrative nightmare with the paperwork and tracking of the legal requirements to avoid being noncompliant. Agents also need to keep up with the date of registration so as to timely renew each year. Furthermore, they need to address issues such as if they are recruiting a player from their base state but are not recruiting at his school, does the agent really have to register in the state where he is playing if the agent does not go there? This was actually a question on the NFLPA test I took in 2014.

I believe that multiple state laws impose an unfair burden on sports agents who try to abide by the law. In practicality, there is enforcement of registration but little or no criminal prosecution because of the difficulty in obtaining any evidence. What athlete is going to testify that he accepted benefits and what agent is going to admit giving benefits? Moreover, any experienced agent who is going to break the law to offer benefits to an eligible player is not going to document such actions. This is why cash would be used and a shell game created as to other benefits that would be offered. A national registration would seem to be the answer, and there actually is a Uniform Agent Act, but it has not been implemented nationwide to date.

University and Team Regulations

Most of the larger educational institutions and teams where the college players play may have their own sets of regulations requiring registration and notification of activities and player contact.

Sparta

The U.S. Congress became involved with sports agent regulation with the passage of a sports agent regulation act called "SPARTA" in 2004. This Act gives the Federal Trade Commission jurisdiction if an agent does not act appropriately when signing a player. It is basically a repeat of the state laws. I have never read of any enforcement of this statue against an agent.

NCAA Regulations

The necessity for most of the laws and regulations is to ensure that the college player does not violate NCAA regulations, which primarily limit a player's contacts with agents so as to maintain the player's "amateur," "student-athlete" status so he can keep his eligibility to play college sports. The NCAA really poses no legal threat to an agent personally, but again the individual state laws, the union agent regulations, and the institution regulations are in large part predicated on enforcing the NCAA regulations and keeping the player eligible to participate in athletics for NCAA member institutions. Accordingly, agents, and arguably even players, do potentially face not only criminal but civil repercussions for causing a player to lose his NCAA eligibility from state and federal laws. This is one of the reasons that most agent violations go unreported and unprosecuted. There are simply no agents or players who want to come forward and report violations, as generally both the players and agents benefit from the NCAA rules being violated. Today many of the NCAA regulations regarding the college players' right to be paid for their enormous contributions to university athletics are under legal attack in such cases as O'Bannon v. NCAA 802 F.3d 1049 (9th Cir. 2015).

The NCAA is a private "voluntary organization" of educational institutions. It arises partly from the actions in 1905 of President Theodore Roosevelt, who became very concerned about the violence that was occurring in college football. During 1905, there were at least eighteen deaths and 150 football players injured resulting primarily from players being kicked in the head or stomach. One article ("The Shame of College Sports" by Taylor Branch, The *Atlantic*, October 2011, beginning p. 81) had the body count from football at twenty-five for the year 1905. As a result of the large number of injuries, New York University's Chancellor Henry MacCracken called for a meeting of representatives from the major college football programs to see if rules could be created to help reduce injuries and save the sport ("Compensating the Student-Athlete" by Michael Aiello, *The Sports Lawyers Journal*, Vol. 23, Spring 2016, No. 1, p. 157).

President Roosevelt was a proponent of athletics but saw the damage being done firsthand, as his son had been injured playing at Yale. Roosevelt intervened and helped force the university presidents to come together and form this "voluntary private organization," which was officially launched in 1910. The rules and guidelines were designed to eliminate some of the physical injuries players were suffering while playing football. Two of the first rules were the creation of the forward pass and kicking the ball downfield to help eliminate the risk of injuries ("Compensating the Student-Athlete" by Michael Aiello, *The Sports Lawyers Journal*, Vol. 23, Spring 2016, No. 1, p. 157).

For almost fifty years, the NCAA had little real authority to regulate college athletics. Moreover, college athletes did receive some sorts of compensation. The *Atlantic* article notes that in 1939, freshman players at the University of Pittsburgh actually went on strike because they were being paid less than the upperclassmen. For years, as the popularity of intercollegiate athletics grew, problems with college athletics arose such as disguised booster funds, allegations of gambling fraud, and even open payrolls. Finally, in 1948, the NCAA enacted the "Sanity Code," which was designed to do away with abusive practices in the recruitment of college athletes by eliminating the concealed and indirect benefits being given to college athletes. Benefits to athletes were to be limited to their scholarships ("Compensating the Student-Athlete" by Michael Aiello, *The Sports Lawyers Journal*, Vol. 23, Spring 2016, No. 1, p. 157 and "The Shame of College Sports" by Taylor Branch, The *Atlantic,* October 2011, beginning p.81). However, the Sanity Code failed because the only penalty was complete expulsion of the offending member. It was not possible to persuade the member institutions to expel each other, and in 1951, the Sanity Code was repealed.

However, 1951 was a landmark year for the NCAA because it hired a college dropout and journalist named Walter Byers as its executive director. Due to several scandals occurring at the time, Byers was able to impanel an infractions board to set penalties without a full meeting of the NCAA, and convinced Kentucky to accept a landmark imposition of a one-year suspension for 1952 through 1953 while the famous Adolph Rupp was the coach. The advent of televised sporting events at this time further cemented Byers's power as he was able to successfully take charge of negotiating a $1.14 million deal with NBC to televise college football games through the NCAA. Byers was able to get a cut of the profits for the NCAA and to fund setting up an NCAA infrastructure complete with a headquarters in Kansas City, Missouri. Accordingly, after being in the job for about a year, Byers had the power and money for the NCAA to begin its growth and domination of college sports.

As executive director, Walter Byers introduced the term "student-athlete" to the NCAA and made sure it was used repeatedly in the NCAA rules and the interpretation of those rules. A key legal decision came by the Colorado Supreme Court in 1957 when it held that the widow of a man who was killed while playing football could not collect worker's compensation benefits since the college was not in the business of playing football. Since the Colorado decision, the NCAA has continued to maintain that student-athletes are not employees.

Mountains of articles have been written about what many consider the unfair exploitation of student-athletes by colleges and the NCAA. It's important to remember that the NCAA is a voluntary organization and its members voluntarily subject themselves to its rules and regulations. Moreover, as an agent, state law and the NFLPA and the NBPA both prohibit the violation of NCAA rules by agents.

The NCAA rules that concern agents most are the NCAA's regulations, which are set up to ensure and maintain a player's amateur status. A player or his family can receive no type of benefit, or his college eligibility could be forfeited. This would be true even if the player did not know that the family member received the benefit. A benefit in NCAA terms could be anything of value, which could even mean something like transportation to a desired destination. Likewise, a player cannot agree to be represented by a sports agent even orally and remain eligible. A player is considered an amateur in the eye of the NCAA—someone who competes in sports for personal satisfaction and not monetary gain. According to the NCAA Division 1 Manual, an athlete is considered no longer an amateur when he accepts a promise of pay, signs a contract of professional athletics, uses his or her athletic skill for pay, or enters into a contract. A good rule of thumb for any agent is that until the player is ready to sign, you should not give him or his family anything of value, even a ride around the block, or you could risk his eligibility. Of course, avoiding giving someone a ride around the block is easier said than done under many of the circumstances agents find themselves in.

In the last several years, there have been a number of legal cases filed in various jurisdictions on behalf of college players, past and present, seeking monetary damages for the time and effort college athletes expend in playing college sports and the use of players' likenesses for profit by the universities and the NCAA. These cases have been viewed more favorably by the public because of the huge amounts of money made by the NCAA, college coaches, and others from revenue produced by college sports. In 2019, according to the *USA TODAY*, 16 head football coaches made an annual salary of $5 million dollars. The LSU football team made a profit of $56.6 million in the 2018-19 academic year according to an article in the *Baton Rouge Morning Advocate* on February 28, 2020. Of course, these cases have centered on college football and basketball players where the real money is produced in college athletics. These cases have been successful to some degree and have produced allowances for players to receive more benefits from their respective college schools and maintain their eligibility to play college athletics.

In numerous states passed legislation allowing college athletes to make money from their intellectual property rights such as the use of their likeness. A bill was filed in February 2020, here in Louisiana, which would allow college athletes to make money from their likeness and hire agents as long as the agents are registered in Louisiana and comply with state and federal law. The NCAA has realized that the players will have to be allowed these rights in the future and will have to implement new rules in this regard for as early as next year. Accordingly, more compensation for college players is on the way in the future. Naturally, this will be an avenue where agents will be more involved with college athletes in the future. However, we will have to wait and see what long-term effect these new rules will have on college athletics.

THREE

The Agent Business—Signing a Player

———————•.•———————

After becoming certified by the NFLPA and trying to become legally compliant, I focused on the problem of becoming an actual sports agent with a client, a real client that someone would recognize. This is because whenever you tell someone you are a sports agent, the first question they ask is "Well, who do you represent?" If you don't have a client, you sound like a liar. If the client is some unknown free agent whom the person has never heard of and who is not in the NFL or NBA, you're still just a "pretender."

Signing a Real Player

Sports agents provide many types of services for their clients, the primary being negotiation of the player's contract with the team that either drafts him or attempts to sign him as a free agent. However, the real heavy lifting in the business is the actual signing of the client. There are plenty of willing attorneys, accountants, and businessmen interested in sports who could all handle the agent duties after signing a client but not many who have the contacts, personality, power, and resources to actually sign a player and maintain a relationship with the player. This is why many of the legal problems with sports agency occur in the signing process.

Signing your first client is difficult not because negotiating the team-player contract is difficult, but because it is not easy convincing a player you can handle the job when there is so much experienced competition willing to do anything to sign the player. It's problematic from the beginning to convince the player and his "adviser" or "advisers" to let you actually negotiate a sports contract for him when you have never actually negotiated a sports contract.

While I was finishing up this book, the federal indictment, and now convictions and guilty pleas, of several college coaches, several Adidas employees, and a prospective agent, confirmed what I had already written about the involvement of coaches and shoe companies in the signing of players for agents. Of course, the amount of money being used has gone up, but even back in my agent days, you had to contend with shoe companies, coaches, and family members getting involved in steering players to agents. When I refer to coaches, it is not just college coaches but AAU coaches, high school coaches, and anyone who had an influence on the player while he grew up.

You might ask, if payments to players to sign with agents has been going on for this length of time, why haven't there been any other convictions like we have seen recently with the federal indictments? The answer is the evidence obtained for these indictments and prosecutions was discovered accidentally and the FBI was able to gather actual evidence of payoffs and agreements while under cover. The NCAA has no power to compel evidence and enforcement of its rules other than through its members, so it is very difficult for it to gather evidence. The NFLPA and NBPA really do not have any power to compel testimony of any who want to be certified agents.

The players who receive money are members of the NFLPA and the NBPA organizations would have no motivation to provide evidence. Finally, state and local law enforcement might have the power to enforce state law, but any case involving the local university would cause the basketball and football stars to become ineligible. Do you think a local Alabama D.A. proving that one of Alabama's star players is ineligible would increase his popularity?

There are several key elements common to the strategy of actually signing a player. There is also a difference between signing a basketball or a football player. In basketball there are fewer agents competing, but there are fewer players and the competition starts at a much earlier age through a variety of sources. This is true because a great basketball player can generally be recognized and targeted at a much earlier age.

Initial Contact

Generally, the NFLPA and NBPA regulations require you to deal truthfully with a player and his family when recruiting him and ensure that he knows that he will forfeit his college eligibility if he signs a player-agent contract, which all players should know already. The Union regulations prohibit paying a player, his family, or any other person to induce or recommend that the player use the services of the agent. However, I believe this regulation has been violated by many agents who routinely would pay players, players' families, or others to recruit the player. For example, see the book *Illegal Procedure* by Josh Luchs, who was a football agent at the same time I was an NFLPA agent, where he details how he would pay players.

The Union regulations generally do not detail prohibitions on how an agent should go about recruiting other than a prohibition of payment to sign and not violating NCAA rules. The NFLPA generally prohibits the agent from hiring a person to recruit the player. Some agents hire "runners" to go on college campuses, befriend players, and steer them to the agent. The problem is that many times these runners bestow NCAA illegal benefits such as money on the players. The NBPA now requires (since 2018) agents to prepare "Recruiter Disclosure Forms" disclosing any other individual, firm, or organization to whom the agent has paid or given anything of value for recruiting the player. The disclosure form recognizes a long-held practice of having others help in the recruitment of players. I assume this means that a recruiter may be used, but you have to disclose it. The NBPA does prohibit any family member or anyone with a prior relationship with the player from being a "recruiter."

The state laws and university policies prescribe rather unrealistic procedures to follow if you wish to contact a prospective client while he is still playing. You are allowed generally to mail literature to the prospect, but have to notify some school officials if you actually want to talk to a player before his eligibility has expired. Some schools arrange agent days when you are allowed to speak with interested players. These agent days generally occur after the end of the season when most players have already been recruited by other agents.

While mailing your literature and going to agent day is great, agents who did only those things would be behind their competitors in the recruiting process if it were their sole strategy. Of course, there are times when agents go cold turkey and do not meet a player before his eligibility is up without any kind of already "established in." However, going cold turkey, from my observation, is the exception not the rule. The high-powered agents would have the greatest possibility of going cold turkey in signing a player. The reality is that most agents have some kind of relationship or "in" with the players they sign. This is particularly true in basketball, where most high potential players have been identified by the time they are in high school.

Don't Waste Your Time

You would be wasting your time to try to sign as a client any player who has a longstanding relationship with an agent. You need to try and discover if the player is a lock for another agent as early as possible so as not to waste your time. When Ben Simmons, the projected number 1 pick in the 2016 draft, finished his one-and-done career at LSU, he signed with Klutch Sports, the agency started by LeBron James's friend and agent, Rich Paul, in 2012. According to a newspaper report (*Morning Advocate*, March 24, 2016), Paul had hired Ben's sister to work at Klutch as a marketer/branding employee in 2014, and Ben attended the LeBron James Skills Academy as a seventeen-year-old in 2014. Clearly, even dreaming of signing Ben would have been a complete waste of time.

Ben's signing is an excellent example of how far out you have to begin your recruiting, and of the competition you would face to sign a top draft pick. Can you imagine trying to compete with LeBron James, the best all-around basketball player in the world, in trying to influence a player? Of course, the better the player the more difficult to sign the player.

Early in my career, I wined and dined several football players (after their eligibility had expired) only to find that they had already committed to another agent. It became apparent when I found out that one player's girlfriend worked for the agent and the other already had two BMWs in his garage. We had a great time, but I did waste a lot of money. I won't say I wasted time because I did enjoy myself, met some new friends, and learned some valuable lessons.

Cash

Of course, as illustrated in *Illegal Procedure*, there are agents who think they can avoid actually recruiting a player by just finding a connection to the player by some illegal monetary inducement. There are agents who follow the Walters and Bloom method today, just in a much more clandestine mode. It is nearly impossible to catch illegal payments to a player because you are dealing with a situation where both parties have a great deal to lose by revealing the relationship. Payments are impossible to trace because almost all of the time they are made in cash.

However, remember that Walters and Bloom also proved that cash alone is not enough to actually have a player sign and stick with you as a client. Walters and Bloom only had two of fifty-eight players actually keep their commitments. Josh Luchs not only provided cash but also developed personal relationships with his players to keep them as clients. You can actually do a great job for the player and still be fired, another perk of the profession. Some players will also accept cash from multiple sources and not really worry about it. There are few, if any agents, who would make illegal payments to a player and then file a lawsuit to recoup their losses as Walters and Bloom did.

The only other agent I can think of in recent history who sued a player after making illegal payments to him was Lloyd Lake, who sued Reggie Bush in 2007. Lloyd and his partner, Michael Michaels, had furnished Reggie's stepfather with a house in San Diego and other benefits totaling close to $300,000, while Reggie was a player at USC where he led the Trojans to a record of 35-1 and two National Championships, and won a Heisman Trophy. Reggie reimbursed Michaels but refused to pay Lake what he demanded after Reggie signed with another agent. Lake and Reggie settled in 2010, just before the two were scheduled to give sworn testimony in depositions. The NCAA came down on Reggie hard, taking away his Heisman trophy and then punishing USC. USC received four years of probation, was forced to revoke all of its wins from the 2005 season and two wins from the 2004 season, and was subsequently banned from Bowl Games in the 2010 and 2011 seasons. I could not find any evidence that Lake or Michaels were ever prosecuted criminally for any violation of California's agent act.

Logistics

Obviously, players who are either from where you live or play near your home are easier to come into contact with. It is also easier to find a connection with the player, either through family or some other individual who knows the player, if he is from where you live or work or you have some contacts. If the player is an athlete playing in the state where you live and work, you should have to register with the state if there are player-agent regulations in effect.

Key Connections

The key advantages and strategy in recruiting any player is not only logistics but some connection to the player. There is no per se NCAA violation in talking to a player, his family, or a third person. The violations come when benefits are given to the player before his eligibility has expired, which could end or limit his eligibility. Direct contact with a player in most cases could violate state law and university policy, but not NCAA rules. I would estimate that some of these regulations are in fact unconstitutional, but no one has ever challenged them because they are not really enforced. However, this is not a criticism because it would be virtually impossible to enforce these rules to the letter. Again, the goal is to keep the player eligible, which benefits him, the school, and the agent so if no harm is done there is no reason for enforcement. So, what are some key connections you can discover to try to develop some relationship to the player?

Family Members

Many agents work through family members to get a conduit to the player. In some cases, the player may not even know that a family member has some other connection to the agent than that which is being portrayed to the player. The family member could, in fact, be receiving some monetary reward to steer the player to a particular agent which would be inappropriate.

Unfortunately, some family members look at an athlete's success as a way to cash in, and some agents take advantage of this opportunity. In the recent FBI Adidas-agent Scandal, the *Wall Street Journal* (Thursday, October 18, 2018, issue, p. A16) reported the following:

> Witnesses have described how shoe executives, coaches, sports agents and others routinely make under-the-table payments to the families of prized recruits to lure the players to universities, sheathe them in brand names and sign them as clients when they turn professional.

One father testified during trial that he accepted tens of thousands of dollars to steer his son to play for Adidas-sponsored teams. This is not to say that there are not many family members who are looking out for the player's best interest. One problem is that as the player gains more and more fame and playing potential, family members who never were involved with the player expediently show up and begin to work their way in to influence the player. If a family member is given benefits to help an agent sign a player, it is an NCAA violation and clearly violates NFLPA and NBPA rules. The definition of who is prohibited from receiving payments to influence players to attend particular colleges was expanded by the NCAA when a church, where Cam Newton's father worked, allegedly received donations from an Auburn booster to ensure that Cam attended Auburn University. Cam said he was aware of the gift and that he should not be punished for the actions of others. The NCAA eliminated this loophole, and now even if the player is unaware of the payment of money, sanctions can be imposed on the school. Furthermore, the NCAA expanded the definition of an agent. NCAA Bylaw 12 now states that "an agent is any individual who, directly or indirectly, represents or attempts to represent an individual for the purpose of marketing his or her athletics ability or reputation for financial gain."

Coaches

Other connections to players include coaches, either college or high school and even pre–high school. On a personal level, I had coaches work against me signing several players. Remember that coaches need favors in recruiting, and an agent in the business can be a good source of recruitment for college players. Once the coach has finished, he can hand the player back to the professional agent for representation. This was demonstrated in the Adidas FBI case described earlier.

It's not uncommon for agents that represent college coaches to sign players from that college. What a break in creating connections, representing the player's college coach! Was it a coincidence that the celebrated and powerful agent, David Falk, signed all the great Georgetown players when he was representing their coach, John Thompson? Of course not. David is most famous for representing Michael Jordan and had access everywhere most of the time, but it certainly helps to represent coaches in the business to gain access to players. When Nick Saban was at LSU, it was no coincidence that his agent, Jimmy Sexton was able to sign LSU players. Don't think that I am criticizing David Falk or Jimmy Sexton; if I had a legitimate advantage, I would use it too. I'm just illustrating the level of competition, strategy, and preparation that must be used in the signing process. After I got started, I did have coaches recommend me, which helped me sign some free agents.

In basketball, AAU basketball coaches and others

involved in the AAU team are used as conduits to the players. AAU basketball is notorious for its effect on development and lack of development of young players. AAU stands for Amateur Athletic Union, but it is anything but a totally amateur organization. My son grew up playing basketball, and I coached him in fourth and fifth grade, making sure he grew up around real players. He continued to play into junior high and high school and was involved in AAU. Even on his team, without kids who may have had NBA potential, there was all sorts of drama with players leaving and being added by different coaches. Generally, AAU plays in the summer, but the recruiting of players goes on year-round with all kinds of drama with kids and their parents or guardians being offered money and other inducements such as merchandise and travel. Some AAU coaches become mentors to the kids or close friends of the player's parent(s) and are used by some agents to recruit clients. Likewise, college coaches will use AAU coaches to recruit players to come play for them. AAU teams are usually sponsored by shoe companies, which become involved with the teams, and some AAU coaches end up working for shoe companies.

Shoe Companies

There has also been much written about the involvement of shoe companies with developing basketball players and the monetary incentives and merchandise used to persuade players to sign with a certain AAU team. Over the years, shoe representatives have been and continue to be a major force in influencing the recruiting of players for agents and again for college coaches. Was it any coincidence that Arn Tellum signed players such as Kobe Bryant going directly from high school to the NBA? Of course not. The close relationship between the legendary shoe representative, Sonny Vicaro, and Arn has been well documented.

The recent FBI-Adidas scandal vividly illustrates the lengths to which shoe companies will go to obtain clients and their involvement in recruiting players for not only agents but coaches and their universities. In short, when you set out as an agent, you are up against many well-funded and powerful forces that can take you down; or if you strike a deal with them and have some really bad luck, you may end up indicted and even convicted of a crime.

Clients

Another avenue to players for established agents is to use their current and past clients to recruit new clients. A satisfied client can be a good spokesperson and give an agent an early introduction to a potential draft pick. A simple introduction to a player could actually be prohibited by state and university rules, but there really would be no consequences as long as no benefit is given to the player. Of course, it would be nearly impossible to prove if a current professional player was receiving something from his agent to act as a conduit to university players, particularly if the professional player was an alumnus of the university.

I read a newspaper account of an agent who set up a dinner with several college players through one of his current clients and told the players that his client was taking them to lunch. The client attended the lunch and pretended to pay for the lunch, but was later reimbursed by the agent. Since the agent actually paid for the lunch, an NCAA violation occurred, and the story hit the papers. The agent had figured out the angles but left a trail of his reimbursement to the client.

Of course, one example of client recruiting these days is LeBron James and Rich Paul. In February of 2019, I saw LeBron at the Duke-Virginia game in Charlottesville, Virginia, with Zion Williamson and a host of other NBA players. I actually telephoned my son and joked that LeBron must have been on a recruiting trip. At the time, I only saw him with Rondo, so I was joking. However, the next day I was watching *First Take* and someone else had raised some controversy about LeBron being on a "recruiting trip." LeBron was deflecting, saying it was not a recruiting trip and that he did not "speak with anyone." It was at that time that I learned he was not only with Rondo but with his agent Rich Paul. Of course, this was a fun night out with his friends, but it surely also was meant to highlight that he was with his agent and friend, Rich Paul, to those young players.

I have no criticism of Rich taking advantage of being seen with his client. There was no NCAA violation or anything illegal about LeBron and his agent going to see a game. I'm sure other agents are terrified in having to face LeBron in recruiting players and will do anything to stop him. My experience personally and what I observed during my career was that very few NBA players went out and recruited for their agents simply as an altruistic gesture. Most players want the focus to be on them.

Financial Advisors

I was aware that at one point financial advisors were used to some degree as a conduit for an agent to sign a player. There was little regulation of so called "financial advisors" for many years, and they were able to avoid the scrutiny of universities or the Unions. Financial advisors could also work through family members. However, over the years, regulation of financial advisors in recruiting and competency has now been tightened up, as some players lost significant amounts of money because of agents and financial advisors. For example, the NFLPA now requires that all financial advisors be certified with the NFLPA and post a bond.

The Other Duties of an Agent

Sports Agents often do much more than negotiate contracts. Their influence on young and financially unsophisticated athletes sometimes borders on surrogate parenthood. (*Trial Magazine*, June 1990 "When Agents Pull the Strings," by Albert Gross.)

Once you are over the biggest hurdle of sports agency, signing a legitimate client, you are now faced with the reality of providing a multitude of services for the client other than just negotiation of his contract. These services include physical training and preparation for professional evaluation, accounting, banking, financial planning, insurance coverages, public relations, marketing, obtaining endorsements, and what I call personal transition from college athlete to professional player.

You Are a Bank

The truth is that normally when a rookie player signs with you, you become director of his career and his source of support (and probably members of his family) until he can get through the draft and finally sign a professional contract. Once you sign a player, his eligibility for college athletics is over and you are legally able to help him out financially, so he in all probability will ask you for financial help. Financial help not only includes money but normally a new vehicle for the athlete and even some members of his family. This is when you begin to try to teach him about money and taxes. For example, if you borrow $50,000, you have to make around $85,000 or more to pay it back. Depending on where the player is projected to go in the draft, you have to determine how much you want to go into debt for a potential fee return, which is not a sure thing. Remember, you collect no fee for this contract until he gets paid during the season unless he signs some endorsement deals.

The difference between football and basketball can really make an impact here, as football draft picks tend to slide up and down the board more easily, and basketball draft picks usually remain fairly stable. Basketball players also have the advantage of being able to play overseas, where they can make some substantial money even if they are not a first-round pick. Again, basketball only has two rounds, but football has seven, so even if a player is drafted in the NFL, he is still a financial risk if he is in the lower rounds of the draft. It is also true that inherently, almost every player thinks he is going to be superstar, so he has no qualms, it seems, about borrowing as much as he can get his hands on. By the time I stopped acting as an NFL agent, almost all players wanted a car after signing. During my career I had to take back at least three vehicles from players.

Training

Once signed, a rookie needs to prepare for the draft, and you are expected to help him get the proper training and arrange and help him pick which camps, combines, and/or workouts are needed and which he should attend. You will also be involved in deciding if a personal trainer is necessary and hopefully make sure the player is in top shape before the draft. This will be part of my story later with Stanley Roberts.

The pre-draft training these days has become really expensive, and some agents even front this as one of their expenses. Who will bear the costs should be discussed up front because unless you tell a player that he's responsible, it will probably be impossible to collect these expenses later.

Personal Transition

This is the part of the job in which you try to educate a young man who may have never had a checking account as to how to function independently in the world without a coach or someone from his university helping him with his daily life. You have to explain money, its value, and how you should save for the future when you are only twenty-two and have your whole career ahead of you. You and others need to explain taxes, insurance coverages, and all the financial aspects of life to your player, including things like why not to lend money to the relatives, who in many cases will be asking for loans and/or seeking investment in some business ventures.

You need to explain how, as a professional athlete, the player will be well known to the public and there are those who will target the player for many reasons to get to his money. In addition, you need to try to explain to your player that women, drugs, guns, social media, and fast cars all pose a danger to his career. You need to try to make the player realize that his career will not last forever and that it could end at any moment with an injury and that he should look to the future. You need to try to remind the player that his business is his sport and that he should focus on that and not some other business like owning a record company that someone else wants him to put his money in. Although this all sounds easy, it is not, especially in the fantasy world that some high-profile players live in. The unions do have some programs to help their members adjust to real life after the draft. If a player is not a high-profile player initially, he should have a real-life lesson on saving his money, which may do more good than all the advice you can give.

Accounting and Financial Planning

Most agencies like to keep these services for a client in-house. This gives the agency the advantage of controlling almost all access to the player so as to prevent any poaching from other agents or agencies. A problem with all services in-house is that you really may not have anyone acting as a safety net in the handling of the player's money and you have the potential for conflicts of interest to arise. There are numerous examples of players losing money just like Kareem Abdul-Jabbar, in bad investments and poor wealth management, which are the fault of the agent. On the other hand, there are some players who, no matter what you advise, will do what they want with their money and listen to the wrong people when investing.

The size and structure of my law firm dictated that I had to go outside of my firm for these services, as I never portrayed myself as a financial advisor. I would introduce the players to some financial people who had actually invested my money and/ or whom I trusted. I would use my own accountant, who is still my accountant and did a great job. Preparing a player's taxes is a difficult job, as each state where he plays forces him to pay state income taxes.

Endorsements

Negotiation of endorsement deals is an area where an agent can be helpful. The fees on endorsements are not governed by the unions, so the fee may exceed the maximum fee allowed under the player-agent regulations. However, the reality is that only a handful of athletes are really in line for any major endorsements. I used to charge 10% for endorsement, but some agents used to charge up to 20%. Back in my day, basketball cards were a small source of revenue for most rookies, but I think those companies went under. Shoe companies would give out endorsement deals, and there was big money for a few, but not the rank and file NBA players. I know there is a lot of talk by agents about endorsement deals, but the reality is that if you are a big enough superstar, the endorsement deals will generally come looking for you. This is again illustrated by the FBI-Adidas scandal, as the shoe companies are out looking for the next superstar and are willing to pay him even if he is in high school and a complete unknown.

Insurance

You and others need to help the player establish what kind of insurance he needs to purchase to cover his soon-to-be assets, and protect him from losing everything by an unexpected injury. You need to make sure he has adequate automobile, personal liability, disability, health, and career-ending injury protection. Naturally, insurance will vary from individual to individual depending how much the player is projected to make on his professional contract.

Legal Services

You must be ready to help your client with any legal problems which may arise while you are representing him such as marital problems, estate planning, and criminal issues. You will not necessarily represent him yourself, but must be able to know which attorneys will be able to properly represent him and not overcharge for their services. If your client wants to set up a foundation of some sort, you can always find attorneys willing to do the legal work.

Public Relations

My opinion is that only a handful of players really need public relations firms, although this is talked about by some agents as a big advantage to using a big agency. Generally, I would handle statements issued to the press through my staff and had pretty good relationships with the members of the press who contacted me. Some players want a lot of media attention and some do not. In any event, with the extensive media coverage of sports from back when I was in the business to now, it is not difficult to get a story published. I would caution my players about speaking too freely about some subjects, particularly when negotiating a contract.

Other Agents

In the agent business there is really not much, if any, comradery among agents due to the intensity of the competition. The agent business is a world of paranoia, subterfuge, and its own brand of espionage. The adage, "knowledge is power," is particularly true in the agent business. Which member of a player's family does he feel closest to? Which member of his family, if any, helps him make his decisions? Who are his "friends," and does he listen to them? Does he have a girlfriend or wife who helps guide him? All of this type of information can make the difference in signing a player. You have to obtain this kind of information, and the more you know, the more power you have toward the goal of signing the player. Since you are in intense competition with other agents, you do not want to share your knowledge or even be on too friendly a basis with those working against you.

I once sat by David Falk in an NBPA agent seminar in New York. I knew he did not need to actually be there, but it is part of the requirements for continued certification by the NBPA. I sat there, admittedly a little bit in awe, and waited for an opportunity to introduce myself. By this time, I had several players in the League (this is how the NBA is referred to by most), and truthfully, if he had recognized my name it would have been a bit of an ego boost. We sat there for several hours and then broke for lunch. He never turned my way or acknowledged me in any way, and I never could get an opportunity to actually speak with him without looking obviously anxious to meet the famous David Falk. I never had the opportunity to meet him again, and he obviously had no desire to interact with me, but why should he? I was a no-name want-to-be agent and he was David Falk.

This highlights one of the big differences in actually practicing law and being a sports agent. If I had been at any legal seminar next to another attorney for several hours, I'm sure David Falk and I would have at least introduced ourselves. Throughout my legal medical malpractice on the side of both the defense and plaintiff, I have been able to remain friendly with the opposing counsel generally, and actually made many professional friends with whom I have gone to dinner and interacted at legal social occasions. Maintaining your professional reputation and being courteous to your opponent usually works to your and your clients' advantage. Of course, in over forty years of legal practice, there have been a few unprofessional assholes whose word you cannot trust and who try to obstruct the course of the litigation. You keep these attorneys on a short leash and rule them into court if necessary. I did meet some friendly and intriguing characters over my sports agent career, but few were other sports agents.

FOUR
My Agent Beginnings

———————— • ————————

The first year of my certification (1988), I did not sign any players. I did attempt to get my name out in the sports community as an officially certified NFLPA agent. I was just trying to see what would happen and was not overly concerned about signing any players right off the bat. I had an advantage in that I was also involved in a very successful law practice and did not have to depend on signing a player for my livelihood. This was always the case throughout my career and was the way that I wanted it. Being an agent and having my livelihood dependent on the decision of a young man twenty or so years old was not something I ultimately wanted for me and my family. They say desperation leads to desperate measures, which is the reason for the over-the-top and sometimes criminal methods used by some agents to sign clients.

The only "sports figure " that I knew in Baton Rouge when I decided to become an agent was Collis Temple Jr. Collis was the first black athlete to play basketball for LSU after he signed with the Tigers in 1971. Collis was not only well known as an LSU athlete but also a strong African American state leader in politics and economics. He was and continues to be a highly successful businessman in the state of Louisiana and a most interesting friend.

I had met Collis way back in 1974, when I was studying at Abilene Christian University (ACU). I had attended ACU in 1972, because at the time my parents were members of the Church of Christ, and there were two colleges within driving distance to Shreveport, where the Church recommended members send their children for a Christian education; Harding College and Abilene Christian. Because then I was planning on attending LSU Law School, I thought that going to any school for seven years would be too much. This eliminated LSU as an option and prompted my choice between the two schools recommended by the Church. I decided to attend the "larger" school, Abilene Christian (3000 students), to make my parents happy.

Abilene is in the beginning of west Texas, 350 miles due west from Dallas, where the wind constantly blows and is home to three colleges, one of which was Abilene Christian University. The other two colleges were also church schools and the county where Abilene is located was dry. ACU was not a "party school," but you could get an excellent education which was fine by me. Because of its size, it was easy to get to know people even if they were not in your class.

In 1972 we did not have many African American students at Abilene and most of those were athletes. We did have a good NAIA football team featuring a running back named Wilbert Montgomery who went on to have a very successful career in the NFL. I used to say hello to a lot of students after eating at the school cafeteria. Because I recognized Wilbert, I would always say hello to him and some of the other athletes. One of the other students I befriended was an African American student on the school basketball team named Robert Bates.

After speaking with Robert, I found out he was from Kentwood, Louisiana, which is near Mandeville, Louisiana, where my parents had moved after I graduated in 1972 from Captain Shreve. My first year of college I did not have a car, so I had to find rides to and from Abilene and Mandeville (a 12 hour drive) if we had a school break. As a result, I only went home for Christmas and at the end of the first semester my first year. My second year of college my father gave me his old business car to make the drive to and from school. When Robert found out, he asked me if I could give him a ride to Hammond, Louisiana when I went home. He would get a family member to pick him up in Hammond, when he rode with me. As a result of our twelve hour drives together, Robert and I became good friends while we were students at ACU.

One day in 1974 when I was at my apartment, I received a call from Robert. He said he had a friend in town he wanted me to meet who was on his basketball team in high school. He brought the friend over and it was Collis Temple, who at 6' 8"was hard to forget. Collis was on his way to San Antonio. He had just been drafted in the old ABA and was going to play professional basketball in San Antonio. At the time, I was not a huge LSU fan since I had not started law school there and really did not know anything about Collis at the time. The only basketball player I knew about from LSU was Pistol Pete Maravich. I can't remember much from our first meeting other than Collis seemed like a cool guy and was very friendly.

When I moved from New Orleans to Baton Rouge in 1983, Collis was living in Baton Rouge and somehow our paths crossed. He remembered me from those years ago and we became friends. Of course, Collis went through some unbelievable experiences when he came to LSU and I've enjoyed hearing those stories throughout the years. Collis has a strong personality and I've always enjoyed our encounters whether they are for a meal or meeting at a sporting event.

When I first decided to get into the agent business, I met with Collis to get any advice he may have since he played professional basketball and was close to the LSU program. Collis was not very encouraging to me in the beginning of my quest to become an agent. I remember him telling me he did not know "why anyone would want to be a sports agent." He warned me about some of the pitfalls of dealing with other agents and professional athletes. I appreciated his advice but decided to plunge ahead anyway. After I actually got going as an agent, he was always there to offer some insight and advice if I asked him.

I actually represented Collis's oldest son, Collis Temple III, after he played basketball and graduated from LSU in 2003. Collis III had a lot of talent, was extremely intelligent and a hard worker, but injuries hampered his try at a pro career. He already had a master's degree when he graduated from LSU, so he went straight into business where he has been highly successful just like his father.

Living in Baton Rouge I would have many random meetings with Collis over the years especially when my son and his son, Garrett, were playing basketball. Little Oscar and Garrett are the same age and would end up playing against each other when they were young. As I said previously, I actually "coached" Little O's teams in 4th and 5th grade though my assistant coach, Marianne McKeithen, was the brains of the outfit.

Garrett and Oscar went to different high schools and didn't meet up during those days, except at some AAU games. I enjoyed following Garrett's career at U High where he played with Glen (Big Baby) Davis and won a state championship. He then played with Glen at LSU with LSU advancing to the final four. After graduation in 2009, Garrett went on to play in the NBA until the present time. Recently, when I was in New York with my wife Lin

I saw him playing for the New Jersey Nets.

One avenue I considered to try to meet some players was to become an LSU jobber. A jobber is a person who provides employment for college athletes while they are still in school. This system is approved by the NCAA, but it is heavily regulated with various NCAA requirements. The NCAA is not only worried about agents giving benefits to players, but also interested alumni and even coaches. The main emphasis of the requirements is that the player works legitimate controlled hours with a non-inflated pay scale. This system has been subject to abuse throughout the years, as illustrated by the old story of a player turning on a sprinkler in the morning and coming back hours later to turn it off in the afternoon, and being paid for a full day's work at an exorbitant rate.

I called the LSU athletic department and made arrangements for my law firm to begin to employ LSU football players or other persons related to the program during the summer. In exchange, I was allowed the opportunity for the firm to purchase LSU football season tickets in a great location, and was also invited to the closed-door spring game. I told LSU I was an agent and we were always very careful not to violate any NCAA rules. I made sure the participants worked and were paid a commensurate rate. I must say we had many great employees over the twenty-five-year period that I was a jobber. The workers included one player's wife who was a first-class secretary, one player's brother, and even an ex-Tiger who was washed out by Katrina. Well-known NFL player and leader of the NFLPA for four years, Kevin Mawae, worked for me for two years. He did not sign with me, but we saw each other over the years and always had pleasant conversations. Kevin has also given several excellent speeches to my sports law class at LSU since he has retired to Baton Rouge.

The first LSU player at my law firm was Jamie Bice. Jamie

was a six-foot, three inch white defensive back who grew up in Lake Charles. Jamie had been blessed with speed, good looks, and size even as a youth and came to LSU as a prized recruit. His brother was a lawyer and he wanted to work in a law firm. Jamie was pre-med at the time, so he was able to help me with some medical aspects of my cases. He was a confident young man to say the least. When he introduced himself, he liked to say, "Hi, I'm Jamie Bice, number forty-one in your program and number one in your heart." My feeling was that Jamie was quite a heartbreaker around the LSU campus.

I was only about twelve years older than him, and we became pretty good friends. I was working on cases against several drug companies and took him to New York for a document production. A document production in drug litigation is similar to a game of hide-and-seek by the drug companies. You request documents, and the company is compelled to produce the document, but they do not have to search through their records to find the relevant documents. As a result, you end up in a room filled, literally, with thousands and thousands of documents that you have to spend hours, and at times, days reviewing to find what you actually need. It can be laborious, but when you find the "smoking gun" key to your case, it is quite exhilarating. Bringing Jamie saved me an enormous amount of time and we enjoyed eating at some fine restaurants while in the city. We also had the opportunity to go on a firm fishing trip. On this trip, I became terribly seasick, and had to be dropped off on an oil platform, much to Jamie's entertainment.

I had jokingly told Jamie that in legal circles I was known as the "assassin." This caught his fancy, and he still calls me that to this day. After the end of his employment, we remained friends and he invited me to his birthday party at his apartment. At the party, I met "Nacho" Joe Albergamo who was an All-American center and a well-known LSU player. Joe and I became friends, and today he is my doctor. Joe was super intelligent and had offers to play in the NFL, but instead went to medical school. It was fun getting to know some of the LSU players whom I had read about and watched play throughout the years. These were the type of initial contacts I made in the sports world. I began to get some references for when I would meet and recruit players and insight on potential players to recruit in the future. I did not realize at the time that I was also making some great friends with whom I would continue my relationship until the present day.

Even though I did not have any clients, I still followed all the legal maneuvering of the NFLPA as a now certified NFLPA agent. In 1987, at about the time I started as an agent, the NFL's CBA expired. This led to nearly five years of legal maneuvers and litigation between the NFL and the NFLPA, and I had a front row seat to most of it. I was busy with my day job, and did not become too involved with the ongoing NFLPA litigation, but did try to stay abreast of the developments as they occurred.

I was not really disappointed by not having signed any players prior to 1989, but really wanted to give it a try in 1989. All the legal maneuvering by the NFL and the NFLPA did not really affect me because I had no clients. However, I still began to read draft prediction literature to get a feel for some of the potential players whom I might recruit. I came to the realization that I was not going to be able to sign any top draft picks, and looked for some guys who may not get the attention of most agents. However, the reality is that in the football agent business, there are always many more agents than the legitimate players who will be drafted or sign as free agents. Moreover, about twenty percent of the agents represent about eighty percent of the players.

Ricky Warren—My First Client

*My first client Ricky Warren
from Grambling.*

Ricky Warren, an offensive tackle from Bogalusa, Louisiana, who had played at Grambling University was the first player I ever signed to an NFLPA player-agent contract and then to an NFL contract. I was able to gain an introduction to Ricky through Thomas "Shadow Man" Kates, whom I had met in the political campaign of U.S. Senator John Breaux in 1996. Thomas and I crossed paths again during the campaign of U.S. Congressman Billy Tauzin, who ran for governor of Louisiana in 1987. I had mentioned to Thomas that I was trying to become an NFL agent and he told me he knew of a potential draft pick who had played at Grambling.

I did some draft research and found out that Ricky had made second team All Southwestern Athletic Conference, and I thought that, with his size and mobility, he had a shot at possibly signing an NFL contract. Grambling was an easy university to deal with, and I told Shadow Man to see if Ricky was interested in talking to me. Thomas discussed this with Ricky and vouched for me personally. Ricky said he was interested in meeting with me, as he was getting some attention but not a great deal. I contacted Ricky and set up an appointment to go to Grambling to recruit him after his college career had ended.

Ricky was a very low-key individual, as is the tendency for most offensive linemen, in my experience. Offensive linemen protect their quarterback, and defensive linemen attack the opposition quarterback, which I feel may play into personality differences of the positions. I played offensive line in high school, but consider myself somewhat atypical for the position. I was very fast but also very uncoordinated. I started out with the hopes of playing running back but was moved to linebacker and offensive guard because of my speed. At Captain Shreve, we were running the old Green Bay sweep with two pulling guards. I ended up having to start as an offensive guard the second game of my junior season and never gave the position up. I really enjoyed my time on the offensive line, especially when we pulled or trapped, because I was in line to deliver a blow to one of the opponents, a trait I carried into my career as a trial lawyer.

Ricky dealt directly with me and produced no go-between coach, family member, or other interested party to assist him in his decisions. We did have ground for common conversation since I had played on the offensive line in high school. I was and have always been grateful that Ricky decided to give me a chance to act as his agent. It was a great feeling to sign Ricky, (a player whom we both thought would get a shot to play in the NFL), to an NFL player-agent contract. It was a small step but made me feel that I was at least making some progress on the road to becoming a real agent.

Ricky just wanted a chance to make a team and was not overly demanding. However, I did spend a lot of time working up his profile for NFL teams, and even did a demonstrative video so teams could see him since he was not invited to the NFL Combine. I thought the idea of the video based on the videos that we, as attorneys, would produce for injured clients at trial. I hired a videographer and worked up what I thought was a quite professional video showing him lifting weights and performing other drills. I sent the video along with all his information to every NFL team. I received a few calls before the draft, including from the New Orleans Saints, my favorite team. The calls made me feel that I might actually be on the verge of negotiating my first sports contract, which was exciting.

Immediately after the draft ended, the Saints called and wanted to sign Ricky. Since I had told Ricky about the pre-draft call, I was ready to come to terms quickly so I could ensure that Ricky got his shot to play pro ball. Since New Orleans was the only team that called me following the draft, I quickly negotiated the contract with a signing bonus in line with what other free agents were being paid. I really had no leverage in the negotiation, since I had no other offers from other teams. The Saints' terms were acceptable to Ricky, and he, of course, was happy to be getting a shot, especially so close to his hometown of Bogalusa. Just as I had learned at the NFL Players Association seminar, I made sure to call the association to run the numbers by a contact I had made during my certification process. The numbers checked out, so I called the Saints and accepted the contract and reported Ricky's numbers to the NFLPA research department, which is required by NFLPA agent rules. The NFLPA was extremely helpful with all the contracts I negotiated throughout the years. Ricky's contract was a simple deal, but it was my first NFL contract!

I did a press release to the Grambling, Baton Rouge, and New Orleans newspapers, and Ricky's hometown paper in Bogalusa. Issuing my own news release helped ensure that his story was published, and hopefully that his agent, Oscar Shoenfelt, would be mentioned. Publicity, as for almost any business, never hurts when you are in the agent business. Truthfully, it was really cool to see my name in the sports section of the paper for the first time.

In post-draft football free agency signings like Ricky's, you generally have little leverage and you have to keep in mind that the primary goal is to get the player into an NFL camp. If you string out the negotiations or get too cute in trying to play teams against each other, the offer could dry up and then your player may not get into camp. Teams usually have a predetermined number of slots to fill, and once those are filled, it's extremely hard to get into camp. Free agents are looking for the opportunity to show the team that they can contribute and possibly make the team's fifty-three-man roster or sign with the six-man developmental squad after the final cuts are made at the end of preseason. Naturally, the odds are generally more against the free agents making the team than draft picks, but every year some free agents beat the odds and make an NFL roster.

Football draft-pick contracts are negotiated over a longer period of time generally, from the time of the draft even up to training camp. At times, a high draft pick may even hold out from training camp for a period of time; however, this is a rarity. Generally, you want to get your player into camp so he will have every opportunity to make the team. High draft picks are generally guaranteed to make the team the first year, because of the amount of money given the player as a signing bonus and the fact that no general manager wants to look like he made a mistake in his pre-draft evaluations. However, lower-round draft picks can be cut and not make the team.

The information compiled by the NFLPA, which includes salary and length and terms of the contract, including the amounts and terms of bonuses from the seasons prior to the draft, are all available to the certified football agent. Football draft pick negotiations are geared to slotting your player so as to make sure he receives a better deal than players taken after him, and a deal as close as possible to the player taken before him. The first pick's deal in the draft is usually negotiated before his selection, and the rest of the slotting takes place after that time. Of course, there are no absolutes, and many variables such as the team, general manger you may be dealing with, and the number of draft picks the team may have made that year. The NFLPA's research staff, including attorneys, are glad to help with information and the validity of any offer being made by a team.

During my tenure as an NFLPA agent, I generally represented low draft picks or free agents. I did do one substantial free agent contract for Rufus Porter in 1995 with the New Orleans Saints, which I will discuss later.

1990—I Continue Building

The successful signing of Ricky Warren to an NFL contract gave me some street credibility as an agent and renewed my confidence that, if I kept working, I might actually sign a player and make some money as an agent. Thus far, though I had enjoyed the beginning lessons of the agent business, I had made no money and expended considerable time and some financial resources. Fortunately, things at the firm were going well and I was still able to pull my weight, and my understanding partners, to some degree enjoyed having an agent in the firm.

For the 1990 draft, I turned my attention to my home university, LSU, which had several players who were potential draft choices. I also recruited at some smaller schools including Louisiana Tech, located in Ruston, Louisiana. The fact that I had a statewide legal practice made it convenient for me to set up appointments with players in other parts of the state. I revised my recruiting materials to include the newspaper clipping of my signing Ricky with the Saints, and emphasized my legal and business background. I also pointed out that having an agent in

Baton Rouge could be very convenient for meeting with clients and helping with preparation for the upcoming draft.

In 1990, there was obviously not the TV coverage and public build up for the draft there is today. I intended to hire a local speed coach, and let the players work on strength and performance of the draft drills at LSU. Today, agents and/or players will spend in the neighborhood of $10,000 to $30,000, if not more, in attending various sports training centers to prepare for the draft. I say agents and/or players because some agents ask the players to reimburse them for the expenses and some don't, using the pre-draft preparation as a recruiting tool.

I researched the potential draft picks at LSU and sent them my recruiting literature and, after the season, asked for a chance to meet some of the players. I was able to get in touch with some of them personally and decided to invite them out for dinner. My partner, Ed Walters, had just finished building a large, impressive house, and I asked him if he and his wife, Norma, would host the dinner at their house. He said that would not be a problem, and Norma, who is a great cook, agreed to prepare the food. We hosted a good group, which included Kenny Davidson, not an LSU starter but an athletic defensive lineman; Eddie Fuller, an excellent running back; Clint James, a defensive lineman who started; Verge Ausberry, a starting linebacker who is now an associate athletic director at LSU; and Karl Dunbar, a defensive and offensive lineman. I can't remember what Norma cooked, but a good time was had by all, and I secured the contact information for all the players and continued to stay in touch to see if I had a shot at signing anyone. Ed and Norma enjoyed the dinner and it certainly made the firm feel like part of the process.

I sent the rest of the players literature and set up meetings with some of them, including Alvin Lee, a senior receiver from Beaumont, Texas, who played at LSU and was projected to be a free agent. Alvin was receptive, and I met with him and kept in touch with him. I also kept in touch with some of the other LSU players, called to check in with the players, and even took some out for another meal. I thought I had a shot with Clint James and Eddie Fuller, and I remember meeting Clint's girlfriend at some point. Kenny Davidson performed remarkably at the draft and his stock shot way up, so I thought I probably would not have a realistic chance at signing him.

The draft was upcoming, and I had been in touch with Eddie Fuller quite regularly. He was one of my favorite players and is still a legend around LSU for the catch he made to end the LSU-Auburn (ranked #4) game in Tiger Stadium (Death Valley) on October 8, 1988, at which I was present. The clock was running down with 1:47 to go in the game and LSU had a 4th down on the Auburn 11-yard line. Quarterback Tommy Hodson hit Fuller in the end zone to tie the game 6-6, and the effect of the crowd afterward moved a seismograph; it was so loud! LSU went on to win 7-6 after making the extra point, and the game is famously referred to as the Earthquake Game at LSU.

Eddie Fuller was projected as a potential fourth-round draft pick for the upcoming 1990 draft, and I was extremely excited to even be in the running for such a high draft pick at this point in my career. I knew he was talking to other agents, but he was also taking my calls and I felt like I had built up a good rapport with him. Several weeks before the draft, I was in Monroe, Louisiana, for a deposition in one of my legal cases. That night, I was in the hotel after the deposition, making use of my time by phoning potential clients, and reached Eddie. We talked, and at the end of the conversation, he told me he was going to sign with me. I told him great, and that we would get together the next day when I returned. My sales background told me to seal the deal as soon as possible, and I regretted not being in town but told him that we would get together the next day when I returned. Naturally, I was ecstatic, and when I hung up the telephone, I jumped up and pumped my fist and yelled. I was so excited about my newfound success! I was about to hit the big time, possibly signing a potential fourth-round pick and one of my favorite players who had participated in one of my fondest LSU memories. Life could not be much sweeter at that moment! I'm sure I made at least several calls to my family and my partners to spread the great news but cannot remember specifically. As I tried to sleep that night, I could barely control my glee, and my mind churned with thoughts of actually signing a player-agent contract with Eddie and preparing him for the draft.

As I drove back to Baton Rouge the next day, my thoughts were on getting in touch with Eddie to seal the deal. When I returned, I called him several times with no answer. I thought this was a little strange and tried to track him down. I believe I called one of the other players, but in any case, I learned that he and one of the other draft picks had left town with an agent the day after he told me he was going to sign with me.

Of course, I was disappointed not signing Eddie, but reconciled myself with the knowledge that the agent business is a tough business, and that as an agent your clients are young kids who can many times be as capricious as the weather. This aspect of the business would be brought home to me many, many times, and it is something inherent in dealing with the players themselves, who come from all types of backgrounds and circumstances, which many cannot imagine. The truth is that these young men are at the peak of their career when they are the least prepared to understand how to deal with the financial and business implications of beginning a high-paying career, which, particularly for football, can have an extremely limited life. As an agent, part of your job is to help educate your clients on how to conduct their business professionally, but many times it is difficult, if not impossible. I never heard from Eddie again and have never seen him since; I never harbored any ill will, though a phone call telling me he had changed his mind would have been nice.

Eddie ended up being a fourth-round pick of the Buffalo Bills that year and I followed his career, always wishing him well. As it turned out, though I negotiated approximately fifteen NFL contracts, I was never destined to represent an NFL draft pick higher than round six.

I did have some success in the 1990 draft. I signed Alvin Lee as a client and was able to sign him as an undrafted free agent with the Seattle Seahawks. After signing him, I had sent his information to all the NFL teams and received a call from Seattle after the draft ended. Alvin was a great person, and I am glad I could assist him in getting a chance to play professionally. He was subsequently cut by the Seahawks, but he gave it his best shot.

In addition, I ended up representing Glenell Sanders from Louisiana Tech on a free agent contract with the Chicago Bears. I flew to New York to see him play against the New York Giants in the 1990 playoffs. He obtained a ticket for me; it was high, and I remember how cold it was in the stadium. It was a good experience but could not compare to the games I would later see as an NBA agent. Of course, at the time, I had no idea that I would end up representing two first-round NBA draft picks and several NBA second rounders and free agents. Later, Glenell would obtain a new agent, which happens quite often, as I was to learn in the agent business.

I did enjoy the recruiting that year and can say that I felt like I became a friendly acquaintance of all the players, and it was really a thrill at this point in time just to get to know some of the LSU football team, which I enjoyed following closely. Most of the players were drafted at various levels, and some kept in touch. I stayed friends with Verge Ausberry since he remained in Baton Rouge and am Facebook friends with Karl Dunbar, who is presently defensive line coach for the Buffalo Bills. I found that a sporting adventure of almost any type made for instant conversation around Baton Rouge. Frankly, when you live in Baton Rouge, one of the biggest sources of entertainment is watching LSU sports, and this is one of the reasons I have enjoyed my adopted hometown.

During this time period, I also had occasion to meet Mickey Guidry, who had played quarterback at LSU. He had finished his playing career in 1989, had no eligibility, and was trying to get a look by an NFL team. I signed him and tried to get him some NFL tryouts. Though I never was able to sign him to an NFL team, I did give him exposure, and Mickey eventually played in the NFL developmental league from 1991 to 1992 with several teams, including the London Monarchs and Sacramento Surge.

I helped Mickey get a book published, which he had been working on for some time. The foreword in the book, *Through the Eyes of Number Two,* describes how we met and went about publishing it:

> As I am sure many LSU fans will recall, Mickey Guidry received a shoulder injury in his final LSU game against Syracuse in the 1989 Hall of Fame Bowl. Although he was invited to the National Football League Combine, he could not participate and was never given the opportunity to play in the National Football League in 1989. Despite being out of football with his injury, he still wanted to fulfill one of his lifelong goals of playing professional football.

In the early part of 1990, Mickey Guidry and I first discussed my becoming his agent, and I decided to work with him. I was excited to be helping a player that not only contributed so much to the LSU Football program on the football field, but also contributed off the field by the fine manner in which he represented the University. After becoming Mickey's agent, many people expressed to me the same feelings I initially had about him. I wanted the best for this young man who, though relegated to a secondary role at the quarterback position for LSU, contributed so much to the winning programs at LSU under Bill Arnsparger and Mike Archer.

Mickey worked hard, got into shape, and I arranged several tryouts with professional football teams, both in the CFL and in the NFL. Several times we were very close to signing professional contracts; however, the opportunity never came in 1990. Despite his being disappointed several times by failing to sign a contract, Mickey continued to work hard and to fulfill other goals he had set. One of these goals was to tell the story of his career at LSU. It was a pleasure to work with him to accomplish this goal.

While working with Mickey both in football and in producing this book I have grown to appreciate Mickey's character which I see reflected in this book. Mickey's book reflects the fact that college football is not all glitter and glamour for the athletes. It reflects the fact that many times athletes face a peculiar set of trials, temptations, and struggles which many of the fans fail to appreciate.

Oscar L. Shoenfelt, III, 1990

Though the book did not sell out, I thought it was well written and I did enjoy the process of helping to edit and publish it. My partner, Ed Walters, was one of the editors, as he is an excellent writer and has for years edited our local bar journal. One of the local writers in Baton Rouge wrote a great article about the book, and this gave the book and my agent business some publicity.

Mickey Guidry and I discuss his book.

Big Willie Time

The year 1990 proved pivotal in my agent career, as I soon had an opportunity to represent my first drafted NFL player, Willie "Top Cat" Williams, also known as "Big Willie." Willie is African-American, stands six feet, six inches tall, was a tremendous athlete, and was and continues to be quite a character. Willie was never an NFL star, but he did play enough to become vested with four credited NFL seasons to obtain his pension. His career is typical of most NFL players, mixed with injuries and some lost chances, some due to the luck of the draw, some to others, and some due to his own inexperience.

He was born in Houston in 1967. Willie and his brother, Bingo, were raised by his grandmother after his parents were killed in an automobile accident when he was five years old. He and his brother had to move to a rough area of Houston, but his grandmother kept them grounded. His grandmother's primary corollary in raising the boys was that they would not end up in prison as many of the young African-American men growing up in the neighborhood did. Due to economic necessity,

Willie had to start working at the age of eleven. His grandmother saw to it that he attended church regularly and even sang in the church choir. To this day he still has a great voice.

Willie's grandmother did a good job of keeping him on the straight and narrow, but this is not to say that he never was involved in any mischief growing up. As a boy, Willie was given the nickname of "Top Cat" by his friends after the cartoon character Top Cat. The character was the leader of a group of cats who always got his friends in trouble but would usually avoid the blame himself.

Willie was a two-sport athlete playing basketball and football at a public high school in Houston called Phillis Wheatley. Some of his contemporaries and friends in high school were NFL players Alfred Williams and Knavis McGee, who both played on Colorado's national championship team in 1990. I would meet and recruit, but not sign them.

Willie was recruited out of high school in both sports and even was offered a scholarship by John Thompson to play basketball at Georgetown. At one point, we considered sending him overseas to play basketball at the end of his career. He did not start playing football until his junior year in high school as a tight end. His motivation was that the basketball coach had implemented a new program requiring each basketball player to finish two cross-country meets. Willie started one meet but was caught deviating from the course by cutting through the woods. He was told by the quarterback who played point guard on the basketball team that he could avoid the cross-country rule by playing football. Willie decided to play football and chose the position of tight end.

By 1986, his senior year, Willie was a blue-chip tight end football recruit out of Houston along with Charles Arbuckle. Willie loved basketball and Georgetown, but was convinced by football recruiters that he only had average size for basketball and would eventually, due to his size and athleticism, be a star football player. The sales hype by the football recruiters influenced Willie to choose football. Willie was talking to several schools, including UCLA, but when Arbuckle chose UCLA, Willie decided to attend LSU in Baton Rouge, which was only a four-hour drive from Houston.

While applying for college, Willie had taken the ACT. He had prepared for the test and did well, especially for a student coming from Phyllis Wheatley high school. After he arrived at LSU, the NCAA arbitrarily challenged his ACT score. His freshman year, Willie was red-shirted, but he played the 1988 and 1989 seasons. He made a huge fourth-and-nine catch the series before Eddie Fuller caught the winning touchdown in the 1989 LSU-Auburn "earthquake" game.

The NCAA challenge to Willie's ACT score dragged on for three years, and he was approaching his senior season and would have been LSU's primary tight end with the departure of Todd Kinchen and Ronnie Halliburton to the NFL. LSU assured him that he would be eligible for the next year, so he bypassed the upcoming NFL draft and combine, where without a doubt he would have done well. After the draft, he was told he would be ineligible unless he retook the ACT. He retook the ACT and did not make a sufficiently high score and was declared ineligible after the draft. There was a supplemental draft, but it was only two to three weeks off, and he needed immediate representation. That was the twist of fate that led him to me, a dedicated, eager, but somewhat inexperienced NFL agent in 1990.

Willie came to me because I knew LSU offensive coordinator Ed Zaunbrecher. Ed's brother, Alan, and I had practiced law together in New Orleans from 1979 to 1983. Ed suggested that Willie call me. Willie was my first potential NFL player with a shot at being drafted. Willie came over and we talked, and he agreed for me to represent him, primarily because of the short time before the pending supplemental draft.

Willie was naturally in shock, having been arbitrarily denied his senior year of play, especially since LSU had reassured him that he would not lose the opportunity. He kept his head up and, as he said to the papers the day after the draft, he knew he "had to keep a positive attitude and keep working hard." I researched the draft, obtained all his pertinent statistics, and faxed a factsheet to every team in the NFL. I spoke to numerous teams, and Willie fielded calls from approximately twenty teams before the draft, but he did not have workouts with any of them.

Despite the short time frame, Willie was drafted in the ninth round of the supplemental draft on July 10, 1990 by the Phoenix Cardinals. Willie was excited and several ex-LSU players were on the roster including Lance Smith, offensive line, and his friend, former LSU linebacker Eric Hill. Eric had been the number ten pick in the draft in 1989 and was a great player and so had great job security with the team, which Willie would not have until he proved himself. Unfortunately, Willie initially failed to realize that management generally will put up with more non-football issues with a superstar that they have an investment in, than a player just trying to get his foothold in the League.

I began negotiations immediately after contacting the NFLPA and discussing our goal for a reasonable contract since training camp was beginning in the near future. Willie needed to get to camp to have a chance at making the team, which is the overriding goal of low draft picks and free agents. Willie was my first drafted player and I was naturally excited and wanted to gain as much experience as possible. He was supposed to report on July 21, 1990 with training camp starting on July 23, 1990 in Flagstaff, Arizona. We had not completed the contract by July 21, 1990, so I decided to fly to Phoenix and finish the contract there to get some firsthand experience.

Phoenix was extremely hot. It was really hard to be outside during the day. Literally, as I recall, it was hot enough to fry an egg on the sidewalk. I was trying to push the envelope and get all I could on the contract, but wanted to get Willie into camp on time. We finished the contract, and had it completed and signed by July 23. I even drove to Flagstaff to check out training camp and send Willie off to camp. Flagstaff was much cooler, and I enjoyed seeing the countryside and witnessing Willie beginning his career. During those last few days before he signed his contract, we talked a great deal and developed a lasting friendship.

Willie had an up-and-down career, but he never fired me or blamed me for any misfortune, which happens with some professional athletes. Willie was a natural talker and entertainer, and I enjoyed hearing many stories about him growing up and his exploits on and off the field. His nickname of "Top Cat" came well-deserved. He was one of those people who could convince you of anything, if you gave him long enough. Over the years, he not only kept me entertained but actually tried to help me with my career.

During those days before he signed, he told me that he was a member of a fraternity. The name of the fraternity is Omega Psi Phi, which is a historically black fraternity with some pretty intense initiation requirements. The subject came up one day when he was changing into some workout clothes and I noticed two brands, one on his chest and one on his arms. These brands are the final stage of initiation: you are branded with the omega sign on some part of your body. Omegas will give the fraternity salute after scoring a touchdown by placing both hands above their heads to look like antlers. After Willie moved, he left some of his things in a box including a book outlining the history of Omegas, which was founded in 1911 at Howard University. It was the first fraternity to be formed at a historically black university. I noted that one of the founding members, Oscar James Cooper, shared my first name. I would learn later that Thomas "Shadow Man" Kates was also an Omega. I would continue to enjoy meeting Omegas throughout my career; usually a group of great guys, who were generally surprised with my knowledge of the fraternity.

Willie did pretty well in training camp, but was waived on August 27, 1990. He did not panic and was signed to the new developmental squad by Phoenix on October 1, 1990. As his coach Joe Bugel said in a newspaper interview, "Willie was really coming along. You don't find too many tight ends at 260 pounds."

Willie showed his loyalty after he was waived. Many players fire their agent when they are cut by a team as if it's the agent's fault that they did not make the team. Other agents will also come in and convince the player that his agent did not do a good job placing the player, or that he can re-sign with another team with his connections or knowledge of the game. Of course, this is nonsense, but a panicked inexperienced player may fall for this ploy. Some players, if they do not make it in a sport, will blame their agent.

In truth, the agent does not control if the player make the team. A player is cut in sports, not because of his agent but because of his talent level or the fact that he does not fit within the team's scheme at that time. Professional sports teams spend tremendous resources in finding and evaluating talent, and do not cut a player because of his agent, especially those players who are under contract.

While on the developmental squad, Willie began to add weight as he continued to look for a position where he had a legitimate chance at making the team. He continued to improve on the developmental squad and was signed to the active roster toward the end of the 1990 season, and played some as an offensive guard. He was on the active roster for three games in 1990, sufficient to earn one credited season toward vesting in the NFL retirement system, which is extremely important to the player's future security. Most of the football players who get a shot at the League play less than four years and never really make sufficient money to help set them up for life. Several hundred thousand dollars or a million might sound like a substantial amount of money, but does not provide a real foundation to place the players on the road to economic success. Furthermore, young players feel like they will play forever, have no experience with money, and have numerous family members and others trying to get a piece of the action. Many football players spend a few years in the League and never vest in the retirement system and never receive their retirement benefit, which can really help when the player is old enough to collect the benefits (fifty-five). Time on the Developmental Squad is nice to keep the player making some money and training, but the active roster is where he makes a real salary and begins to accrue credited seasons toward retirement. Willie had done well during the 1990 season and showed he had the potential to play in the League, and we were looking forward to the 1991 season.

I had no idea of the many adventures and exploits Willie and I would share in the future. Handling his contract provided me with additional experience, and helped to some degree to prepare me for my next client, Stanley Roberts, a basketball player whom Willie knew at LSU.

FIVE
Stanley Roberts, 1990

Stanley and Shaq at LSU.

Big Stan is a mountain of a man, even more so now than in 1990, when he signed with me and changed my life. He stands seven feet tall, and in 1990, he was probably the most talented big man playing college basketball. And yes, that would include his teammate Shaquille O'Neal. He had come to LSU in 1988 as a Proposition 48 player along with his high school basketball coach, Jim Childers, from Hopkins, South Carolina.

Stanley had nimble feet and amazing agility and moved on the basketball court as smoothly as a deer running through a dense forest. Despite his size and thick body structure he could move with incredible fluidity. I have seen him do things on the basketball court that I've never seen men his size ever match, and I am talking about basketball greats. I truly feel he was one of the most naturally gifted individuals to play the game of basketball in many respects. I asked him once how he came to perfect one of his basketball moves and he said, "Oscar, I didn't perfect it, I just do it, no thinking about it."

Stan is a great individual with a heart as big as a house, and he would give a friend or even a stranger the shirt off his back. None of these qualities would necessarily make you a great basketball player. In fact, those attributes can run counter to the attributes that I feel make a player with all the physical tools great: the natural born desire to win, willingness to do any amount of work to be great, the willingness to impose your will on others through your physical play, and a real love of the game you are playing. And yes, it even takes a certain amount of arrogance for most superstars to rise to the top.

Stan was and still is a person with a big heart, and God blessed him with tremendous physical talent, but Stan, deep down, lacked the love of the game and a real desire to win at the point in his life when he had his opportunity. I care for him like a member of my family, but that is my appraisal of why he never really lived up to his real basketball potential.

Unfortunately, professional athletes, unlike most of the rest of us, usually are at the peak of their earning and job potential when they know the least about the lessons that come with living life itself. People in their twenties may not understand the realities of finances, relationships, and limited opportunities. The combination of inexperience and the temptations that professional sports can bring has led many a young man down the wrong roads, and Stan had his share of dead ends. But ultimately, he found the right path. We had some highs and lows, and I can say that representing Stanley was challenging and at times frustrating, but never boring.

Stan did not even play basketball as a young man. He grew up as one of two boys of Isabella and Robert Lee Davis. His mother gave him a choice for his last name. Stanley chose Roberts after his mother's father, Robert Davis, who was a truck driver when Stanley was young. As he became older, Stanley and his father grew apart because his father had a problem with alcohol addiction. Stanley would help keep the trailer and cook while his mother worked long hours as a custodial supervisor for the University of South Carolina.

Because he was raised in a trailer, there was not always a great deal of room for big Stan. As he grew, he had to curl up in his bed because he was so tall. His mother loves to laugh and is a naturally sweet person, and Stanley inherited much of her personality. When she talks of Stanley, she still laughs and refers to him as "her boy." Although he is great in size, he has a personality more like a big teddy bear than a grizzly bear.

Stanley's brother, Wayne, played basketball for coach Jim Childers at Lower Richland High School. One day, Wayne mentioned to Coach Childers that he had a brother who was taller than he was at the time. Wayne stood six foot five, so Childers tracked down Stanley to have a look for himself. When Coach Childers first saw Stanley, he was in the eighth grade. Even at that time Childers knew Stanley had the potential to be a big-time player. Of course, this was not too difficult since Stanley already stood six foot seven at the time. Stanley was reluctant to play basketball but continued to grow, and in the ninth grade he reached six foot nine. Stanley is built similarly to Karl Malone, and at six foot nine, I'm sure he was an intimidating sight even in the ninth grade.

Coach Childers persisted and was finally able to persuade Stanley to come out for the team to play his sophomore season when he stood six foot ten. In order to prepare for the team tryouts, Stanley worked out with his Uncle Dale, Wayne, and a cousin. Naturally, Stanley struggled at first, but with each game and drill, Stanley, with his height and natural ability, improved at an amazing rate. He not only made the team but made the varsity team his first year. Childers was a natural teacher of the game, and Stanley absorbed the basketball fundamentals quickly. The coach worked with Stanley on all the moves he would need as a big man, and Stanley blossomed. He was an All-American by the end of his first season. Stanley continued to gain height and by his junior season in high school he stood seven feet. Stanley never sought to play basketball, but when he did, basketball enveloped him, and he was a real natural, with the physical and skills portion of the game.

Stanley became an acclaimed player and won numerous awards including more All-American honors. He began to be recruited by many universities and was, of course, recruited hard by South Carolina. On April 21, 1987, his older brother, Wayne, was assaulted by a group of young men. Wayne unfortunately, pulled out a pistol and killed the assailant, who was only eighteen years old, and wounded two other assailants. This event overshadowed Stanley's senior season and became a national story. It was an emotional rollercoaster for Stanley, as his recruitment could become a factor in whether his brother could obtain a fair trial. Threats were made by South Carolina fans from various directions that Stanley had better sign with South Carolina or things would not go well for his brother in his upcoming trial.

Coach Dale Brown of LSU, a national sports figure, made some calls in an attempt to help Stanley's brother. The LSU staff courted Jim Childers and his wife, Cindy, to come and work at LSU. Jim was offered a job at LSU, and in November 1987, during his senior season, Stanley announced that he would attend LSU. This did not sit well with many of the local South Carolina fans, and Stanley felt the brunt of those emotions. There were also threats from the families and friends of those killed and injured by Wayne. Coach Childers coached Lower Richland to another state title, but Stanley's senior season was anything but gleeful.

Wayne's trial was in February 1988, and even Jesse Jackson came down to speak on his behalf. Wayne was acquitted to the relief of Stanley's family, but Stanley still faced threats until he graduated. He even had to have armed guards for a period of time. After he graduated, he immediately left for LSU and Baton Rouge and did not return for well over a year when things had calmed down.

I did not meet Stanley until the day before I signed him, but I was friends with Jim Childers. I met Jim, who is a good friend to this day, through coach Dale Brown. I had contacted Dale on behalf of one of my amazing clients, a young black man by the name of Jonathan Shaw. Jonathan had been born with only one arm, three fingers, and no legs. He was in his teens when I met him. When I joined the law firm of Moore and Walters in 1985, his case had been pending for some time and was given to me to get it moving. It was a complex case involving the prescribing of medications while his mother was pregnant. Since I had extensive experience in medical and drug cases, I was given the file.

Jonathan's good arm was actually very strong, and he could move himself from the wheelchair to a car seat with little difficulty. My partner Ed told me when he first met Jonathan, he was on a skateboard and actually swung himself from the skateboard to a chair. Jonathan said he would talk about the case but did not want anyone to feel sorry for him. I began to move the case and arranged a meeting with Jonathan and his mother. I still remember him coming into my office (with his mother) in a wheelchair with a big smile on his face. He was and still continues to be an inspiration to me when I feel things are not going my way. Jonathan had obvious reasons to be bitter but was not, and really enjoyed his life despite his physical handicap. One thing I always think of was a conversation we had about what he liked to drink. He did not drink alcohol, and I asked him what he liked to drink. He said he liked milk and water but he "liked water the best because God made water." I thought, here is a man who could have chosen to be bitter about the circumstances of his birth, but he loves all things that come through the Creator.

Jonathan and I became quite close. He was a huge basketball fan and really liked LSU. He watched basketball on TV, and we would talk about the LSU games. He wanted to go to the games and perhaps see a practice. I was also a huge LSU fan and had started following the team when I went to LSU law school in 1976, but I was not as big a student of the game as Jonathan, who watched all types of basketball games, college and pro.

I was a big fan of Coach Brown, and had read about how he had been raised by a single mother in North Dakota, overcoming a great deal of adversity to gain his success in life. As a result, he liked to help individuals who were underdogs in one way or another. He was an outspoken critic of the NCAA and the many rules and regulations placed on a coach's ability to help his players and their families. He seemed to always have the time to promote many causes, and still lead the LSU basketball program to national prominence. I read about the many individuals he had helped throughout the years. Jonathan and I discussed it, and I thought that he would help get Jonathan into games and perhaps allow him to watch some practices. Jonathan would really enjoy this and perhaps it would get him interested in attending college.

When I called Coach Brown, he was eager to help, as usual, and put me in touch with Stanley's old high school coach who was now at LSU. Jim Childers is a first-class individual and was a highly acclaimed high school coach, having won three state championships in South Carolina. I should note, he won the first championship with limited talent.

Though I have no proof, I'm sure that Jim had been led to believe by Head Coach Dale Brown that at some point he would be coaching at LSU. He stayed at LSU for eight years but never officially coached for LSU. When I met him some time in 1989, his job title was administration assistant. I never saw Jim coach, but I'm sure he would have done a great job at LSU, if he had been given the chance.

I liked Jim immediately. I had not met a lot of people associated with athletics at the time, and I was pleased that Jim was very down to earth and somewhat quiet. We are almost the same age. He had not been in town long, and we soon became good friends. His wife, Cindy, has more of an outgoing personality. She is quite a talker, is funny, and can really tell a story. If you really want to know what's going on, you ask her because she won't mince words, whereas Jim sometimes tries to sugarcoat adversity. They are a fun couple and are each equally enjoyable to be around. Both can produce serious and funny conversation, which is not something you can always find in friends.

Jim and Cindy had their share of adversity. Their oldest child, Amy, had suffered an anoxic brain injury at birth and as a result had cerebral palsy. She is confined to a wheelchair, and even though her mind is sharp, she has no use of her legs and limited use of both arms. She is a delightful person and despite having some communication problems, loves to laugh, and one gets a warm glow just being around her. Stanley has a special relationship with her, and she really enjoyed his periodic visits throughout the years.

When I met Jim and Cindy, I could see they had done a great job raising Amy along with their son, Jay, who was a devoted brother and helped take care of his sister. Having interacted with several families with special needs children through my law practice, I knew the stress both physical and mental that caring for such a child can produce. Jim and Cindy made no complaints, but I could see concern in their eyes when speaking about her future medical care and particularly medical insurance. This was particularly stressful when Jim lost his job and the family moved back to South Carolina several years after I met them.

When I spoke to Jim about Jonathan, he was very eager to help him in arranging to go to LSU games and to get him in some practices. Jim understood perfectly the issues facing a person using a wheelchair in public spaces and took care of Jonathan. Coach Brown also said he would look into helping Jonathan gain entrance to LSU as a student.

Stanley had come to Baton Rouge as a Proposition 48 player, which means that the NCAA required him to sit out the 1988–1989 season. He only played one season at LSU, 1989–1990. The team that year had amazing talent, which included not only Chris Jackson (Mahmoud Abul-Rauf), Stanley, and Shaq but also Wayne Sims, Geert Hammink, and Vernel Singleton.

Naturally, I had been looking forward to seeing Chris Jackson play with Stanley and Shaq after attending games during the 1988–1989 season. That season, Chris put on one of the more amazing individual performances in college basketball history. I remember watching the Florida away game on TV when he scored fifty-three points, and thinking, like every other fan, that I could not miss another game. After the fifth game of his career, the Florida game, the attendance at the Maravich Center went from half-full to packed for the remainder of the season. Chris was named SEC Player of the year and a First Team All American, so expectations were naturally high for the next year when he would be joined by high school All Americans Stanley Roberts and Shaquille O'Neal.

I really enjoyed the 1989–1990 season and watching the talent that Coach Brown had assembled. I saw Jim and Cindy regularly, and it was, of course, cool to discuss the game with people who knew the game of basketball so well. Jim was quite popular around LSU and made the best of the fact that he was not doing what he really wanted to do, which was coach. His son, Jay, was an LSU ball boy, which he enjoyed, and Amy and Cindy attended all the games.

LSU had many exciting and memorable moments that season, including the Texas and Loyola Marymount games. I was excited about the NCAA tournament and watching LSU potentially reach the Final Four with all the talent on the team. Jim managed to get me two tickets for the NCAA Round of 16, which was taking place in Knoxville, Tennessee. My ex-wife very graciously gave me the okay, and my brother-in-law, Dicky Palfrey, and I drove the twelve-hour trip to Knoxville to see the games. We had a great time hanging out with Jim when he was not working, Cindy Childers, Craig Crase's wife, and the rest of the LSU fans. I even attended a pep rally for UC Santa Barbara and met the entire cheerleading squad.

1989 NCAA tournament in Knoxville; Me, Cindy Childers, Dickey Palfrey and Jim Childers; LSU lost to Georgia Tech.

LSU won the first game, beating Villanova 70-63, but lost in the quarterfinals to a very strong Georgia Tech team. Coach Brown received some criticism for the loss with the talent we had onboard, but in his defense, Georgia Tech was loaded with future NBA stars Brian Oliver, Kenny Anderson, and Dennis

Scott. Early on, LSU had a fifteen-point run, and it looked like we might blow out Georgia Tech. However, Georgia Tech stormed back and LSU only maintained a slim 41-40 lead at halftime. Georgia Tech shot the lights out in the second half and beat LSU in a 94-91 nail-biter. Chris Jackson did not have his best game but played with chest discomfort and shoulder pain. He had only thirteen points and missed ten of fifteen shots, which was not his typical game. Chris fouled out with minutes left in the game and LSU ended up ahead 88-87. Stanley had twenty-one points, fifteen rebounds, and four blocks, and Shaq had nineteen points, fourteen rebounds, and four blocks. Georgia Tech went on to play UNLV in the finals, losing 90-81.

After the game, Chris Jackson announced that he would enter the 1990 NBA draft. Chris hired a Mississippi attorney from his hometown as his agent. He was drafted by the Denver Nuggets as the third pick of the 1990 draft after Derrick Coleman, who was the first pick and Gary Payton, who was the second pick.

Unknown to me until recently, Coach Brown had spoken with Stanley after the Georgia Tech game as to whether he should stay in school or turn pro since he did not really like school. At that time Coach Brown had introduced Stanley to Leonard Armato, an attorney from Los Angeles who had negotiated a reported $300,000 shoe contract with Coach Brown for LSU to wear LA Gear shoes.

Leonard Armato played basketball for University of the Pacific as a guard averaging 12.8 points per game. In the mid 1980s, he had started working with sports companies as an outside attorney for such companies as Fila Sport and LA Gear Inc. Leonard had helped Kareem Abdul-Jabbar handle near-bankruptcy in 1987 after his representation by Collins referenced earlier. He had also helped found the AVP pro beach volleyball league in the 1980s. He had good timing with the

LA Gear contract gaining access to LSU basketball with Chris Jackson, Stanley Roberts, and Shaquille O'Neal on the roster.

Stanley needed to attend summer school in order to stay academically eligible. He really liked LSU and decided he would like to try to stay in school. Whether he would pass summer school and stay on the team was in question heading into the summer of 1990.

I was not aware of these developments at the time but would become aware of them sometime in the summer of 1990. The sports agent basketball information pipeline had this information because at some point in the summer, one agent had learned of my relationship with Jim and telephoned me inquiring as to Stanley's status and if my intent was to try to represent him. He also informed me that Stanley would have to go to Europe if he became ineligible because the NBA draft had already taken place. Jim and I may have had a short discussion at some point that summer about me representing Stanley, but the other agent's conversation was the source of my information.

I did have another connection to Stanley, as his girlfriend Ida Henry was working at our law firm. I had mentioned to Jim that I was a football jobber and that the players only worked in the summer. He asked if there was an opening. There was, and Ida was hired. She was a sweet and capable girl, and the entire firm really liked her work. Having two connections to Stanley did give me at least a chance, I thought, sometime in the future, to get into basketball representation, but that seemed like a hope for the future, as I had never even had a conversation with him at this point in time.

I was, in fact, looking forward to seeing Stanley and Shaq play together in the upcoming LSU season. However, the conversation with the other agent had peaked my curiosity about the thought of negotiating a contract in Europe. I had only been to Europe twice before, once on an extended trip between college and law school, and then again in the late 1980s. In college, I had studied some European history, and the thought of another trip there as an agent sounded glamorous and exciting. I began to read articles on European basketball and studying the legal requirements of being an agent there. The prospect seemed a little daunting, but at this point in time was only a far distant ambition.

My initial research showed that the agent business in Europe was less regulated than in the United States. There was no agent certification required by any union, so the contract between the player and the agent was the sole necessity to bind representation. There was no set fee, but I did read that the agent was normally paid ten percent of the contract, which was paid by the team at the time of signing. In fact, European representation could be very lucrative at ten percent, which was higher than the four percent maximum allowed by the NBPA. The fee was paid up front and not by the player over the course of the contract as required by the NBPA. Having been in the business now for a few years, I could just imagine the competitive nature of the business.

Europe had several levels of markets for U.S. basketball players. The top markets at the time were in Italy, Spain, and Greece for U.S. players who could not quite make it in the NBA or who were not offered guaranteed money by NBA teams. Only two foreign players were allowed on teams, and big men were always a valuable item.

European contracts normally came with guaranteed money; however, enforceability could be an issue since you would be dealing with FIBA, the governing body for basketball worldwide and potentially the jurisdiction of foreign courts. I did fortuitously read an interesting article about Real Madrid and its basketball team. Real Madrid with its premier soccer team is one of the largest sports corporations in the world.

The article concerned a player who had apparently agreed to a contract with the team and suddenly died. The main point that I took from the article was that Real Madrid paid the contract off even though there had been no official signing. This impressed me and stayed with me as I began to think about the reality of actually negotiating a European basketball contract.

I read that European contracts typically included housing, an automobile, and other perks to help the American player acclimate himself to his foreign environment. Normally, the money was tax free because the team would pay all the taxes. Though I wasn't sure of the mechanism of how this was accomplished at that time, it sounded like a good deal to me. I was to learn later that the team actually pays the foreign taxes due, which are usually at a high rate, and the player can get a tax credit for those payments on the U.S. taxes owed.

During the summer, I was practicing law and had the big break of signing Big Willie, so I spent considerable time on that venture. I also had three children: Katie, my oldest was six, Little O, my son was four, and my second daughter Mimi was only one year old, so it was a busy time and the summer passed quickly. I must add that my ex-wife, Elizabeth, was an excellent mother, and did take most of the pressure off of me as to the actual day-to-day care of the children so I could work.

Sometime in August, I received a call from another agent inquiring as to whether I'd heard anything about Stanley and whether he would be eligible for the upcoming season. I had not and told him to my knowledge he was eligible. I was not really concerned with Stanley at the time; however, the call did remind me that the issue of Stanley's eligibility was still in play.

It was about this time that Jim telephoned and told me that Stanley had not made his grades and was ineligible. Jim further related to me that Stanley wanted to hire an agent as soon as possible, because he was already receiving telephone calls about going to Europe and that his intent was to play in Europe for the upcoming season. Apparently, the European season was starting in a week or so, and time was of the essence. Looking back, I underestimated the amount and type of attention this situation would create. Specifically, I never anticipated the number of agents and associated persons who would want to become involved and the media attention that would be generated by Stanley leaving LSU to play overseas.

Since Stanley had lost his eligibility and wanted to sign with an agent to negotiate a professional contract, I figured I might as well take a shot at signing him, though I really thought I had no shot. I obtained Stanley's phone number and asked him if he wanted to meet. I was somewhat surprised when he said yes and that he would come over to the office. I knew that he had already been contacted by numerous agents and others, but one thing I did have going for me was my proximity and that I knew Jim. I know Jim had told him that I was trustworthy and that I had represented some football players. Jim later told me that he had recommended me over others because he knew me and he "knew that I would be honest and not take advantage of Stanley." I'm proud to say that to this day Jim still feels that I always had Stanley's best interest at heart after all the years of me representing him. Most importantly, Big Stan knows that I always looked out for him. We are still close to this day, even after many years of crazy experiences and ups and downs. Stanley was an honored guest at my sixtieth birthday party in 2014 and my second wedding in 2017.

Stanley came over on August 21, 1990, and we talked for over an hour. Besides Jim and Cindy, Stanley knew Willie and had worked with him on a construction site along with Shaq. No, they were not really working construction. Their job was to man a trailer out of the hot sun. Apparently the three hung out in the trailer the summer of 1989 and talked quite a bit.

Willie had told me at some point that Shaq was perfecting his rapping at the time.

At the end of our discussion, Stanley said he wanted to sign with me and begin the process of negotiating a contract. I really liked Stanley when we met, and I was now at the point of actually signing a big-time player. I took the signing of Stanley as a serious proposition. I knew I would do my best to represent him but wanted him to be sure of his decision, so I told him to take a night to think it over, and if he felt the same the next day, we would sign the papers. This shows how green and naïve I was at the time. I had already been stood up once with Eddie Fuller, but I did want Stanley to be sure of his decision. Besides, I'm not even sure I had the player-agent contracts ready at the time.

I was really wound up and could barely sleep Tuesday night. This is one of my biggest flaws, not sleeping well when I have a big event the next day. My mind just keeps working during the night even though I'm trying to sleep. I arose on Wednesday and went to the office and made sure the contracts were in order. Much to my amazement, Stanley did come in and sign the contract as he had promised, and we were off and running.

Running to where, I was not sure, but it was a thrilling race from the beginning. I did not realize it at the time, but signing Stanley really changed my life and brought me many adventures, new friends, and also a great deal of stress at times. Events began to unfold quickly that would ultimately be good for me in my efforts to retain Stanley as a client, which was going to be a huge challenge in the sports agent world. Just because you sign a player doesn't mean that he will be with you long enough to negotiate a significant contract.

Stanley needed to get some clothes and other items before he could travel to Europe, so I lent him some money and he took off. He did not even have a passport. I talked to Jim and told him Stanley had signed with me and I would give it everything I had to get him a good contract. I went to Stanley's apartment and met his Uncle Dale, who was in town. The apartment was a typical college student's apartment, complete with a beer keg in the middle of the living room.

Coach Brown was out of town when the news broke as to Stanley not being eligible. When Coach Brown came back into town, Jim told him that Stanley had already signed with me. According to Jim, Coach Brown said, "who is Oscar Shoenfelt?" I guess Coach Brown had forgotten that we had been introduced when Jonathan came to practice.

When Jim told me this, I was a little disappointed that my hero, Coach Brown, did not remember me, but I knew he was always quite busy. Eventually, we spoke, and he suggested that I let Leonard assist me with the contract. This suggestion seemed to make sense since I had never done a European basketball contract, and apparently Leonard had already been in the process of contacting teams about Stanley's availability before he actually became ineligible, which is pretty typical in the business, I would come to learn.

I had also begun to receive calls from several agents who were familiar with international basketball and had done European contracts. I listened to whomever called and gleaned information as to the European market. One theme was that the season was starting soon and there were not that many teams that had an opening and could pay big money. The contract had to be done as soon as possible, as the season started the next week and almost all the big paying jobs were filled. The agents all had European contacts and wanted to assist me in signing Stanley to a European team. Of course, they wanted half the fee for their help. I was careful because I had learned that haste in decision-making usually benefits those with the most knowledge. I also knew that if I turned over the negotiations to someone else, then I would lose part of my personal relationship with Stanley. Further, this was not just about signing a European contract, but also about representing Stanley when he was a top NBA draft pick next year. He had signed a player agent contract for international basketball and the NBA.

Like all agents, international basketball agents are aggressive, and some may even offer the player to a team even though he was not under contract with them. The stealing of clients was a common practice, a fact I did not know at the time. An agent would obtain the offer and then either work through the real agent or go straight to the player with the hope that the player would fire the real agent. With the amount of money involved and how quickly it can be delivered, there were those who had no problem with this tactic. The agent fee of ten percent is paid by the team normally upon the execution of the contract. For example, with a million-dollar contract, the fee could be as high as $100,000. The key, as always, is control of the player and being able to deliver him to the team.

My real knowledge of agents' business practices in basketball was limited at this time, and it would take me a year or so to get up to speed. My prior football experience was helpful but being a basketball agent is a different animal in many respects. There are only thirty NBA teams with fifteen players on the roster, and this includes players worldwide, whereas the NFL has thirty-two teams and fifty-three-man rosters with up to six practice squad players. The NBA is a much more exclusive worldwide club, so clients are generally much harder to sign than in football. Furthermore, the agent fees are guaranteed after the player is signed to a guaranteed contract.

By Wednesday afternoon, my signing of Stanley had spread to the news media, and I was being contacted by them for interviews. I had completely underestimated the amount of interest that would be generated by Stanley's turning pro.

I spoke with newspapers and gave a TV interview.

I also spoke with Leonard Armato or Gary Uberstein, a sports attorney who worked with him, about them assisting with Stanley's contract. This was per my conversation with Coach Brown. Gary and I discussed a sub-agency agreement, which he drafted and sent to my office on Thursday. I learned that Leonard had been aware that Stanley's chances of making the team for the upcoming year were not good, and that he had been in contact with some Italian teams.

I was also told that Armato was sending an employee, David Spencer, who had been a basketball coach, to Baton Rouge on his way to Italy to further advance the deal. This sounded a little strange, but seemed like a way to get a quick deal done for Stanley with some help with experienced agents. I really was not concerned with the money, and I felt that if Coach Brown recommended him, Armato would be a trustworthy partner or the best partner I could find. I really wanted to gain experience and make sure that Stanley was well taken care of for his first-year contract. Spencer's hectic arrival would of course put pressure on me to go ahead and do the deal through Leonard since he would have a man on the ground, so to speak. I recognized this type of sales move from my days as a door-to-door salesman.

Doing the deal with the other agents seemed out of the picture now since I would be meeting with Leonard's emissary shortly. Gary's agreement looked very professional and well written. I could tell from our conversation that Gary was super intelligent, and he seemed like a great guy. This was confirmed when I reviewed his academic and professional background. I wanted to review the agreement in some detail and discuss it with my law partners, but did not have time to with the speed of the recent developments. This would ultimately be a good thing because, looking back on it now, I realize that if Armato had done the deal, I would have lost control of the process and probably Stanley as a client.

David Spencer arrived Thursday afternoon and came to my office. He seemed to be a really nice person and was a "basketball guy," not a business guy like Gary Uberstein. In the sports agency world, there are people who are experts in the sport but not the legal and business sides of the sport. There are other people who are experts in the legal and business aspect of sport but not so much the sport. Of course, there are those who know both the law and the sport. Often those are athletes who played the sport and later attended law or business school. When dealing with basketball, I knew the legal and business side but not so much the sport side, since I did not play the game on a competitive level. I would learn a great deal about the sport over the years but still never felt like I knew basketball the way I knew football. David Spencer, having been a player and basketball coach at one time, was a sport guy whom Armato had apparently enlisted to work with him in what appeared to be recruiting, training, and taking care of players.

David was full of interesting news such as the fact that the Italians had been in town sometime in August and either worked Stanley out or watched him work out and felt he was out of shape. It seemed that the Italian deal was shaky now. The amount of money they were willing to offer had decreased and was not what I had projected and hoped for from my research. He also had brought Stanley a couple of pairs of basketball shoes, probably from LA Gear. We arranged to meet for dinner at Juban's restaurant. After our initial meeting, I believe he went to meet with Stanley and possibly Coach Brown.

At dinner that night, David and I had further discussions about basketball and Stanley's future. Interestingly, David was originally from Philadelphia and told me that he was courtside when Hank Gathers died in 1990. Ironically, that night, one of our waiters at Juban's was Dennis Tracy, who played basketball at LSU when both Stanley and Shaq were playing. Dennis would later become Shaq's personal assistant when he turned pro. David told me that he was leaving for Italy the next morning to try to further cement a deal, which seemed a little strange, but who was I to argue with an employee of Leonard Armato? During the course of our conversations, he told me that Armato would like to be able to sign Shaq when he turned pro.

I went home Thursday night thinking about what would be best for Stanley. It now sounded like the Italian deal was going down the tubes, or at least it would be less than the money I thought would be sufficient, based on my research and my conversations with other would-be agents. I wondered, should I sign the sub-agency agreement with Armato now that the sure deal seemed to be in doubt? If I signed that agreement, I would in effect be punting to Armato, not something my competitive nature was comfortable with at all. I felt like that would be letting Jim, Stanley, and myself down. I began to have some doubts as to whether I really had the experience to do an international contract with the sums of money at stake. I also weighed the option of the other agents who had promised big deals using their connections with various teams.

I slept very little Thursday night, pondering the options again and again. When I awoke, I went down to the office. I consulted some of my partners and the other attorney in the firm, Steve Thompson, whom we had recently hired. Steve was exceptionally bright and had come over from a big defense firm in town, Kean Miller. He had practiced some employment and labor law, which would prove to be valuable later, but really did not help with this quandary. I was still in the process of reviewing the sub-agency agreement when I received a telephone call.

The caller spoke in a foreign accent and introduced himself as Jamie Ibanez. He said he was in the country with the basketball general manager for Real Madrid, Jose Luis Lopez-

Serrano. Jamie said that he had talked with Coach Brown, who had told him that Oscar Shoenfelt was the agent for Stanley Roberts. He wanted to make sure that I was Oscar Shoenfelt and that I was Stanley's agent because he wanted only to deal with Oscar Shoenfelt. I was thrown for a loop initially, as I was not quite sure if the call was real or not. "Why would the general manger for Real Madrid be in the United States to make a deal when the news about Stanley had just been made public?" I wondered.

Jamie continued to talk and explained that the team (Real Madrid) was anxious to make a deal as soon as possible to sign Stanley. Jamie, I later learned, was originally from Medellín, Colombia, but he had grown up in Miami, so his English was very good, and he talked a mile a minute. His father apparently had a connection to the board of Real Madrid. Jamie is a real character, and we are friends to this day. He came to the United States to play soccer for Houston Baptist University and had become involved in the Houston college and professional basketball scene. On Friday August 24, 1990, all I knew was that he sounded legitimate and that he had to be somewhat legitimate because he knew Coach Brown, who had given my information to him.

We continued to talk, and I mentioned that other agents were interested in assisting me, but we had not come to terms. He insisted that he and Mr. Serrano were ready to deal now and that he only wanted to deal with me, the legitimate agent. I felt this could be a good move to make a quick deal, keeping in mind the article I read on Real Madrid and the fact that the Italian offer had been lowered after a workout. Jamie ended the conversation by saying that he and Mr. Serrano would fly to Baton Rouge and meet with me before day's end to discuss the contract. "Wow," I thought, "this is happening amazingly fast!" I suddenly felt like this was going to be a real chance at a great deal for Stanley with one of the best teams in Europe.

Since Jamie only wanted to deal with me, I put the sub-agency agreement on the backburner. I called Stanley and told him of these developments, and he sounded happy and ready to move forward. I also called Jim and told him that he should come over and meet the Real Madrid representatives. I went to lunch and talked over the developments with some members of my firm. At this point I thought about the fact that I had never even negotiated a European basketball contract. However, I had obtained some samples and knew what the basic considerations were from my previous discussions with other agents.

The most important consideration, of course, was the salary, which was to be guaranteed with taxes paid. This was different from NFL contracts at the time, where the only guaranteed money was the signing bonus, and no taxes are ever paid. Monetary bonuses based on playing time, honors, team performance, and statistics could be included. The player would also be guaranteed housing, automobiles, and other perks including airline tickets.

I decided it might be beneficial to have someone review the contract before we signed it, so I telephoned an agent who was not far from Baton Rouge to see if he would look at the contract for a fee. Of course, he agreed so he could get involved. He said he would arrive the next day. This sounded fine to me because I was sure we would take a day or two to negotiate the contract.

Jamie and Mr. Serrano arrived sometime in the midafternoon, flying in from Dallas, Texas. They did not go straight to my office but instead went to pay a courtesy call on Coach Brown.

Jamie and Mr. Serrano turned out to be quite an interesting pair. Jamie was five feet, six inches tall with a large head and a moustache. He was wearing a jacket without a tie.

He was and has always been a person who is very enthusiastic about what he believes in. He was there to interpret for and aid Mr. Serrano, the general manager. Mr. Serrano was of average height and wore a suit and tie. He appeared to not be feeling well.

Jamie did the talking, and he was really fired up about the prospect of signing Stanley. He knew a great deal about American basketball and had followed the LSU team and Chris, Stanley, and Shaq. Jamie relayed how they had been traveling for the past two days and had originally flown to Dallas to sign Larry Johnson, who was playing at UNLV. Apparently, they thought they had a done deal, but it fell through at the last minute, and Jamie had read the news about Stanley becoming available. They had immediately changed plans and contacted me to try to sign Stanley. Mr. Serrano had apparently been up for around two days and had developed a painful toothache.

Jamie and Mr. Serrano had spoken to Coach Brown, and while he was not complimentary of Stanley's work ethic, he did say that, at that time, Stanley had better basketball skills than Shaq. Jamie was very familiar with Shaq because of his notoriety and the fact that Shaq had played high school ball in San Antonio. Jamie had helped arrange for Carl Herrera to leave the University of Houston and sign with Real Madrid. He would be a teammate of Stanley's, if Stanley signed with Real Madrid.

Of course, Jim and I began to pump Stanley up and had a "Stanley highlight tape" that we showed them, which was impressive. When Stanley showed up and entered the room, Jamie and Mr. Serrano both kind of gasped—in a good way—at his size. Stanley had impressive size when he was at his ideal playing weight, which was 280 and even up to 300 pounds. He had reported to me that he had gained twenty to thirty pounds since the end of LSU's season, but his huge frame carried it well. Up to this point in time, there had been no mention of him working out before the contract would be negotiated, which I took as a good thing considering the lowering of the Italians' offer.

Stanley talked for a while with Jamie and Mr. Serrano, with Mr. Serrano understanding little and still looking like he was very tired and in pain. Stanley left, and Jim and I invited Jamie and Mr. Serrano to grab a bite to eat at Ruth's Chris Steak House. Jim's wife Cindy joined us. During the meal, I was able to further size-up Jamie and Mr. Serrano. Jamie again was carrying all the conversation, and he seemed to be convinced that Stanley would do great at Real Madrid. We did talk about the general outline of an overseas contract such as base salary, home, car, and bonuses, which confirmed my earlier research. I also knew I was dealing with a very powerful and honorable organization based on my previous reading.

It became evident that Jamie and Mr. Serrano had been depending on signing Larry Johnson since the season was to start next week, and Mr. Serrano had flown all the way to the United States to close the deal. This translated to me that they would be willing to get a deal done for Stanley coming to Spain. Mr. Serrano was tired and had the ongoing tooth pain even at dinner. Fortunately, Cindy was a dental hygienist at the time. Cindy called the dentist she worked for and he agreed to see Mr. Serrano right after dinner. Cindy took Mr. Serrano over for a quick-fix dental appointment immediately after leaving the restaurant. I thought Jamie was a real character and liked him, so we had developed some rapport to begin the negotiations. He stayed with Jim and me, and we headed back to the office.

When we arrived back at my office, we had not really discussed any terms, just that it would be great if Stanley could go to Spain. I had thought that we would begin discussions that night and hoped to come to an agreement the next day, Saturday, or even Sunday considering the late hour and

Mr. Serrano's condition. Stanley came back to the office to be available when I needed to confer with him. Mr. Serrano was delivered back to the office with his tooth feeling much better, and he was grateful for the dental attention. However, he naturally was still quite tired and jet-lagged.

We sat down to begin discussions and I began to try to feel out what they would be willing to pay. I had knowledge of the general market and the numbers that Armato had solicited from the Italians initially. I had discussed the numbers with Stanley, and they were in line with our goals for the contract. I kept in mind how the Italians had substantially decreased their offer after seeing Stanley's present conditioning. In addition, we had no other firm offers at the time and with the season beginning the next week, it might be difficult to find another top-level job with a great team. Finally, I knew Stanley was not in shape and was carrying twenty to thirty extra pounds.

Since graduating from law school in 1979, I had been negotiating settlements for lawsuits on both the defense and plaintiff side. Some of these negotiations had involved millions of dollars and some as little as thousands, but the principles of negotiation are generally the same. You need to prepare and be as knowledgeable as possible of the prevailing market; be aware of your goal and devise a strategy to accomplish that goal; give yourself the greatest leverage possible and exploit that leverage to the fullest in attaining your goal; assess your opposition and find out what their goals are and how you can turn that to your advantage; and not take a position that you ultimately cannot live with because, on occasion, you may be called on to live with that position.

We began to talk, and I was intent to let them give us their first number to see if they were even in the ballpark of the Italians. Then, out of nowhere, Jamie announced that they wanted to come to an agreement that night. He threw out a salary number that was twice as much as the prevailing Italian number and was considerably higher than the number the Italians were originally going to pay when they thought Stanley was in shape. It was also higher than any number that any other agent had said that he could get a team to pay.

My adrenaline began to flow, as I could see that Real Madrid really meant business and it was of the utmost importance to them to come to a deal immediately. I could feel that the fact that Mr. Serrano had been up for days and had a toothache that needed treating played right into our hands for a quick deal. Clearly, Mr. Serrano and Jamie felt it was of prime importance to get a deal done as soon as possible that night. I felt that now was the time to get a deal done and strike while the iron was hot, so to speak. In every negotiation there is a turning point, and this was it. I felt that to delay the deal would reduce our leverage, and that we had to go with the flow and push the terms of the deal to the max in order to keep our leverage. Real Madrid was not so concerned with the money but securing a great player and getting the deal done.

I went into a separate room and conferred with Stanley. He felt like the offer was low, even though it was the most generous we had heard, and I felt we would not be able to top it. He later confessed to me that in reality he knew it was a good offer but was really not that anxious to go to Europe. I had just known Stanley for three days, so I felt like I had to prove myself to him at this point. At this moment, it struck me that I should go for an outrageous figure to satisfy Stanley and get him committed to play. I decided to counter with a doubling of Real Madrid's initial offer and press Real Madrid to commit to that salary if the deal was to be completed that night. At that point in time, completing the deal as soon as possible seemed to be the most important condition for the team. Stanley agreed to the figure, although I felt that there was no way the team would pay it. If the deal was not done immediately, we still had a great offer on the table to resume with the next day, and I had the other agent coming to review the contract in the morning.

I went back into the room and thanked Mr. Serrano for the offer and politely said it was a good offer we would consider, but if we wanted to speed negotiations so we could reach a deal that night, we would need twice that amount! As I said this, I brought my hand down on the desk to emphasize tonight. Jamie and Mr. Serrano looked stunned, then looked at each other for several seconds and then nodded in agreement to pay the amount demanded to complete the deal as soon as possible. The basic consideration of the contract was agreed on that quickly! All money paid would of course have taxes paid. We then spent another hour or so adding on the housing, automobiles, and all kinds of bonuses that Real Madrid was willing to pay based on team and player performances.

The only flaw in the negotiations was that I had failed to discuss the agent's fee beforehand, which I had heard in foreign contracts was ten percent. When I brought this up, Jamie quickly said that it was only five percent, which struck me as odd; however, I had lost my leverage on this point because we had already agreed to the tremendous contract for Stanley. I felt like my client was the important thing, and that I was getting a substantial fee, which I had no idea I would be obtaining at the beginning of the week, so I accepted Jamie's statement without questioning it. My later experiences confirmed that the agent fee for foreign contracts is normally ten percent, but there were no set rules at the time. I was very happy with the five percent but always discussed agent fees before the beginning of negotiations thereafter. Lesson learned.

I did not know Stanley really well, but I was impressed with his street smarts in negotiations. After we had the salary in place, Stanley and I pressed for many considerations from the team, which it agreed to, such as several airline tickets for friends. I asked and received several first-class airplane tickets to Spain to visit Stanley, which were added to the contract. I was thinking that I needed to stay as close to Stanley as possible even though he was in Spain. I was also eager to finally use the Spanish I had studied for two years in college. I agreed to travel with Stanley to Spain to complete the contract in Spanish and to keep him company.

We wrote the contract out in detail, and Stanley, Mr. Serrano, and myself signed the contract to seal the deal. We had to go to a hotel to make copies for everyone. By the time we finished, it was almost 1 a.m. I believe everyone felt satisfied, as Real Madrid had their man and Stanley had a great contract.

The next morning, the other agent showed up to "help" with the contract. I related to him what had happened and informed him that the contract was already completed. He looked at the contract and said it looked great. I felt bad that he had wasted a whole day coming to Baton Rouge just to look at a completed contract, so I gave him a check for several thousand dollars to smooth things over. He accepted the check and left. I was told some years later that he was taking credit for the contract and showing the check as proof that he actually negotiated the contract. It proved the axiom that in the agent business no good deed goes unpunished, especially when it comes to other agents.

I began to prepare for my trip to Spain. The news of Stanley's signing had hit the news media, and I gave a television interview, which was something new for me. I received a call and was told that Stanley had somehow been bitten by a spider and had had a reaction for which he was hospitalized. Stanley's spider bite slowed our departure for several days. After he was released from the hospital, Stanley and I flew to Houston with

Jamie and Mr. Serrano. Wherever we went Stanley always caused a stir with people staring at the seven-foot, 300-pound plus basketball player. I admit it was an ego boost to feel I was part of such a newsworthy event and that I was now an actual agent involved in an international deal.

We stayed in an upscale hotel near Houston's Galleria for several days while Stanley obtained a passport. I had managed to dig mine up and was set for the journey. I had someone cover my schedule at work and had explained to my wife that the trip was unexpected, but I needed to complete the contract and get Stanley set up in his new job. Stanley and I flew first class on the trip over while Jamie and Mr. Serrano went coach. Jamie joined us on the trip over, as he wanted to help Stanley settle in and see Carl Herrera, who was to be Stanley's teammate. Each European team was allowed to sign two foreign players at the time.

Up in first class, Stanley and I had a great time eating, talking, and drinking some champagne. I fell asleep and woke up when we were preparing to land in Spain. The sun was just coming up, and as I saw Spain from the air, I was thinking what an unbelievable adventure I had stumbled into. When we landed, Jamie and Mr. Serrano were able to get us through the airport without going through the official customs. It was at the airport that I first realized just how crazy Spain is about sports, particularly about the famous Real Madrid organization. The primary interest in Spain is of course soccer, but basketball also has many fervent fans. When we arrived at the airport, there were about twenty reporters and photographers present. Spain has several daily sports newspapers, and Stanley was big news even before he arrived.

Over the course of the next several days, we tried to get Stanley up and moving. He was of course jet-lagged, but he had also become ill and was somewhat homesick. Jamie thought it would be a good idea to see if Jim could come over and help Stanley acclimate himself to the European scene. This sounded good to me, so Jim came over for several days to support Stanley and help him get mentally ready to begin his pro career.

Stanley had gone from being a college basketball player playing in his own country to being a pro player on an internationally known team in little over a week, which would be a big change for anyone, much less a twenty-year-old. Stanley used one of his travel tickets to bring his girlfriend, Ida Henry, over to keep him company. We were waiting on his apartment to be readied for him to occupy it. Stanley needed a translator to help communicate with the coach and most of his teammates. However, Carl Herrera was from Venezuela and had lived in Houston, so he spoke Spanish and English well. I became acquainted with Carl and enjoyed discussions with him about Venezuela and America.

While Stanley was spending a lot of time resting in the hotel and acclimating himself to play, I was meeting with Jamie and others to ensure that the contract was being implemented properly. Jamie introduced me to Arturo Ortega, an attorney who worked as the Spanish agent for an international group of basketball and soccer agents headed up by Luciano Capicchioni, who was based in San Marino, Italy. Arturo was the agent that drafted Carl's contract with Real Madrid. Arturo is a first-rate individual, and he is one of the few agents that I could actually trust. I consider him a friend and still keep in touch with him on occasion. He has since left Capicchioni but I believe is still working as an agent.

At the time, Arturo was representing the big Russian and NBA player, Arvydas Sabonis, who was then playing in the Spanish League. Stanley would play against Sabonis when he began actually playing for Real Madrid. Arturo and Jamie seemed like a good team because Arturo was extremely low key with a mild temperament in contrast to Jamie, who at times could be overly enthusiastic in evaluations of players and teams. With Arturo's help, we converted Stanley's contract from English to Spanish and made sure everything was in proper order.

I got to know Jamie and Arturo really well. They were not only showing me around Madrid, but introducing me to some great Spanish foods in various restaurants. Jamie was enjoyable to hang out with because of his constant enthusiasm over everything, but especially Spain, Real Madrid, and basketball. He could talk about these subjects nonstop at an incredibly rapid pace, using numerous hand gestures to emphasize his points. Jamie, as Jim and I would joke, could sell snow to an Eskimo. Jamie informed me that he had a lot of connections in the Houston basketball community and that we might be able to do some business in the future.

Arturo Ortega and client in Spain.

During my stay in Madrid, I enjoyed getting to use some of the Spanish I had learned in college. I did get stuck many times listening to Jamie making a usually lengthy point in Spanish to another party that I did not understand. This really instilled in me a desire to bring my Spanish to a higher level. I vowed to understand more when I returned in December to check on Stanley's progress. I kept this vow to some degree, but I would still need years of practice to really feel comfortable speaking Spanish.

Jim returned to the United States after a few days, but I stayed several days longer. During that time, Jamie and I went to a Real Madrid soccer match. I had heard about the world's love for the real "football" but was still in awe of the number of fans and their enthusiasm for the team. The crowd of over 100,000 was very loud and loved to sing and chant for their team, Real Madrid. I would also experience the fervor of the fans and their singing and chanting at a Real Madrid basketball game when I came to see Stanley play at the end of the year.

After approximately ten days in Madrid, it was time for me to depart, as I needed to get back to my family and my real job. I was reaching the point of some burnout after the sequence of events of Stanley's signing, negotiating the Real Madrid contract, our trip to Houston, and my extended stay in Madrid, but it had been an amazing experience. Jamie told me he would be staying there for several more weeks to help Stanley get acclimated and move into his apartment. Stanley had not begun to play when I had to leave. My plan was to keep up with Stanley by telephone on a near day to day basis, and to return some time at the end of the year or the beginning of 1991, so I could actually see him play and monitor his progress. I already had the airline ticket guaranteed in Stanley's contract. On the plane ride back, I recounted the events of the past several weeks and really felt like God had blessed me with all that had occurred and that I might have a chance to turn my agent business into a full-time occupation. I have told big Stan many times there are few people that actually change your life, but he did change mine by trusting me to become his agent.

After my return to my normal life in Baton Rouge, things had changed, because every sports fan in Baton Rouge knew me not as an attorney but as a sports agent. It seemed that wherever I went, people (men primarily) wanted to discuss Stanley and his departure from LSU. It was kind of cool, I must admit, to actually have people interested in my work, but I kept my ego in check somewhat, remembering that I was making a living not as an agent but as an attorney. The actual fee I had earned with the Real Madrid contract did not nearly justify the time and money I had spent on the adventure; however, I finally had broken through and actually made some money with the sports business. Besides the several thousand dollars I had given the agent that reviewed Stanley's contract, I had also spent a portion of the fee on some of my expenses while in Madrid. However, the team had picked up part of my hotel bill and my plane ticket. I did not charge Stanley for any of those expenses that the team failed to pay but still came out in the black.

I did come back from Spain with a new Rolex wristwatch, which I had obtained as $4,000 of the contract fee. It was partly gold and silver with Roman numerals, which I really liked. I knew that I would never go to a store and actually buy such an expensive watch as some of my personal injury attorney friends would have done. Jamie had suggested that I could get a good deal on the watch because I would be obtaining it directly from Rolex, which was a team sponsor. He had such a watch and I was swayed by him to go ahead and just get the watch as a reminder of the Real Madrid deal. I really liked the watch and wore it for over twenty years, until I developed hand problems and could no longer handle the weight on my hand. I recently gave the watch to my son "Little O" who is now a physician. I actually looked to determine what the price of such a watch would be when I returned to the United States, and it was a little more than $4,000. So even though the watch was not such a great deal, it was a fair deal and I really enjoyed it. Ultimately, I was grateful Jamie talked me into getting the watch.

My law partners were understanding and excited about my seeming breakthrough into the sports agent world. All the publicity had created some excellent public relations for the firm. The law business was still going well, and the firm was in the process of building a beautiful new office. I put an advertisement out to hire an assistant to help me with my law practice and the sports practice and requested that the person be bilingual. Shortly afterward, Angela Gary applied for the job and was a perfect fit. Her father, a physician in Houma, had seen the ad given it to her. Angela was tall, intelligent, attractive, and spoke fluent Spanish. She had lived a year in Spain and was familiar with Real Madrid and thus would be the ideal person to work with Stanley on some of his personal needs while he was in Spain. Angela was athletic and had been involved with sports most of her life. She was an excellent tennis player and even had attended a year of law school. Angela was also extremely mature and poised and could handle all kinds of people from team owners to professional ball players, which would be crucial in the job. I placed her on my letterhead as in charge of "public relations."

For the next several weeks, I continued to chat with Stanley and Jamie to see how Stanley was doing. Angela was constantly in contact with Stanley and was even helping him with problems like getting appliances installed. Stanley was sick for several weeks after I left and working on losing his extra weight.

Several weeks after my return, I was surprised to receive a bill from Leonard Armato for close to $5,000. He was demanding payment for the expenses he had incurred for sending his employee to Italy to "work on Stanley's deal." I had not instructed Armato to send his employee, David Spencer, to Italy and had never signed any type of agreement with him. Of course, I was not inclined to pay any part of the bill. I knew that Leonard and Coach Brown were close, so I met with Coach Brown and asked for his opinion about the bill. He suggested that perhaps Stanley should pay the bill because it was his contract around which the bill had been incurred. I remember talking to Stanley about it. He, of course, did not feel like he owed it and was not going to pay it, and I agreed. I thought about it and really did not want to get on Coach Brown's bad side, so I went ahead and paid half of it to show my good faith. When I told Stanley that I had paid half the bill, he said something to the effect that me paying Leonard anything was really stupid, because Leonard was "trying to get me to fire you right now." Stanley's statement hit me in the gut, but again taught me the valuable lesson that in the sports agent world almost anyone will try and poach your client. The stealing of someone else's clients is how many notable agents made their start and is of course portrayed vividly in the film *Jerry Maguire.*

This lesson was brought home to me again in several months when Stanley had actually begun playing and had moved into his apartment. I was on the telephone with him when he told me that an agent, Joel Bell, showed up at his house with pizza. Joel was then employed by Advantage and was in Spain visiting with a client. I had information that Joel had begun to court Stanley as a client. I could hear him in the background, and he told Stanley to put him on the telephone. Stanley did, and I introduced myself and said I would be coming to Spain around May first. I told him that I appreciated the professional manner he was exhibiting around my client and he said, "I'm talking to him." I asked him if he was trying to get Stanley to sign with him and he responded, "we're talking about different things." I asked him if he knew that Stanley had signed with me; he responded that he knew and "I really don't care." I asked if he was a lawyer and he said yes. I asked if he considered it ethical to approach other people's clients when they are under contract, and he retorted "absolutely." This statement really disheartened me and put me on high alert as to what I would be facing in trying to retain basketball clients. Subsequently, I researched Joel's background and learned that he had graduated from Duke law school, which of course is a major accomplishment. I remember thinking how pitiful it was that a Duke law school graduate was in Spain bringing pizza to my client in order to get him to fire me. "Oh well," I thought, "this was my welcome to the real world of sports agency," a thought that would prove prophetic to actions of others during my tenure as an agent.

Jamie, Stanley and I arrive in Madrid in August 1990 where I met Carl and his son.

SIX

1991: The NBA Draft

———·•·———

As 1991 rolled around, I was beginning to feel that I was on my way to establishing a real career as a sports agent. I felt like Stanley's signing and the successful negotiation and implementation of the Real Madrid contract gave me some street credibility in the world of basketball. Stanley was projected as a potential lottery pick for the next draft, which made me feel I had an exciting year coming up. By now, I realized the cutthroat nature of the business and keeping Stanley as a client was my top priority. Joel Bell's stated intention to steal my client and Leonard Armato's apparent move to dislodge Stanley had impacted me, and I realized that I was in a business now that was even more competitive than football agency, which had made the plaintiff's personal injury business seem tame. Basketball was the wild, wild west of client-signing with slicker, more intense competition, but more of an upside if you could complete the contract. This was an arena where espionage, secret contacts, counterintelligence, and disinformation were really in play, just as in the political campaigns in which I have been involved. I did enjoy these components of the job, although it did bring with it a new type of stress.

By this time, I had a letterhead with "SHOENFELT SPORTS MANAGEMENT" on it with my name listed and the fact that I was NFLPA certified and NBAP and CFLP registered. For good measure, I listed my father on the letterhead with his address and the fact that he was a CLU or certified life underwriter to advise clients on insurance issues.

I made a mid-season visit to Madrid to visit with Stanley, to check on his progress and continue to build our relationship. I stayed in his apartment and had a great time seeing him and Carl play basketball for Real Madrid. Stanley had lost weight, was playing well, and was a huge star in Madrid. I visited with Arturo Ortega and also with Miguel Soler, a former Spanish gymnastics champion whom I had met on my first visit. Miguel was working in Madrid with a gymnastics show, and we would remain friends for years to come. He moved to Las Vegas with his show years later. Madrid was very different in the cold of winter, but still a lively city, and having some friends there made it very enjoyable. The basketball games were a real experience, with fans chanting, waving flags, and really getting into the games.

After the success of my mid-season visit to Spain, I felt like Stanley and I had been through a great deal together, and consequently felt more secure in our client-agent relationship. My parents vacationed in Spain with a friend and were very excited to meet Stanley and see him play for Real Madrid. However, Eddie Fuller's commitment and next-day disappearance had taught me that client relations can change quickly. Now with a genuine realization of the nature of the business, I anticipated that it could be even more difficult to keep Stanley as a client when he returned to the United States. Back in the States, Stanley would be open prey for numerous other agents, their runners, and anyone else whom they might convince to become a co-conspirator to poach Stanley, including the powerful shoe companies.

I knew that I had done a great job for Stanley thus far by relying on my previously acquired skills, the resources I had available, and the series of lucky events that had made his signing and the Real Madrid contract possible. It was now up to me to continue to be up to the job of properly representing Big Stan and even to try to obtain some additional clients to finally begin making some real money as an agent. This would help justify the time and resources I was spending on my sports agency practice as opposed to my successful law practice.

After a background check, I became a certified NBA agent, which consisted of paying the $1,500 annual dues and attending a seminar. The NBPA has its own set of player-agent regulations, which was in booklet form in 1991, and remained the same until a recent change in 2016. Some of the major recent changes included raising the dues to $2,500 a year and requiring a test if you were not currently certified. I remained a certified NBPA until 2006 and then became recertified in 2014, and still am as of June 2020.

At the agent seminar, each agent was given a player-agent booklet containing the names of all certified agents and whom they represent. I remember reviewing the list and thinking that perhaps someday my name would be on the list with several high-profile clients. The prospect seemed exciting, but I did not get my hopes too high. The booklet also contained contract information for every NBA player, including information on all current player contracts such as salary, signing bonus, length of contract, and amounts and types of guarantees. The booklet included various charts with one showing where each player ranked in the league in salary.

My observations as an agent were that the NBPA, though

extremely helpful, did not obtain free agent and draft signing information from agents nearly as rapidly as the NFLPA. I thought this was the case because the few powerful basketball agents generally were not as willing to give up information to aid other agents in negotiating draft and free agent deals. My impression is that the NBPA does not have the teeth or will to really bite powerful agents who do not report information quickly. However, basketball draft information is probably not as important, because of how the basketball CBA deals with first round draft picks. Further, there are so many fewer players drafted in the NBA than in the NFL. In dealing with free agents, the information would of course be helpful, but it is reported in the media, which helps in setting the range of a potential deal along with the salary information and salary cap information available through the NBPA. A salary cap basically is the most that each team can spend on all of its players combined. There is a salary cap in both football and basketball, which is negotiated by the Players' Union (NFLPA and NBPA) with the team owners in the CBA.

I began to study the NBA CBA in detail so I would be an expert in its nuances when the 1991 draft rolled around. After some study, I became familiar with the terms of the CBA and called the attorneys at the NBPA with any questions I still needed answered. I also began a study of the potential draft picks for 1991 to see who would be Stanley's competition in the draft. I really wanted to deal from a position of knowledge and power when I negotiated Stanley's contract. My legal practice had taught me that knowledge is power in negotiations from a substantive view, but also from a procedural point of view, which in this case was outlined in the CBA.

A significant difference between the NFL and the NBA, that was immediately apparent, was that because of the number of players normally on an NBA team (fifteen), there were only two rounds in the NBA draft as opposed to the twelve rounds in the NFL. The NFL currently has seven, and the NBA still has only two. Because of the number of players involved in the NFL, players contracts were not guaranteed; whereas in the NBA, first-round picks and some high second-round picks normally had contracts that were guaranteed for the entire length of the contract, which for first-round picks could be up to three years. The NBA has what is called guarantees for skill, which means if the team cuts a player because he is not good enough, he still receives his entire contract. An NBA contract is also normally guaranteed for injury, which means that if a player is injured and can't play, he still gets his contract paid out. If an NFL player is injured and can no longer play, he does receive a portion of his next year's salary, but not his entire contract.

An NBA contract usually does not contain any significant signing bonus. High-round draft picks in the NFL receive guaranteed money, but it is paid in the form of a substantial signing bonus, which the player receives when he signs his contract. The amount of the signing bonus decreases with the player's place in the draft.

I had not given up on football and was still recruiting some potential 1991 draft picks during this time frame. Willie had grown up and played with two highly rated draft picks from Houston, Kanavis McGhee and Alfred Williams, who had played on Colorado's newly-crowned national championship team. Willie had been moved from tight end to tackle at Phoenix, and was a really big guy weighing over 300 pounds on his six foot, six and a half inch frame. However, he really did not seem that large to me, because I had been spending so much time with Big Stan. My brother and I had met Willie in New Orleans for the Sugar Bowl, and we had talked about Colorado's success and his friends on the team. I figured it was a long shot to sign either Alfred or Kanavis, but asked Willie to see if his friends wanted to come down to visit in Baton Rouge and see some of New Orleans.

Willie agreed and arranged for Alfred and Kanavis to come down. I picked them up with a limo at the airport. Norma and Ed Walters were again nice enough to host the two Colorado Buffaloes at their house, and Willie came over to Baton Rouge to help entertain his friends. We had a great meal at Ed's house, and the players told us that one of their teammates, Charles Johnson, was going to be on the *Johnny Carson Show.* We watched the program and Charles gave a great interview. C.J. (Charles) had been the second-string quarterback until an injury knocked out the starter, Darian Hagan. C.J. took over and led the Buffaloes to the national championship with a win over Notre Dame. He also scored the winning touchdown in the famous fifth down game at Missouri on October 6, 1990. I did not know that C.J. and I would later become good friends. He is currently an assistant athletic director at Colorado.

Willie and I took Alfred and Kanavis to New Orleans for a night of entertainment after the big meal at Ed's house. New Orleans was fun, and as the two were departing to go home, they invited me up for a visit to see Colorado. Kanavis said I could stay at his condo. I thought about it for a while and then accepted. I had been to the University of Colorado on one prior occasion, a weeklong trial seminar, during summer when I was a second-year associate at Adams and Reese. I thought it was an amazing campus and wanted to see it in the winter. Colorado had several other potential draft picks, and I thought I might sign someone. Furthermore, it couldn't hurt to befriend a number of potential NFL players.

I flew up and stayed at Kanavis's condo, just as he promised. Boulder was really beautiful in the winter, and I had a nice stay. I met the quarterback, Charles Johnson, who told me to call him C.J. He was a bright young guy and not interested in playing any more football. He was thinking about becoming an NFL agent, and I cautioned him about many of the pitfalls. He certainly knew a lot of potential players, having played at Colorado; however, one thing I learned was that not many NFL draft picks are willing to put their future in one of their teammates' hands, no matter now close the relationship. In any event, we kept in touch and discussed him coming to Baton Rouge, which he did some time later. I thought perhaps he was someone who could be a potential football partner in the future.

C.J. was a member of the Omega fraternity, just like Willie, which led to some interesting conversation since I had read Willie's book on the fraternity. While up in Colorado, I did get to meet some of the other players, including Eric Bieniemy. Eric was really funny, with a big personality, and I enjoyed meeting him and getting to know him for a short while. I did not sign any players from my trip, but did enjoy the visit and following the careers of the players with whom I had become acquainted. I stayed in touch with Alfred and Kanavis through Willie and C.J., and we have remained friends to this day.

One great source of information and potential help in my newly-developing basketball business was my newfound friend, Jamie Ibanez. Jamie had been involved with the ins and outs of college and professional basketball for several years, especially around the basketball mecca of Houston, Texas. He was a member of a large Baptist church that had a huge gym where many of the pros worked out, including Hakeem Olajuwon. He had great seats for the Rockets game and was on a first name basis with Steve Patterson, the general manager of the Rockets.

Jamie always maintained that same enthusiastic attitude that had been on display when we did Stanley's contract. When he talked, he made it seem as if the sky was the limit with my agent potential. Jamie was a real character and I enjoyed his company, but I did keep in mind his natural tendency for some exaggeration, depending on what he was trying to accomplish. I was lucky to have met him when I did. He seemed to be looking for an agent he could trust to work with some potential pro basketball players, and I was glad to oblige.

As I had learned while in Madrid, Jamie was very close to Carl Herrera and had mentioned that I could probably represent Carl when he made the transition from Real Madrid to the NBA (the League), which could happen in the near future. Carl was six-foot nine and 215 pounds and had been a second-round pick (thirtieth pick) of the Miami Heat, but had gone to Spain to play for Real Madrid. Jamie had contacts with another 1991 potential draft pick who was playing for the University of Houston named Álvaro Teherán. Jamie introduced me to Álvaro, and it was clear he had some potential to play in the League.

Álvaro was seven foot one and originally from Cartagena, Colombia. He played at Houston Baptist from 1987 to 1989 and then at the University of Houston from 1989 to 1991. Álvaro was a little taller than Stanley, but did not have his size, weighing around 235 pounds. He was laid back, like Stanley, had a big smile, and was a lot of fun to be around. He told me that when he came to the United States, he could not speak English, so he watched TV all day to help him learn the language. By the time I met him, he spoke English well enough to communicate, and we had some interesting conversations. I met Álvaro on a visit to Houston, and Jamie and Álvaro came over for a tour of New Orleans. We toured the French Quarter and spent part of a night at Pat O'Brien's, the famous bar located in the Quarter. Álvaro had a good time, and we developed a good rapport for my future representation. Álvaro agreed to my representation and signed a player-agent contract, so I had not one, but two players signed for the upcoming 1991 draft. Álvaro was not projected as a first-round pick, and would most likely be playing in Spain the next year. He would be represented there by Arturo, but it certainly did not hurt for me to be listed as his NBA agent in terms of furthering my sports career.

Angela and Alvaro at our office 1991.

Jamie and I were now in communication on a regular basis, and he knew that I was planning a spring trip to visit Stanley with a ticket I had from the Real Madrid deal. Jamie was bringing Álvaro over to check out a potential Spanish team in Málaga, Spain, an interesting city that I had never seen. We combined the trip, and Jamie, Álvaro, and I flew into Madrid where we were greeted by Stanley and Carl. By now, Stanley was ready to come home, and was leaving Real Madrid to get ready for the draft. Real Madrid had made it to the finals of the Koraĉ Cup, a FIBA (Federation International Basketball Association) trophy, with Stanley and Carl on the team, but both would be heading to the NBA for the next season. Stanley would be staying in Baton Rouge, and Angela was ready to set him up with accommodations.

After meeting with Arturo, whom I now considered a good friend, Álvaro, Jamie, and I proceeded to tour a bit and went to Málaga, Spain, where we met with team officials and saw a basketball game. There was even a photograph in the local paper of me sitting with the general manager at a game. This proves again that, in Spain, there is very close media coverage of all sports. We finished the trip by going to Barcelona for some sightseeing and came back to the United States. It was a nice trip, and it was easy to travel in Spain since Jamie and Álvaro spoke fluent Spanish. I continued to study and practice my Spanish during the trip.

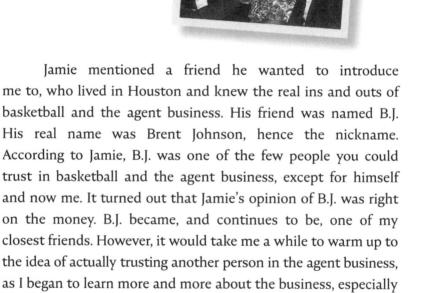

Alvaro and I in Malaga Spain.

Jamie mentioned a friend he wanted to introduce me to, who lived in Houston and knew the real ins and outs of basketball and the agent business. His friend was named B.J. His real name was Brent Johnson, hence the nickname. According to Jamie, B.J. was one of the few people you could trust in basketball and the agent business, except for himself and now me. It turned out that Jamie's opinion of B.J. was right on the money. B.J. became, and continues to be, one of my closest friends. However, it would take me a while to warm up to the idea of actually trusting another person in the agent business, as I began to learn more and more about the business, especially given Jamie's periodic leaning toward exaggeration. B.J. and I would not connect until late 1991 and the first part of 1992, after I had gotten to know him better and needed someone with his experience to help me.

Stanley's return to the United States now put him in close proximity to old friends who would not only do his bidding, but wanted to take advantage of his newfound potential wealth. While in Spain, he had met some of these hangers-on, but now more people had ready access to him. Since Stanley is an incredibly nice person, he became an easy target for these "friends." These people included not only women but also those who would give him access to all the temptations that have brought many an athlete down. I was there to give him advice and help him with his professional and personal needs, but I could not really shield him 24-7 from those he chose to associate with.

Upon returning home, I threw myself into preparing for the upcoming NBA draft, which was scheduled to be held on June 25, 1991, in New York City. I had already sent some preliminary information on Stanley to all the NBA teams, indicating that I was his agent. In truth, basketball players are normally well-scouted, and Stanley had played at LSU and professionally at Real Madrid, so he was well exposed. However, I put together a highlight film from LSU and from Real Madrid with statistics and information on Stanley. According to the 1991 early draft publications, Stanley was a projected lottery pick in the 1991 draft, which meant he could go in the top fourteen picks. Most publications had him in the top ten based on his basketball skills, athleticism, and physical presence. Two of the other potential best big men in the draft were Dikembe Mutombo and Luc Longley. Having seen Stanley play, I certainly felt that he belonged in the top ten, and I felt he could compete with those two, particularly offensively. However, there were concerns by the teams about Stanley's work ethic and his ability to control his weight, which could overshadow his actual playing ability.

Since Stanley had just finished a pro season that lasted longer than the college season, he did not wish to participate in any of the pre-draft camps. I understood his wishes and felt that his ability to play was not the real issue in a decision to draft him. Also, I was in a position where I could not really order Stanley to do anything. He was now twenty-one years old, had played a year of professional basketball, and weighed over 300 pounds.

We had become close, but he, at times, had his own agenda and would listen to my advice, but not necessarily heed it. Very few people, except his mother, Ida, could make him do anything he was against. I did learn early on, after Stanley's return to the United States, that yelling at him not only had no positive impact, but in fact, caused him to react negatively. I can say with certainty that though Stanley chose his own path, he did not blame others for the consequences of the road he had decided to travel. I always respected that about him. I can say, throughout the years, he had several opportunities to heap blame on me for events that occurred, but he never did that.

Stanley and I after his return from Spain.

There were numerous teams that wanted to fly Stanley in for pre-draft interviews. NBA teams do not want to waste any draft pick, much less a first-round pick, on a player with question marks, no matter how talented. The teams do a lot of detective work on each player and interview as many people with connections to the player as possible. This was even true in 1991. I fielded calls from many teams and attempted to set up as many interviews as possible. I told Stanley that I would take off work to go with him on the interviews, but he did not want me to go along. Instead, Stanley elected to take along one of his "friends," Dwayne, whom he had hired to run personal errands for him.

Angela was assisting me in keeping up with Stanley,

arranging his visits, and taking care of some of his personal matters. She and I worked on setting up Stanley's visits and were in contact with most of the NBA teams who wanted to see Stanley work out and meet him face to face. He was a no-show for an arranged visit with the New York Knicks, because of an automobile accident. Stanley reminded me that he did complete visits to Golden State, Washington, Atlanta, Los Angeles, and Minnesota. Unfortunately, during his tour he was eating hotel food, and the teams were gathering intelligence from his friend, Dwayne, about his training and work habits.

Over the several weeks of the tour, Stanley gained at least twenty pounds. Dwayne, not a professional agent, gave out information on Stanley. At least one article appeared describing Stanley's pre-draft tour, detailing his weight gain, and containing quotes from Dwayne that did not paint a favorable picture of Stanley's work habits. It was reported that while Stanley was in a meeting with Don Nelson, Dwayne interrupted the meeting so Stanley could take a telephone call. Furthermore, at one stop, when asked about Stanley's workout routine, Dwayne commented to the effect that Stanley had actually run a whole mile at some point in time like it was a major breakthrough, and that he was "not joking" and serious. Stanley told me recently that at the Golden State visit, Don Nelson had him scrimmaging and requested that he play down low, but Stanley was shooting three-point shots instead.

As a result of Stanley's "draft tour," his projected draft position began to drop. He was invited by the League to come to New York where the draft was being held, but declined, stating he was tired. Stanley knew that his stock had fallen, and he was not going to be caught sitting, waiting on camera while the TV analyst discussed this. Initially, I had planned to go with Stanley to the draft and bask in the glory of his being chosen a top pick, partly as a result of my own genius. Now I was faced with the truth of the sports agent business, which many forget when they talk about "super agents": the player makes the agent and gives him his power and not the other way around. Of course, it is true that the agent can assist the player with his sound advice, but the player himself provides the agent with the negotiating strength, and his skill only assists in completing the deal. Professional sports teams spend countless hours researching and evaluating potential draft picks during live workouts, at games, and on film, and do not rely on the agent's "sales puffing" when signing players, in my experience. However, it is true that the teams may at times look at the agent's handling of other client contracts to determine some pattern of his negotiation tactics.

I was disappointed that Stanley's draft stock had dropped, but came to the conclusion that I had done all I could to help Stanley and that attending an NBA draft when I was representing a first-round pick could be a once in a lifetime opportunity. I also knew that ultimately Stanley, in my opinion, had as much if not more talent than any other potential draft picks, and where he went in the draft would ultimately not determine the outcome of his career. I decided that I would fly to New York with my brother, John, and enjoy the city for a few days, attend the draft and get the experience of being at a live draft. John was thirteen years younger than me, but we had become very close when he came to live with me and my family in Baton Rouge in 1986. He was taking a break from college, and he came down to help me work in the senatorial campaign of then-Congressman John Breaux. Breaux won the campaign, and John had then moved to Washington D.C. to work as his intern.

After finishing his draft tour, Stanley returned to Baton Rouge and shut down, as far as meeting with any more teams. About a week before the draft, Stanley was not answering my calls, as usual. Angela then alerted me to a developing situation with Stanley. Somehow, he had come under the influence of a local boxing promoter named Dana Pitcher. I had never heard of him, but was told he was the cousin of a Baton Rouge judge who was a good friend of mine and our law firm.

Apparently, Pitcher was making an aggressive move on Stanley to fire me and hire him as an agent, even though he was not certified by the NBPA at the time. This type of move had been expected, and now the threat was here. Pitcher without my knowledge was sending out information to some NBA teams that he was representing Stanley, because he had some connection to the teams (as I recall). I may have been contacted by the teams, but Stanley had refused to go on any more trips after a certain point in time. Stanley told Angela that he was meeting with Pitcher, and she was keeping up with the process. Stanley had not fired me yet, but I was, of course, very upset and concerned. This was like a scene right out of *Jerry Maguire* when Jerry thought he was representing the number one projected football pick, Cush, and was fired by Cush's dad the night before the NFL draft. No agent contract had been signed, because Cush's dad did not like to sign contracts, but he told Jerry "you have my word, and its stronger than oak." I thought of this scene many times throughout the years when, after working hard for a player, I received the certified letter firing me.

Several days before the draft, I was told by Angela that representatives from Denver were actually flying into Baton Rouge to meet with Stanley and this fellow, Dana Pitcher. Angela was to be included in the meeting. I was livid, but kept my cool and immediately called a private investigator who did some work for our law firm, and put him on the job. He was to follow the parties when they met and obtain photographic evidence of the meetings and Pitcher's activities. I wanted to have documented evidence in case Stanley actually did fire me, to form the basis of a contractual interference lawsuit and a complaint to the NBPA regarding this potential agent's conduct.

The meeting did take place and the private investigator obtained photographs of Paul Westhead in the Baton Rouge airport with Stanley and Pitcher. It seemed incredible to me that NBA teams, knowing that I was representing Stanley and having a contract on file with the NBPA, would fly all the way to Baton Rouge and meet with Stanley and a non-certified agent claiming to represent Stanley, without me being present. In the legal world, an attorney would be sanctioned and perhaps disbarred for meeting with another attorney's client. However, negotiations are very different in the world of sports, particularly basketball, where huge deals can be cut informally, and the communications between players and management do take place through channels other than the player's agent.

Angela attended the meeting and continued to inform me as to Stanley's movements after the meeting. Following the meeting, Stanley did not fire me, a decision that Angela, I am sure, influenced. Stanley recently told me that Dana Pitcher was in fact working with Don King during the big coup attempt. Years later, I had an opportunity to attempt some sort of payback on Dana Pitcher, when I was appointed to the Louisiana Boxing and Wrestling Commission for four years under Governor Kathleen Blanco. I chose to let bygones be bygones since he had been arranging reputable boxing matches for some years. We actually had a shared smile on several occasions when he appeared before the Commission. At one point, I met Don King when he was in Baton Rouge to speak with the Commission. I'm sure Don had no recollection of any of the events surrounding Stanley and the potential grab of my client. Again, the only information I had about his involvement was secondhand through Stanley.

Surveillance photo of meeting with Westhead before draft.

My brother and I along with one of his friends who was a sports enthusiast did attend the draft, which was held at Madison Square Garden, with one of his friends who was a sports enthusiast. The draft was quite a spectacle, with many fans along with the players and their families gathered to see the players take their place among some of the most elite athletes in the world. It is truly an elite club, as there are less than 400 players on an NBA team during a year. Statistics show that only about 1.3% of college players make it to the NBA, a fact that I wish more basketball players would realize when they fail to obtain a free education at a university or college while playing college basketball.

A player does not usually make it to the NBA without working extremely hard, and making use of all the talent that God has given him. A player, no matter how talented, does not become a long-term player in the NBA without continuing his hard work and developing his talent. Some very talented players can get a shot with an NBA club, but talent alone will not keep someone in the League. Players need to constantly press themselves and develop their game. Players who have gotten by in college by being talented will be weeded out quickly in the NBA. Unfortunately, it is hard to learn new work habits when you hit the NBA, and talented, but lazy players, will soon be exposed. This is why NBA and NFL teams doso much research into players' backgrounds and work habits before the draft.

I was at the draft and saw Stanley slip to number twenty-three in the first round, when he was selected by the Orlando Magic. I felt relieved that he had not fallen further, and that he would get an opportunity with a guaranteed contract. Before the draft, I had spoken to Orlando management, which consisted of the well-known general manager Pat Williams and his assistant John Gabriel. Both of these guys were really professional, and I enjoyed meeting them. In fact, I must say that all the NBA management personnel that I met throughout my career were fairly easy to deal with, and I enjoyed the experience. It was the same with the NFL, but I never really developed the relationships with NFL personnel that I did with the NBA, except for a few members of the New Orleans Saints management. This was partly due to the sheer number of players that NFL personnel deal with compared to NBA personnel, and the fact that I represented Stanley and Ervin Johnson, who were both first-round picks and had lengthy NBA careers. This is also framed in the context of my work as a trial attorney, both as a defense attorney and a plaintiff's attorney. As an attorney, at times, you have to deal with some real jerks who are opposing you, but I really did not find that problem in the sports world.

Pat Williams was known for his humor and quick wit, and I found him quite an engaging individual to deal with when negotiating Stanley's contract, and all my dealings thereafter. I would consider him a friend, and did miss working with him after Stanley left the Magic. Pat had played minor league and college baseball, but had moved into basketball management in the late 1960s. He was one of the founders of the Orlando Magic, and was there when the Magic started playing in the NBA in 1989. He and his then-wife had five children of their own, but were well known for having adopted a large number of children of many races and nationalities.

Because of the draft tour and the publicity that ensued, Stanley's weight became a public sports topic. While at LSU, Dale Brown had also spoken publicly regarding Stanley's "struggle with his weight," though at LSU I do not think Stanley had really struggled with his weight to a great degree. In any event, Pat was not one to pass up the opportunity for a witty quote, and he was often in front of the media. He was and still is an excellent and interesting speaker with a wild sense of humor. In 1994, he wrote a "jock joke book" and sent me a copy with the inscription "To the Big O—Go for it and have fun. Pat Williams."

I believe Pat's quips about Stanley's weight started even before the draft. The one I remember most vividly, having read the poem by John Donne that says, "no man is an island unto himself," was that Pat said at one point that "no man is an island unto himself except for Stanley Roberts." Another quip was that the Magic had told Stanley "to start eating from the six basic food groups, and a month later there were only two."

Stanley and I did not really appreciate that Pat joked about Stanley's weight. I had been overweight as a child (in fourth and fifth grades) and still remember the taunting and being called "fatso." Stanley, like any person, did not like being made fun of by anyone, particularly his potential future employer. Some people tend to lose sight of the fact that professional athletes have feelings and emotions just like anyone else. They don't get paid to be abused, but to play their respective sports. I demanded, while we were in the process of negotiating and afterward, that Pat stop making jokes about Stanley's weight. Pat probably felt like he was trying to motivate Stanley with his quips, but it had the opposite effect, and I tried to impart this to him.

After the draft, I had spoken with Stanley about our contract negotiation strategy. Stanley and I both knew he had been drafted much lower than his potential to play in the

NBA. He had already played professionally one year in Europe against players such as the previously mentioned giant Arvydas Sabonis, who would later star in the NBA. Both he and I knew he would be successful in the NBA, if he was willing to use even a portion of his potential talent. He did not sit around and feel sorry for himself. He was now determined to show what he could do and try to get a much better contract over a short period of time. The safe bet, and what most, if not all, first-round NBA picks would sign in 1991, was a three-year guaranteed contract. This would give the player a good living, and allow him time to develop his skills while on a guaranteed contract to make it in the League. However, since we knew Stanley would be a star when he played, he suggested, and I agreed, to just go for a one-year deal, which would be guaranteed, but would make him a restricted free agent after one year. If he played well, we would have the opportunity to take offers from any other NBA team, sign a contract, and then the Magic would have only fifteen days to match the offer by agreeing to the exact same terms as the signed contract with the other team. The matching team (Orlando) would have no right to add or change the terms of the contract signed with the other team. If Orlando did not match the other team's offer, then the contract that had been offered and signed for the other team would be in full force and effect.

Being a restricted free agent could give us much more negotiating leverage than just being a draft pick. The restricted free agent status does not give great leverage at all times, but Stanley and I felt that in this case, if he proved himself, there would be other teams willing to put Orlando on the spot and offer Stanley a large contract at the end of the 1991-1992 season. I knew my NBA agent career was riding on this, my first contract, as Stanley was a first-round draft pick and the contract would be under a great deal of scrutiny when we went for the one-year. If Stanley did not do well and was out of a job with no negotiating power, I would look like an idiot for obtaining only a one-year deal. I knew other agents would get the contract and show any potential players what a terrible contract I made for my first client.

I began preliminary discussions with Pat sometime shortly after the draft. I had all the salary information from the prior year's draft and could see what the twenty-third pick had signed for the year before. In addition, I would have access to the contracts that would be negotiated for all the 1991 draft picks as they signed through the NBPA and the news media. I had some leverage in suggesting that Stanley might return to Europe, but in reality, he did not want to play again in Europe at that time. A main concern and top priority for Pat was to have some type of weight and conditioning clauses in Stanley's contract. He talked about Stanley's weight and conditioning a great deal and, of course, wanted him to be in top shape when he arrived at training camp.

Personally, I always wanted Stanley in top shape and would try to motivate him, as would Jim and Cindy Childers and the other coaches at LSU. He was able to use the facilities at LSU as an alumnus if he so desired. Stanley was a well-known sports personality in Baton Rouge, and because of his easygoing nature had many friends in town, some trying to influence him positively and some negatively. Stanley wanted to stay in Baton Rouge to train, and the consensus was that a personal trainer might be able to get him into shape. The hiring of the trainer would also help in the negotiations, as I could reassure Pat that Stanley was working and would come into camp in shape and ready to play, which would benefit him in preparing for his restrictive free agency for the next year.

I cannot recall the exact mechanism, but somehow, I was referred to a "holistic trainer" from Chicago who would come down and train with him until training camp. The difficult part was not finding a trainer—the sports world is filled with many such "gurus" of fitness—but to find a trainer who could connect with and motivate Big Stan. Frankly, I think any player who really wants to play in the NBA and NFL, if properly motivated, should be able to find the support necessary to train in many places, including his old university and large cities where many professional athletes work out, as in Houston, Texas. However, many agents now sell the player on their services by shipping a player off to an exotic site where he can "train" with some guru.

The ingredient, which mandates the agent be involved in a young player's training, is financing. Obviously, it is much easier for an athlete to train if he does not have to work and has his expenses of living and training paid for by an agent. I'm sure, as was my experience, that agents incur untold dollars in losses in financing training and living expenses for players who go bust and never make a professional team, or never earn sufficient funds to reimburse the agent for the money fronted. Of course, this risk does not come into play if you are representing high second-round and first-round NBA picks or high round NFL picks. At times, when a player jumps ship to another agent, conflicts can arise as to what expenses the player was to reimburse, and what expenses the agent was to bear. In the early days of sports agency there were some agents who filed lawsuits on such issues, but now this conflict would be resolved exclusively through an arbitration when an agent would file an agent–player grievance with the Player's Union. In order to be certified, the agent has to agree that this is the sole means by which he can pursue legal action against an ex-client. Fee disputes are also subject to this means of dispute resolution.

Most agents like to have a personal trainer in house or one they work with on a regular basis. This can be a big selling point when some players choose their agent. The key for the agent is not only to have a competent trainer, but also to have someone he trusts training his clients, so when the hopefully close bond between trainer and agent develops, the trainer will not be used by another agent to lure the client away. A close relationship between a client and another person, whoever he may be, can be an Achilles' heel through which another agent can obtain a foothold and steal the client. My experience was that most agents would not hesitate to grease anyone's palm for access to a new player and potentially big payday.

The holistic trainer was a very pleasant African-American gentleman who had trained several athletes. I never really figured out exactly what it meant to be a holistic trainer, other than that he ate natural foods and did not drink alcohol. The trainer seemed qualified and sold us on what he was doing. Stanley's team all felt it would be a great idea to have someone in charge of his training, and Stanley agreed to hire him. In retrospect, Stanley was probably going with the flow to avoid rocking the boat, so he could continue with his own game plan. He knew in his own mind, I'm sure, that the holistic trainer was no match for him in determining his own course of action. Stanley had a unique ability, which I would later term his "rope-a-dope" (after Muhammad Ali), that when a person was imploring him to do something, such as getting in shape, he could look that person in the eye, and convince the person that he was going to do exactly what that person said when his true intent was to do what he wanted as soon as the conversation was over. He used rope-a-dope to great effect on various persons throughout the years, including team owners, general managers, coaches, and yes, his agent. Stanley never would do anything malicious to any other person, but he had his own mind and would take some advice, but rejected advice as he saw fit. Angela met the trainer at the airport, and he gave her a rundown of his game plan. He had some type of special diet and emphasized mental discipline as part of his training program. I was anxious and a little nervous to see how successful the program would be with Big Stan.

Top Cat Update

During 1991, I was of course still keeping in touch with my other clients, including Willie "Top Cat." Willie was on the active roster for the Phoenix Cardinals, and was now projected as an offensive guard or tackle. Willie was feeling pretty comfortable, perhaps too comfortable, out in Phoenix after having made it the first year. He had grown his hair long and purchased a red Jeep, which he enjoyed driving around with rap music blaring. It seemed like harmless fun, but it's always better when you are on the bubble in making a team, to get attention from how you play, rather than your flamboyant lifestyle. Riding with him in the Jeep on many occasions was Eric Hill, who was rock solid with the team and could afford to have a more flamboyant lifestyle. I emphasized to Willie the difference between his status and Eric's, but he is a naturally friendly talker and enjoyed his time with his old LSU teammate. (Since his football career, Willie has had a great career as a bartender, working for the Ritz Carlton for many years.) Willie felt all would be well as long as he took care of business on the field. Apparently, Willie made frequent trips to Arizona State University where he became friends with several of the cheerleaders who enjoyed riding in his Jeep.

One night around 10 p.m., Willie pulled up in his Jeep to a light next to a car that was being driven by his head coach Joe Bugel, with his wife as a passenger. Willie apparently had the music blaring, his hair flying, and had as passengers a pair of Arizona State cheerleaders. Nothing was said that night, but the next day at practice Coach Bugel called the team up and gave them a reminder about acting like professionals when they were out in public, describing Willie's actions as a way not to behave.

Willie also had one other minor incident as a result of his joy riding. One Saturday afternoon around the summer of 1991, Willie was out in his Jeep with Eric Hill with the music blaring, cruising through Arizona State University. When Willie pulled up to make a stop, some words were exchanged with a faculty member in a vehicle next to his. At some point, Willie and Eric exited their vehicle and the campus police were summoned. A police report was written up, and Willie was given a summons. Naturally, Willie asked me to review the matter. My most salient memory of the report was the complaining party's description of Willie getting out of his Jeep, which stated that "the largest human being he had ever seen got out of the Jeep." Willie was huge at the time, and I'm sure the mere sight of him and Eric must have terrified the individual, but there was no physical contact between the parties.

We were able to smooth over the incident, but I told Willie that he had to remember he was not Eric, and he had a lot less of a margin than Eric as far as making the team. This is one lesson that all players should realize: the difference in making the team can at times be something as nebulous as whether the player is low maintenance, a good teammate, or a person you want in your locker room. In Willie's situation, I was worried that Coach Bugel would get the impression that Willie was a troublemaker, or that he was bad influence on one of the stars of the team, Eric Hill.

Usually, management's tolerance of a player's baggage off the field is proportional to the player's talent and playing contribution to the team. Later in my career, Stanley was playing with Minnesota and I was discussing some issue about Stanley with Kevin McHale. Kevin was making a point about player baggage when he commented to the effect that "Oscar, most players come with some baggage, but Stanley comes with a whole moving van of baggage."

Willie survived his little legal skirmish and went on to make the fifty-three-man roster in the fall. He played in all sixteen games at guard and tackle and started three games. He even scored a touchdown on a tackle-eligible play. I flew out to Phoenix and spent a weekend with him, took a Jeep tour, and watched him play. I saw him study his thick playbook before the game, and thought that he had really matured as a professional, and already had two credited seasons in the NFL. Willie's playing career seemed to be on the verge of really blossoming as we headed into 1992; however, the athlete's nemesis, injury, can occur at any time and in many circumstances.

Willie and me in Phoenix.

SEVEN

Big Stan Signs with Orlando and the NBA Life

Stanley at Orlando.

As the summer of 1991 was coming to an end, I was busy practicing law and working on negotiating Stanley's contract with Orlando. Pat and I had numerous discussions about various proposals including two- and three-year deals, but Stanley and I insisted on a one-year deal as planned. In July, I had talked with some teams in Europe that had some interest in Stanley, particularly one in Greece. I put this information out in the media, citing some big money numbers for the potential contracts, but the Magic and the media were not buying our interest in Europe. When he had visited, following the draft,

Stanley had commented to the media that he did not want to return to Europe, and this had been reported in the paper. In truth, both Stanley and I were ready for him to begin his NBA career. As I focused on the one-year deal, I attempted to get Pat to pay me more than what could be expected for the twenty-third pick in the draft, based on the previous year's signings. My argument was that Stanley could go to Europe, and he had already played professionally. I pointed out to Pat that he would, in fact, be taking a pay cut from the previous year when he played for Real Madrid.

Naturally, Pat was not sympathetic. He argued that Orlando had also drafted Brian Williams (later Bison Dele) out of Arizona, with the tenth pick in the draft, and Chris Corchiani in the second round and that he only had so much room under the cap to sign draft picks. Pat's argument had validity, but I would concede nothing at this point in time. I would later meet Brian Williams on several occasions, and found him to be a hard worker and quite an interesting individual whose background and interests were not typical for an NBA basketball player. He played several musical instruments and seemed more pensive in some ways than most players. I met his mother several times, a very elegant lady. I was, of course, saddened by his bizarre death in the Pacific after he had retired from the NBA. Stanley, was too, as he had Brian as a teammate for a year with the Los Angeles Clippers. Prior to training camp starting, Brian developed a medical condition that would delay his actual signing until November. I looked at Brian's illness as an opportunity for Stanley to get some additional work when he arrived at camp.

Initially, the primary disagreements on the terms of Stanley's contract centered on compensation, number of years, and a weight clause that the Magic adamantly wanted included in the contract. The weight clause would contain language that would allow the Magic to monitor Stanley's weight, and include financial penalties if he did not maintain his weight at certain benchmarks. Based on Stanley's past weight and conditioning issues, Pat was arguing that to include some kind of weight and workout requirement would be good for Stanley and the team. As much as the Magic wanted the clause, Stanley was equally determined to have no type of weight or conditioning clauses in his contract. As I had learned by this time, once Stanley made a decision on a subject, it was extremely difficult to get him to change his mind. Stan wanted a contract with as little control as possible over him personally, particularly his weight and conditioning. He was my client, so I was determined to come through for him on this point, even though staying in shape would obviously benefit Stanley too.

Meanwhile, Stanley was still in training with the holistic trainer, although I could never get any definite answer on how much weight he had lost. Frankly, I always had my doubts as to how the trainer would affect a change in Stanley's diet in such a short time frame. Jim Childers also mentioned to me that the trainer was waking Stanley up in the morning, and that he was now eating breakfast, which prior to the new training regime, he had skipped. Pat was constantly questioning me about the status of Stanley's conditioning and weight when he reported to training camp. I would respond that he now had a professional trainer and should be fine, which was my hope; but I did have my doubts, because the trainer and Stanley were both vague as to his weight, and what he was doing to get in shape. I visited some training sessions, and saw Stanley working out and completely drenched, wearing some kind of plastic sweat outfit. I finally had to just concentrate on the negotiations, and trust that Stanley and the trainer were really getting some work done.

As the negotiations wore on, I was in touch with the Player's Union and checking all the information available when other draft picks signed. I would now receive regular calls from different NBA sports writers, and writers from Orlando and Baton Rouge as to Stanley's signing status which did provide me with another source of information. Barry Cooper of the *Orlando Sentinel* kept in touch on a regular basis. Pat offered various deals with up to three years guaranteed, but Stan and I had decided on the one-year deal. I became confident that a one-year deal was not a problem, but Pat kept insisting that there be some type of weight and conditioning clause.

By early September, the European leagues were underway, and our threat of going to Europe really had evaporated. I was still throwing out numbers based on Europe as an alternative, such as a two-year deal averaging a million a year, which was way out of line for what the twenty-third pick should receive and the money that the Magic had in place to sign Stanley and Brian Williams. By now, it appeared that Corchiani would be offered a minimum contract of $130,000, which would not count against the cap. Based on the money that the Magic had to sign Stanley and Williams and the slotting for the twenty-third pick, it appeared Stan's contract should come in at around $600,000 for the first year.

Training camp was slated to begin on October 4, 1991. I really did not want Stanley to miss any of training camp since I had questions about his real shape and weight, and knew it would be better if he had a fast start to begin the season showing what I knew he could do on the basketball court. Our one-year strategy was based on him playing really well during the season, and I did not want him to be behind at the beginning of the season like he had been at Real Madrid. I also knew that Stanley would be better off out of Baton Rouge and in Orlando, where he would not have as many personal distractions and could focus on basketball. I was getting an ominous feeling with the lack of information coming from

Stanley and the trainer that it would be better to get Stanley to Orlando where he would have professional help from the Magic on his training. Angela was trying to keep me updated on what she could learn of Stan's true shape, but she was not getting a straight story from either the trainer or Stanley. She, too, was developing misgivings, like mine, about the holistic training situation.

The Magic had set a three-week voluntary conditioning program to begin on Monday, September 9, 1991. I took this as an opportunity to try to get a more realistic offer on the table, with the hopes that Stanley might make some of the conditioning. I decided to fly to Orlando to have a face-to-face with Pat, to get to know him better to aid in our negotiations and determine his bottom line. I flew down around September 4 to see Pat and discuss the contract in more detail. I enjoyed meeting Pat in person and our discussions aided me in evaluating where we were going with the negotiation. The meeting confirmed my thoughts that he was fine with a one-year deal, but again was determined to have the weight and conditioning clauses. No deal was struck, but I did gain some great background information for further negotiations. Again, when asked about Stanley's current condition and weight, I just retorted that he was working with his personal trainer.

After my return from Orlando near the end of September, I began discussing the ongoing negotiations with another attorney in the firm, Steve Thompson. Steve is very intelligent, very competitive, and was a great sounding board. He had met Stanley several times and had a good relationship with him.

As I explained the situation to Steve, it was nearing the end of September, and training camp would officially be starting on Friday, October 4. I felt it would benefit Big Stan to move to Orlando and get acclimated prior to the official beginning of camp. I told Steve that the big delay on the contract was Pat's insistence on the weight and conditioning clauses, which did not really give Stanley a significant amount of money, and which he would refuse to sign. It is important to note, as discussed previously, that when negotiating an NFL or NBA contract, almost all of the specific clauses and wording of the contract have already been negotiated by the NBPA and the Owners during good-faith bargaining, creating the Collective Bargaining Agreement (CBA). The actual player contract is contained in the CBA, and the agent and player negotiate more specific details of the contract such as salary amount; term of the agreement; what type of guarantees the player will have as to salary; incentive and bonus clauses; and other allowable restrictions such as weight and conditioning clauses, as Pat Williams was demanding.

Based on his experience in labor and employment law, Steve came up with an idea that we felt would give Stanley what he wanted, and get him into camp within a few days of its beginning. I had confirmed all of Pat's offers in writing, and we already had a "reasonable" base salary of approximately $550,000 on the table. Pat was dangling another $25,000 to $50,000 to get the clauses he wanted inserted, which could have affected payment of the entire salary. Steve suggested that we accept the base salary, and then tell Pat that we would accept the standard player contract that had already been negotiated collectively through the NBPA. The idea sounded good to me, and Stanley was agreeable, since he wanted to avoid those clauses he did not want in the contract. In the overall picture, considering the money Stanley had made and what we hoped he could make in the next year, $50,000 was not a significant figure to prevent the Magic from having the control they wanted over Big Stan.

I telephoned near the end of September and told Pat that Steve was to become part of our negotiating team as my labor and employment attorney. I then told him we were accepting the contract as is without any additional conditions with the base salary he had offered previously. I told him this was based on the advice of Steve and that we would be confirming by fax that this would complete the contract. To put some pressure on the Magic and enforce our position legally, I also told him I would be flying down on Monday, September 29 to complete the contract and prepare for Stanley's arrival. Pat was caught completely off guard by our legal maneuver, and I now felt that legally we had the superior bargaining position. I have to give Steve's knowledge of labor law the credit, a lesson I learned and would use again later. Pat was not happy and told me initially that the Magic could not be forced to take the contract without the weight clauses he wanted. He said he was going to consult his attorneys and get back to me.

I had emphasized to Pat that as far as we were concerned, the contract was completed and we had an agreement. I let the NBAPA know of our contract position and prepared to fly to Orlando to finalize the contract. I had the Orlando reporter, Barry Cooper, calling me regularly, and I let him know our position to put additional pressure on the Magic to accept the contract as it stood. Cooper wrote in the *Orlando Sentinel* on October 2, 1991:

> **Has an agreement-in-principle been reached regarding a contract for Orlando Magic rookie center Stanley Roberts?**
>
> Oscar Shoenfelt, Roberts' agent, insisted Tuesday that he and the Magic have agreed on all major terms, and that a news conference is imminent, perhaps as early as Thursday. But Magic General Manager Pat Williams insists he doesn't know what Shoenfelt is talking about.
>
> Shoenfelt, who canceled a trip to Orlando on Monday, said by telephone Tuesday that the contract is virtually a done deal.

"We have agreed to the length of contract and the amount of compensation," said Shoenfelt, an attorney. "The only thing left to do now is put some of the clauses in writing."

Shoenfelt declined to divulge details of the negotiations. The Magic reportedly had offered Roberts a two-year deal worth $1.2 million.

"The only thing that I am saying is that we have reached an agreement on the two major issues," Shoenfelt said.

Magic officials said Shoenfelt's optimism seemed odd. Late in the day, Williams said he had not spoken with Shoenfelt since Monday.

"I cannot react to any statements he may have made to you," Williams said. When asked whether a deal was imminent, Williams said: "We have a deal when the contract is signed."

Williams refused several times to answer questions regarding the state of the contract talks.

"I don't know that we have a deal," he said.

A news conference would be unlikely for today. Shoenfelt said Tuesday afternoon that he was preparing to leave for Houston. He said he will be negotiating a contract there today for Carl Herrera, whose NBA rights are owned by the Houston Rockets. Shoenfelt said he regretted having to cancel his trip Monday to Orlando.

"That had nothing to do with the negotiations," he said. "I had to cancel because of personal reasons."

Once our position was that the contract was done, my next obstacle was to get Stanley, the reluctant camper, ready to go to camp. Over the weeks of negotiation, Pat had continually preached that Stanley should already be in Orlando working out, and that he really needed to be there for the start of camp. He again kept asking about Stanley's weight, which continued to give me an uneasy feeling in the pit of my stomach. Stanley was aware he would be going, but was of the opinion it should be later as opposed to sooner. Although Stanley enjoyed the thrill of playing a game, he was not one geared to enjoy the rigors of training camp, and liked to play himself into shape at the first of the season.

Now that we had the contract done, Stanley let me know that he did not want to go down to Orlando until several days later during the upcoming weekend. I can't remember the exact reason that he gave me, but I seem to recall it had to do with him attending the upcoming LSU football game, which made little sense to me. I initially said that I was coming down on Monday, September 31 to finish the contract, but I put that idea on hold until we could get Stan geared up for training camp. I had to delay now to give us some logical explanation as to why Stanley was not coming down until several days later. Truthfully, I can't remember the exact details, but Cooper's October 2, 1991 story said I had cancelled the trip and was flying to Houston to work on Carl Herrera's contract, which seems like a reasonable sequence of events.

Pat had been talking to the media about Stanley needing a weight clause in his contract, and this was reflected in Barry Cooper's stories on October 3, 1991 and October 4, 1991:

> On the day that second-round draft choice Chris Corchiani signed a one-year contract for about $130,000, the Orlando Magic were left wondering whether rookie center Stanley Roberts would **agree to a weight clause.**

> Sources familiar with the talks said the only holdup is a weight clause. Roberts weighed about 304 pounds when he visited Orlando after the draft in June. There is speculation the Magic are insisting on weighing him each week.

If the issue regarding the weight clause can be settled, it is possible Roberts will sign today. The Magic open training camp Friday. The team's top draft choice is forward Brian Williams. His agent, Fred Slaughter, has not responded to telephone messages left for him.

The medical conditions of Smith, Acres and Kite are magnified by the absence of the two first-round draft choices. Roberts' agent, Oscar Shoenfelt, arrived in Orlando late Thursday night to finalize the player's contract. Roberts appears ready to accept a one-year, $550,000 guaranteed contract that would include **a weight clause.**

Since Steve was involved in the negotiations, he offered to come to Orlando with me. We flew down to Orlando on Thursday, the night of October 4, 1991. Barry Cooper wrote on Saturday, October 5, 1991:

Roberts and top draft choice Brian Williams, a 6-foot-9 power forward, became the first contract holdouts in the Magic's history. Their absence was immediately felt. With the rookies missing and Kite and Acres being held out, the Magic were forced to cancel some of their drills for lack of enough centers and power forwards.

Roberts' agent, Oscar Shoenfelt, arrived in Orlando late Thursday night, but two face-to-face meetings Friday with General Manager Pat Williams failed to produce an agreement. However, both sides said the deal is near, and Williams confirmed that he and Shoenfelt have agreed on salary and length of contract. The men are said to be haggling over clauses in the contract, possibly including **a weight clause.**

Shoenfelt is believed to have accepted a one-year, $550,000

contract that **includes a weight clause.** Neither side would discuss specifics of the deal. Williams said he hopes a final agreement can be reached today.

"We want to get this done so Stanley can get in here. I don't want him missing any of this," Williams said.

Shoenfelt also suggested that a settlement might be at hand. "I'm looking forward to seeing Stanley here," he said.

I had spoken to Pat, and he had consulted his attorneys and now seemed resigned to our position. Our strategy had worked, and we had gotten the result our client wanted, so Steve and I were feeling good about our unusual move. The local media had gotten word of our "agreement," and Steve and I were greeted by some TV cameras, which did feed my ego a bit. However, I still had at least two days to stall until we could get Stan in position to make the trip. Angela was working on helping make the arrangements and getting his things together. Bringing Steve into the negotiations gave me one more moving part with which to occupy Pat while we readied big Stan for his journey to Orlando. I was still constantly reminding Pat that Stanley had become sensitive to his comical references to his weight and that we had to have a gentleman's agreement that the jokes would stop.

After Steve and I flew down to Orlando on Thursday, we began an almost comical cat-and-mouse game with Pat, trying not to meet with him so as to finish the final details of the contract. This was so that Stanley's failure to arrive on the scene seemed reasonable. At some point, I remember being at my hotel and exiting the hotel quickly so that I missed Pat when he came by to chat. During this time, Pat was again asking about Stanley's conditioning and what his weight would be when he arrived in Orlando. Both Steve and I told him the truth but with the slant that he was so serious about his conditioning that he had hired a "holistic trainer." Naturally, Pat came up with many one-liners to describe the situation. Steve's arrival was great in that I now had someone to hang out with and take some heat off of me. Steve really seemed to enjoy the negotiations and being a part of the team. Despite the increase in manpower, the agent fee would, of course, be the same as previously agreed and even less than that mandated by the NBPA in the standard player-agent contract.

I felt like Stan was almost across the finish line on getting into the NBA and beginning his career. This was the journey that we had begun when he signed with me more than a year before. Angela was back home getting Stan ready to travel. Looking back now, I think the trainer may have pressured Stanley and persuaded him that he needed him as a trainer, and Stanley, being a nice guy, and really having problems telling people no, hired him just to make everyone happy. In any event, we would soon be able to see how effective the training had been when Stan rolled in for his physical. As Stanley's appearance neared, I was getting quite apprehensive since Steve and I had been assuring Pat that Stanley had been really working with his personal trainer.

Big Stan finally rolled in on Saturday, October 5 and we were able to get the contract signed. Pat was still disappointed that there were no weight and/or conditioning clauses. However, we never discussed this matter with the press. We had achieved the goal we wanted for our client by a nice legal maneuver, and Stanley was as pleased as punch, but there was not a need to bring any additional attention to Stanley's weight. I thought there was no need to correct the record in the media that we had agreed to a weight clause when we had not. We had accomplished our goal, and there was no need to raise new questions in the media about Stanley's weight. These types of clauses would play a factor in the negotiation of at least two more of Stanley's contracts.

After the signing of the contract, I went to the gym for Stanley's weigh in and a workout. The local media were present with cameras for the event. The press had reported that Stanley was 304 in June when he had come into town after the draft.

As Stanley headed to the scale, I really could not tell just from looking at him if he was significantly overweight. Stanley is very big-boned and can carry over 340 pounds before it begins to show, especially in street clothes. Stanley climbed on the scale and he weighed about twenty pounds more than before he started with the holistic trainer. Steve and I were sitting directly behind Pat, and as Stanley approached the scale, Pat was already coming up with more one-liners just based on Stanley's appearance. When Stanley weighed in, Pat looked at the scale and rolled his eyes. He then looked at me as if I was complicit in the weight debacle, which I guess I was, since I had helped to hire the trainer.

As the team workout began, it became apparent that Stanley was not in good shape to go with his weight gain. Pat continued to give me all kind of looks, some even comical as Stanley began to move around the basketball court being filmed by the media. Despite all this, Pat kept his sense of humor and Steve and I talked with him while the workout continued. Now I felt like we had at least crossed the first finish line and had Stanley in a position to allow him to do what he needed to obtain a good contract for next year.

As Pat and I talked, both Steve and I put on an outward face as if nothing was amiss, but I was really very disappointed with the result that had been obtained by the trainer and the fact that he had not given me any clue that anything was amiss. The trainer was now in Orlando at Stanley's behest to help him settle in and start training camp. I'm sure that Pat and the basketball staff would have liked to have him gone, but Stanley was the client and had wanted him to come down. I later learned that

Stanley was playing the trainer's game, to some degree, but was obviously not keeping the "holistic diet" as he had his friends smuggling hamburgers to him. When Stan was determined to do something, he usually made it happen, even though it may not have been to his ultimate advantage. Jim Childers used to call Stanley a "rascal "when he would go astray. As our relationship continued, I was amazed at some of the things he did, and no matter what happened, you could not help but love him.

The newspaper never revealed Stan's true weight, although some source leaked 317, which was not accurate. The public never heard any more about the weight clause because there was none. Stan was now in the NBA, the elite world player club, and had a stage to prove himself in one year, as we had planned. During that year, I would become really acquainted with the NBA player's lifestyle, and somewhat familiar with the perks of being an NBA agent. Personally, I much preferred being an NBA agent to being an NFL agent, but then again, I really only had one star NFL player, Rufus Porter, but I was blessed to sign two first-round NBA players and several other second-round NBA draft picks.

Oh, Give Me the Life of an NBA Player and His Agent

Initially, I was unaware of the protocol for how an NBA team handles the additional persons (entourage or posse) that may come with a particular player. For example, Stanley's trainer. There could be an issue as to whether the trainer would be granted access to view team workouts. Stanley's signing really brought me into the world of the exclusive club of those few players who have the pleasure of playing in the NBA.

Generally speaking, NBA teams not only work with the players in accommodating the additional personnel that may accompany a particular player but go to great lengths to ensure that the player has a pleasant work and home environment. In the NBA, even back in 1991, and more so today, the teams go out of their way to make a player feel at home and help him have an amazing lifestyle while making a great living. Naturally, the better the player, the more tolerant and accommodating team management will be to the player and those that surround the player. During the past twenty years, players have gained increased ability to move from team to team with free agency, and this has given players even more power to determine where they will play. This has led teams to continuously recruit players to come play for them.

Of course, many players have family and friends who become part of the network that travels and moves with the player. A wife and children would be expected to come with the player, but many players also have parents or siblings and even old friends that spend most of their time supporting the player or working for him. These additional persons may at times become part of the player's support group. Teams have to deal with the family members and friends, and usually these persons can be granted access to the behind-the-scenes operations of the team. At times, the agent will arrange assistants for the player. As an agent, it's always important to keep an inside track on what's happening with your client and those surrounding him. This is easier said than done.

Over the years, I met many family members and other friends at workout facilities and during and after games. These meetings were enjoyable for the most part. I remember spending a pleasant couple of hours one afternoon when I was waiting for a client, and chatting with some of Allen Iverson's "posse" as they had been called by the media. I was really impressed with these young men, who were quite friendly and entertaining. I had read several accounts of how Allen had helped support these friends from his early rough years after he had made it in the NBA. I always had and still do have great admiration for Allen as a player, but also for his loyalty to the people he knew really had his back and he could trust to take care of him.

Even though I have not had a client in the NBA for ten years, my reading convinces me that not much has changed. I noted recently in a newspaper article concerning a civil lawsuit brought against Derrick Rose by a woman accusing him and two other men of sexual misconduct, that the two men who were accused with him were some of his "childhood pals" who both work for him. LeBron James has successfully included several of his old high school friends and other friends on his management team, including making Rich Paul his "agent." LeBron recently became irritated when Phil Jackson referred to his management team as his "posse," though I'm sure Phil did not mean anything derogatory by the remark. In any event, for LeBron it made good business sense to put friends he could trust in charge of certain parts of his business to help himself and those friends, as long as they can handle the work, which it certainly appears they can. Naturally, the fact that LeBron is the single most influential basketball player in the world goes a long way toward the success of his agent and management team. Again, generally it is not the agent that makes the player, but the player that makes the agent ultimately successful.

NBA players meet many that pretend friendship, but have ulterior motives. This is true of sports agents: you have to be careful who you let close to your players, such as your employees. Many players have been stolen by other agents by hiring employees of their competitors. In addition, some of your employees may become agents and take your clients. A close relationship with each player is important because when your employee becomes closer to the player than you, there is the possibility of that employee leaving with the player. This is particularly true if that employee begins feeling the "juice" of fame and fortune from being in the sports business.

As an agent, you are always introduced as the player's agent, and this shows the reason for your presence. After several years, I did feel a bit of an identity crisis because of just being thought of as an "agent" and not an attorney. This was not a big deal, and it helped in my legal work. As an attorney, I was known for what I had done and my reputation and not just being the appendage of a player. Some agents gain celebrity to some degree, but their power comes from who they can attract as clients and from doing their deals. The recent *Sports Illustrated* article on Rich Paul showed that he has taken what representing LeBron gave him, and gone on to be a success in his own right. Of course, as long as he has LeBron, he has a trump card in his pocket in recruiting and negotiations.

The agent helps to support his prime players as much as possible, and may have assistants who help the player deal with looking for suitable housing, automobiles, insurance coverages, and other personal requirements. Some financial advisors take on some of this work. However, the agent wants to keep as much control as possible in choosing who the player relies on in his daily life, since control helps you to have continued employment as the player's agent, and thus future fees coming in on future contracts. There are always other agents looking for opportunities to step into the void if a player becomes dissatisfied with your services. If someone like a financial advisor is intimately involved with the player, the agent may have in fact lost that close player agent relationship which may ultimately lead to the player firing the agent.

Stanley was not married and unfortunately would end up many times relying on people who were not looking out for his best interests. Angela was very helpful in helping him move down to Orlando and setting him up in an apartment. She and her boyfriend drove down Stanley's cars and brought most of his personal items. However, Angela could not move to Orlando, and Stanley over time found some hangers-on to help him personally. These people were used at times by him to accomplish things that he did not want me to know about. Angela was available to help him with the most personal things he really needed.

Stanley moved into an apartment in Orlando and began his NBA career. He began working hard to get into shape and prove what he really could do on the court. I spoke with him often and went down to visit him, and he started playing well once he began to get into shape. I was enjoying representing him and was proud that he began to prove to the world what we both knew: that he did belong in the NBA and could be a dominating player, if he wanted to be. I now felt as if I had planted a flag on Mt. Everest, having taken Stanley from playing in Europe to the NBA, but I still had plenty to learn.

Teams may have individual real estate agents and others who get involved either directly or indirectly in helping the player settle into a new team and environment. There are always many persons who want to help support a young, well-paid celebrity in town. The sports world and the NBA in particular have an unimaginable number of vendors who show up trying to sell clothes, shoes, jewelry, automobiles, and anything else you can think of to young players who, many times, are convinced that buying expensive items will make them a "real player," which is, of course, a fantasy. I'm not saying that a player, from a business point of view, doesn't need to look sharp and dress businesslike on draft day, but he has to keep in mind that clothes, expensive jewelry, expensive automobiles, and beautiful women do not make you a player. Hard work and the development and use of your God-given talent is what will keep you in the League, not the material possessions that many feel are a necessary part of being a star.

The NBA schedule is set up in many ways to facilitate vendors and others who want to reap economic benefits from the players. Remember that there are eighty-two games in an NBA season, and half of those are on the road. The NBA player travels in a chartered jet to play away games, and is picked up at the airport and then bused to a luxury hotel like the Ritz Carlton. The player then may have free time and then have to go to shoot around the next morning on game day. A typed schedule is given out to each player and his agent for each NBA road trip, which can last a few days to a week. It's during these hotel stops that a great deal of personal business and "monkey business" gets done. It's no wonder that some players can become distracted on away trips with all the family, friends, and salespersons who may show up to see the player. Of course, what the player does in his free time is up to him, but going out to eat, milling around the mall, and going to clubs are popular diversions.

Anyone can look at most NBA players and wonder where and how they find clothes. There is no shortage of private clothes vendors who want to land an NBA player as a client. Naturally, the players will be well outfitted with all the athletic type gear they want from the team and their endorsed equipment partner such as Nike. But where do you go to get a nice suit made when you are over six-foot eight and 250 pounds? Private tailors show up at the player's hotel when they are on the road to do private fittings. A lot of the rookies are introduced to these clothes salesmen by their agents or other players. Car salesmen and jewelry dealers may show up at the hotels along with all kinds of professional autograph seekers who always seem to know where the visiting NBA team is staying. Players' friends and friends of friends may show up to add to the excitement of a visiting team coming to town. There always seemed to be plenty of women milling around the hotel when a team was in town. These women could be sent from friends of the players, friends of friends of a player, or women just hoping to meet a player.

If you spot a semi-professional looking guy in the hotel lobby with some type of small bag who is constantly on the phone, that will likely be a player agent. Some agents follow their client on the road with great regularity. You can arrange to stay in the player's hotel with the team and even get a discount on the room. Your client can provide you with tickets for the game, and in the NBA, visiting teams are usually given fairly good seats. You are seated with other guests of the players on the team, potentially including their family and friends, which always leads to an interesting evening. You have to watch what you say, because you never know who is related to whom, and any criticism of how a player is performing could result in being stared down or receiving a sharp remark. When agents are following the team, they not only bond with their clients but also bump into other players whom they may be able to poach from other agents.

Of course, the mood after the game is better if your team wins. All the friends and family of the visiting team are asked by security to sit in a special area so they can say hello to the players after the game, when the team is usually on the way out to fly home or on the way to another city. All the friends receive a visitor pass from the player, which tells security you are allowed to be there. When your player or players come out, it's always fun to congratulate them on the win (hopefully) and how well they played, whether they win or lose. At this time, you can meet the friends and family of your player who happen to be at the game.

I, many times, brought one of my children or a friend to the game, depending on where I was, and this was always a lot of fun for those who may not get to meet NBA players on a regular basis. I traveled a lot and even brought other attorneys to games and, on occasion, an expert medical witness. You'd be surprised how many physicians are basketball fans.

EIGHT
1992 Begins the Era of B.J.

————————— • • —————————

As the fall of 1991 rolled around, I was living the life of an agent, at least a part-time agent. Willie was on the active roster and playing in Phoenix. Stanley, a first-round NBA draft pick, was now playing in Orlando. Even though I really had little to do with negotiating Carl Herrera's contract, he was a second round NBA draft pick, playing for the Rockets in Houston, and I was his registered NBA agent. In addition, Álvaro Teherán, a second-round NBA draft pick, was playing in Spain, until he developed some medical problems. All in all, I now had some more "street cred" as an agent, and I was thinking in terms of, perhaps, making this more than a part-time endeavor.

My biggest concern centered on my experience with Stanley's personal trainer. If I was going to attract and hold clients, I needed someone I could trust who could work with me, and could help train the players and evaluate their basketball potential.

When I met B.J. on one of my trips to Houston, I had really liked him. He had a very outgoing personality, a very positive attitude, and always seemed to have a smile on his face. B.J. was African-American, six-foot three, about 195 pounds, and had the walk of a basketball player, because he had played basketball his entire life, including professionally, though not in the NBA. B.J., unlike me, had an extraordinary knowledge of the game of basketball, and he knew all the major players in professional basketball, including athletes, coaches, NBA general managers, and agents.

The NBA is similar to a big club with a lot of members who often change roles. The players at times turn into coaches and general managers, and even agents. Those working in the League who don't evolve from a player role, such as Pat Williams, usually come from some type of sports background or work their way up the food management chain. Generally, both players and management move from team to team, so everyone becomes familiar with each other.

B.J. just flat out loves the game of basketball! He loves to play it, watch it, and talk about it nonstop. His enthusiasm would carry over into his training and working with players, and his work with me. When we met, he had the player experience and contacts that would take me years of work to establish. He had played basketball at East Tennessee State from 1976 to 1977, and worked as a graduate assistant there from 1977 to 1978. B.J. was a close friend of Ralph Sampson and had grown up playing basketball with him, since they lived just a few houses away from each other. B.J. attended the Houston Rockets rookie camp in 1979, and just missed making the team. He attended the Boston Celtics rookie camps in 1981 and 1982. Afterward, he had traveled with Meadowlark Lemon from 1982 to 1987. B.J. attended the Houston Rockets veterans' camps in 1983 and 1989. He also played professionally in some of the lesser basketball markets in South America and Mexico.

B.J. was the partner I had been looking for, and was a

perfect match for me. All we had to do was spend some time together, and we became friends and gained a mutual trust. I had the resources of my law firm and my legal background, and B.J. had a tremendous knowledge of basketball and football, since he had also played football in high school. We were a great team, and rather than him working for me, we became partners. The fact that he was African-American was a real positive since it would help with recruiting clients; the large majority of our clients would be African-American. His presence would counter some of the agents who used race against me when recruiting.

B.J. had been working with an African-American agent in Houston named Sid Blanks, who apparently had hit a rough patch. Sid, with B.J.'s help, had signed several good players, but they were becoming dissatisfied. B.J. split with Sid, and this gave us the opportunity to start working together at the beginning of 1992. B.J. and I would have a great time working together, and he really made the agent business fun for me. Working in sports, and particularly basketball, was B.J.'s life ambition, so if we could make it work, he was ready to go. From our discussions, I thought his true goal, at some point, was to work for an NBA team, but this would give him, and me, a good opportunity to work in professional basketball until he could reach that goal.

Since B.J. had been around players most of his life, including such stars as Ralph Sampson, he could relate to the players we would be recruiting. He had helped recruit Olden Polynice in 1986, when he left Virginia, and went with him to Rimini, Italy. The next year, Olden was the eighth pick overall in the 1987 NBA draft. As an aside, while in Italy, B.J. met an Italian basketball enthusiast named Steffano Lotto, whom he would bring by my house later. Steffano and I would become good friends, and are good friends to this day. I have enjoyed many trips to Italy during which I would see and visit with Steffano.

Subsequently, B.J. had helped to recruit several other players who were drafted, including Tony White out of Tennessee, and Cadillac Anderson, and Rickie Winslow out of Houston. He had helped recruit and sign Chris Morris out of Auburn for Sid Blanks in 1988, when he (Chris) was the number four pick in the 1988 draft. After B.J. and I began to work together, I would become Chris's attorney, but never did sign him in an agent capacity.

Once B.J. and I decided to partner up, I had to convince the law firm that this was a good move. Steve Thompson was a partner now, along with me, Charles Moore, and Ed Walters. We had a good young attorney as an associate in the firm named Chandler Loupe, who happened to be my brother-in-law. Chandler had helped me take care of Stanley at times too. The entire firm liked the notoriety of being involved in the sports business, and our firm had received a great deal of free press from our involvement with professional athletes.

Even though I had been an agent for almost four years, I had really not made any money up until this point. I felt like I was just about to be able to demonstrate that we could generate some fees, particularly if Stanley continued to improve, as he was at this point in time. I pointed out to the firm that Stanley's contract negotiation at the end of the season could be huge, based on my hopes and expectations, now that the big man was playing well. The firm was aware of the results for Stanley after working with the holistic trainer. I explained that with B.J., I had a trustworthy partner who could help me recruit and then train and retain clients. My partners went along with my decision, and B.J. and I began slowly, but surely working together. He would continue to live in Houston, which was a basketball sports hub, but we would talk often, and visit each other in either Houston or Baton Rouge when necessary. We would travel when we needed to recruit and visit with clients to maintain our relationships.

Trip to Philadelphia with Álvaro

Álvaro Teherán had returned from Spain with an injury to his left ankle, which had also bothered him his senior season at Houston. Jamie, who was in Houston, was close to Álvaro and spent a great deal of time working with him, and had worked with Arturo in signing him in Spain; however, I was his registered NBA agent. I was working with Jamie to get him a shot in the NBA. Angela worked well with Álvaro because she was fluent in Spanish, and his English still needed work even after his stint at Houston.

At the beginning of 1992, we had some discussions about Álvaro signing with the Philadelphia 76ers, who had drafted him in the second-round of the 1991 draft. Álvaro had been the team's lone draft pick in the 1991 draft. The timing was not great since the team was already packed with centers, but the hope was that he could sign, show some talent, and begin developing for the next season.

A trip to Philadelphia was arranged, and I was to accompany Álvaro as his agent. At the time, Gene Shue was the general manager of the team and Harold Katz, the founder of Nutrisystem, was the owner. I had spoken to Gene Shue when Stanley was going through the draft, but I had never met or spoken to an NBA owner, up until this time. I was excited to learn that during the trip, both Álvaro and I would be taken to Mr. Katz's home to meet him. I read that he had a mansion in Philadelphia and was quite an interesting character.

We flew into Philadelphia on January 31, 1992, and were put up in a hotel. A team physician examined Álvaro and found he had a stress fracture in his ankle. As with any ankle injury, it was advisable for Álvaro to lay off the ankle until it had healed. He and I did visit with Mr. Katz at his mansion. He was a very colorful individual, and I was impressed that he had a full basketball court in his house. All in all, it was not a super productive trip, but I did enjoy the experience and spending some time with Álvaro. At the end of the trip, he returned to Houston, and I returned to Baton Rouge. Álvaro never made it to the NBA, and I never did make any agent fees, but I do have the memories of our travels in Spain, Philadelphia, and Houston. Jamie and Arturo had Álvaro return to Spain for the 1992-1993 season, and he played with the Fort Wayne Fury of the CBA the next year. He spent the rest of his career playing overseas, and we lost touch for the most part, though I did keep up with him at times through Jamie.

I spoke with Álvaro, on Skype a couple of times in the last few years after finding him on Facebook. I really wanted to go to Colombia and was planning a trip there; I thought Álvaro would be a great person to show me around Cartagena, his hometown. We talked and had planned to meet, but the trip never took place. I was saddened to learn, only recently, that Álvaro had medical problems and passed away.

NINE

Recruitment of Tim Burroughs and Portsmouth, 1992

———·•·———

As an agent, you have to continually be looking for potential new players to sign. This is done in order to generate new fees to pay your overhead and make some type of living. Early on, I had been thinking about and preparing for the 1992 draft. I tried to find some type of connection with players who would be graduating in 1992. Working through my current clients, I spotted one in Tim Burroughs, one of Stanley's high school teammates at Lower Richland in Hopkins, South Carolina. Tim was a potential basketball draft pick coming out of Jacksonville University in Jacksonville, Florida. He had played at Independence Community College from 1988 to 1989, Delgado Community College in New Orleans from 1989 to 1990, and Jacksonville University from 1990 to 1992.

Tim was a six-foot six, 240-pound power-forward born on October 14, 1969. Tim had a tough childhood, growing up in foster care. Jim Childers gave me some background on Tim and felt like he would have a shot to play in the NBA. I liked the thought of representing someone who had experienced some rough times growing up and making a positive impact on their career. Jim told me that Tim was so anxious to come to practice in high school that when he could not find a ride, he would run seven miles to get to practice. He seemed like someone who would work and give it all he had to make the League.

Jim arranged an introduction to Tim for me. I received Tim's telephone number and mailing address and sent him some materials. Tim was not slated as a first-round draft pick, but B.J. thought he had sufficient size and ability to make an NBA team; we decided it would be worth the time and money to try to sign him. If he was not drafted by the NBA high enough to obtain a guaranteed contract, he could always play in Europe.

Tim was talking to some other agents, but I did have two connections to him with Jim and Stanley. Stanley was now playing extremely well, and those who doubted our choosing a one-year contract were now eating their words. In addition, I had a new partner who knew not only the game of basketball, but the agent game as well. B.J. was an unbelievable asset and made the recruiting process fun. With B.J. as a partner, I now could offer the players a skilled analysis of their weaknesses and strengths and how they could improve.

Stanley's quick signing as a client and then immediately signing a pro contract was an aberration of the business, not the norm. Normally, the recruitment and signing of a player takes months, if not years. I focused on Tim late, but "in time" since he was not yet committed to any agent. I had made contact with Tim before B.J. came on board; however, now that we were together, he became a real asset in the recruitment of Tim.

B.J. gave me instructions on how most full-time agents spend their time. He told me that there were several pre-draft basketball tournaments that were necessary for an agent to attend not only to recruit players, but also to protect any clients you might have playing in the tournament from other agents. The oldest of these tournaments was the Portsmouth Invitational Tournament (PIT) held in Portsmouth, Virginia. This tournament invites sixty-four players who are all seniors. The camp is attended by NBA scouts from all the teams as well as scouts from European Leagues, and others. Generally, this tournament is not attended by players who are considered first-round NBA picks, but several of the players usually go in the second-round.

Portsmouth is the first of the tournaments and at that time was held in April. It usually started the first Wednesday after the Final Four, with the upcoming draft taking place in June. If the player does extremely well in Portsmouth, he may be invited to one of the later tournaments, which at the time took place in Phoenix and Chicago. The Phoenix tournament was held several weeks after Portsmouth, and many, but not all, potential first-round draft picks worked out there. The Chicago tournament was held shortly before the draft, and was a last-look tournament for players whom the League was still trying to evaluate. The timing of these tournaments has changed, and Orlando has replaced Phoenix as a tournament site.

The NBA scouting service was directed by a fellow named Marty Blake at the time. Marty had been the manager of the Atlanta Hawks and was the first general manger in the NBA to draft a foreign player in 1970. When the ABA and NBA merged in 1976, he had become Director of Scouting. Marty and his crew were responsible for the invites to the tournaments.

Any type of athletic scout is proud of his "discovery players," as I call them. Discovered players are players a particular scout has found in some obscure school, a minor league, or even in a foreign country, with the talent to make it in a major league like the NBA or NFL. Marty and his crew combed many of the smaller schools to find the hidden gem of a potential NBA star. For example, he is credited with playing a role in bringing Scottie Pippen (Central Arkansas), Jerome Kersey (Longwood), John Stockton (Gonzaga), and Joe Dumars (McNeese State) to the attention of NBA teams.

There is always a bit of braggadocio by agents of how they have the "connections" to get a player tryouts with professional sports teams. Although it definitely may help to know some professional general managers and scouts, generally professional scouts comb every possible source for new talent, and they will be the ones who may help get an obscure player into a tryout or a camp. If a player calls an agent asking them to help him get a tryout (although anything is possible in sports) in almost all circumstances, it is a waste of the agent's time.

I had met and spoken to Marty several times when Stanley was getting ready for the 1991 draft. We had talked about Stanley attending a camp. However, Stanley was not going, and I really felt it was unnecessary, since he had played an entire season at Real Madrid. Marty, of course, wanted Stan to attend the camps to give NBA teams more of an opportunity to evaluate him. The decision on what private workouts to hold, and which, if any, tournaments a potential basketball draft pick should attend, is a decision to be made by the player and his agent.

In football representation, the player and his agent will make a decision as to whether a player should attend the football combine, and the degree of the player's participation in the combine before the draft. Generally, if a player is considered a lock for an extremely high draft pick, the player will not work out or will do so in an extremely controlled environment of his choosing after the combine. If the player wants to improve his current draft status, he is naturally more willing to work out and display his physical skills and playing ability. Stanley was the only player that I signed that I felt did not need to go to a camp to perhaps improve his draft status. Of course, in my career as an agent, I was not in most circumstances dealing with high draft picks.

Tim had been invited to the Portsmouth tournament, which was a positive sign that he was on the radar of the NBA scouts. After B.J. worked him out, he felt he was a good potential client and that we should spend further time on trying to sign him. I talked to Tim on the phone several times, but knew I needed a face-to-face meeting to help close the deal and sign him as his NBA client. I arranged a flight to Jacksonville to meet Tim and his wife, Donna, personally. Tim had been married for several years to Donna, an older white lady. They already had two young children. I could tell Donna would be a major player in Tim's decision on which agent he would sign with. The fact that Tim was already married with children indicated that he would probably want job security. This meant that if he could not go high enough in the draft to obtain a guaranteed NBA contract, he would probably want to go overseas to ensure that he would begin making some money as soon as possible.

I had a good visit with Tim and Donna in Jacksonville. Tim was a physically imposing individual, and it was obvious he had the potential to be a physically imposing basketball player. He was animated and charming. He was a strong Christian and was very involved with his church. He had discussed his impending agent-hiring with the leadership of the church, and they wanted to meet me and be involved in the process.

At the time, my parents were living in Lancaster, South Carolina. Though I cannot recall the exact reason, it was determined that Tim would come up to Lancaster with his wife and some of his church leadership, and we would meet again at my father's house. The meeting was arranged, and I am sure that meeting my mother and father helped build Tim's, Donna's and the church leadership's confidence in me. My parents were not only avid sports fans, but very personable people and strong

Christians with years of experience and wisdom. We had a meal at my parents' house, said some prayers and sealed the deal, as far as Tim signing with me. He signed a standard NBA player–agent agreement and an overseas contract player–agent agreement for overseas basketball, which proved to be of some consequence later. After our several meetings and his eventual signing, I felt confident that I had a good relationship with both Tim and Donna.

Tim Burroughs and my Father at Dad's Lancaster house.

Portsmouth was the next step in Tim's representation. By this time, B.J. and I were working together with Tim as a client. I knew B.J. could give Tim help in not only his training and basketball game, but in getting an idea of what he would encounter at Portsmouth. B.J. filled me in on the game plan and what would happen at the tournament. We made arrangements to go, and my father said he would like to go with us. This sounded great to me, as I could spend some time with him, and he would really enjoy being part of the action. He had met Tim, and could help us further form a strong player-agent bond. I can't remember my exact route, but I'm sure that I drove up part of the way with my father, and that B.J. flew up and met us at Portsmouth. At any rate, our party included B.J., myself, and my father, all there to see Tim.

There was another player I had interest in seeing named

P.J. Brown; he played for Louisiana Tech. He had come on my radar when I was reading publications on the draft as a player from Louisiana who might go in the draft. Since I was raised in Shreveport, several of my high school football teammates played for Tech, and I had visited the school on several occasions. I had quite a few cases in North Louisiana, so it was not difficult for me to recruit that area. I knew that P.J. would be playing at the tournament from the list of players participating, and I wanted to speak with him, if possible, to see if he had an agent.

At Portsmouth, the players were initially divided up into approximately eight teams with each team having eight players. At that time, sponsors of the tournament would provide local coaches. The teams would practice and then play a round-robin tournament from Wednesday to Saturday. Every player would play twice, as they had winners' and losers' brackets.

During the tournament, I could see that B.J. was not exaggerating when he had told me he knew all the players in the basketball business. He knew all the NBA scouts, the agents, and the employees of the agents, and he would stop and speak with every one of them. When we were leaving the basketball arena, it would take at least an hour, with him speaking to everyone and introducing me and my father. When he introduced me, B.J. usually mentioned that I represented Tim and Stanley Roberts, and at times, Carl Herrera as well. The whole basketball industry knew Stanley was playing well and would be a restricted free agent soon. Big Stan was now shaping up to be one of the few really great big men who might be available in the near future for a team with a need at that position. I could feel that my representing Stanley and our strategy to sign a one-year deal were paying off and had given me some instant credibility with the other agents and NBA personnel. Because of Stan's pending new contract, my signing of Tim for the 1992 draft, and working with B.J., I no longer felt like I was perceived as a flash-in-the-pan-agent, but a real up-

and-comer in the industry. Of course, this was more my delusion than reality. As I used to joke, "I was a legend in my own mind."

Shaquille O'Neal was the headliner for the 1992 draft and would be the first player taken. I was not surprised in the least to learn that Leonard Armato would be the agent representing Shaq in the upcoming draft. Little did I dream at this point, that Stanley and Shaq might end up on the same NBA team in the future.

B.J. loved this tournament, as basketball was his great passion. Likewise, my father, the ultimate sports fan, was in his own element and loved to watch the games, meet the players, and talk about the game with B.J. and whomever else he might have been talking to at the time. Frankly, one game was sufficient for me in a day, and though I enjoyed the competition of being an agent, the day-to-day public relations with players and NBA personnel grew a little boring after a while. Performing the negotiations and creating the contract were my real interest, and my thrills came with negotiating the deal and securing a good contract for my client. Unfortunately for me, the actual negotiation and positioning for a contract probably only consumes ten to twenty percent of the time that the agent actually spends working for a client.

We spent most of the tournament watching and talking with Tim but also took an opportunity to speak with P.J. Brown when Tim was resting and not in the picture. P.J. proved to be a great guy and B.J. and I really liked him. I was familiar with Louisiana Tech and his hometown of Winnfield, and we developed a bit of a relationship. P.J. had a girlfriend, Donna, who would become his wife; she was from Slidell, Louisiana. I can't really remember if she was at the tournament, but I would meet her at some point in time and liked her too.

We would continue to pursue P.J. as a client after the tournament. I met with him and Donna at La. Tech on at least one occasion. I even went with him to his hometown of Winnfield to meet his mother. He came from humble means but was a classy individual. The more time I spent with P.J., the better I liked him. P.J. was down-to-earth, quite intelligent, and seemed to have a natural peace within himself. I really wanted to sign him, as I could tell he was the type of individual who, once signed, would listen to reason and probably remain a loyal client, even if hard and unexpected events occurred, such as getting cut.

However, it was not to be. I was visiting with P.J. in Ruston at La. Tech, and B.J. was supposed to drive up to help close the deal. For some reason, B.J. could not make it up in time. P.J. subsequently signed with agent Mark Bartelstein, whom I was familiar with, and is one of the few agents that I dealt with that I really respected. Mark had Louisiana connections which he had developed earlier. He represented "Hot Rod" Williams, the basketball player from Tulane University who was taken in the second-round in 1985 by Cleveland and made the NBA all-rookie team for the 1986-87 season, since he could not play in the NBA in 1985. In 1990, Hot Rod signed a seven-year $26.5 million contract, which made him, at the time, one of the five highest paid players in the NBA. Mark had done a good job in the negotiations and done well for his player. In fact, I had read about Hot Rod's contract when thinking about our strategy for Stanley. Hot Rod had rejected an $11.8 million guaranteed contract before his contract expired in 1990 in order to become a free agent the next year. The next summer, 1990, Miami extended an offer sheet of $26.5 million, which Cleveland matched. I was hopeful that some team would follow a similar course with Stanley that summer.

In addition, Mark was a competitor for LSU football players that were entering the NFL. He developed a particularly strong connection with offensive linemen at LSU and signed several over the years. He had represented the beloved

LSU player Eric Andolsek in 1988 when he was drafted by Detroit in round five of the NFL draft. On June 23, 1992, Eric (an NFL starter) was working in his yard when a tractor-trailer left the highway in front of his house, and tragically, killed him. This was a horribly sad day for all who knew Eric, and for the LSU fan base. In 1994, Mark signed Kevin Mawae, who had worked for me in the jobber program. Kevin to this date is very complimentary of the work Mark did for him. I have never heard anyone say that Mark did not do a good job in the representation of a player.

I always felt that if B.J. could have made it to Ruston for the final meeting, we might have signed P.J. I'm sure this is wishful thinking, but we were in the hunt for P.J. until the final bell. P.J. went on to be a great and consistent NBA player after being drafted at the top of the second round by New Jersey. He would go overseas for his first year, but then spend fifteen seasons in the NBA, winning an NBA title and earning all-defensive honors for three seasons. It was no surprise to me when he won the NBA sportsman award in 2004. I have run into P.J. several times over the years, and we have talked occasionally. At one point, he did tell me that Donna really liked me and suggested he sign with me. This made me feel good, but knowing him, he may just have been trying to make me feel better after having not signed him.

During the tournament, Tim proved to be an emotional player who would get really pumped up for the game. He would make ferocious sounds and put on an intense, almost crazy, face at times. I think he was trying to psych the opponents out with his ferocity. As the tournament wrapped up, we all felt that Tim had played well, but not good enough to get an invite to the next camp.

In any event, I enjoyed the tournament, especially hanging out with my dad and B.J. They formed a strong friendship, which would last until my father died in 2009. Of course, B.J. and I formed a close friendship beyond basketball that continues to this day. I formed a good bond with Tim, which would last for a while and prove interesting for the rest of 1992, but not afterward until recently. Leaving the tournament, I felt like I had learned a great deal about the agent business and basketball. I felt like we had a shot at P.J. and that Tim would probably not go in the first round, though anything was possible. I was looking forward to the draft and seeing what would happen with the rest of my clients but particularly Stanley.

I stayed in touch with Tim with pending draft news. I think we negotiated at least one card deal, as I had done for Stanley the year before. The draft cards were a big item at that time, and several companies were producing them. Stanley had done several deals, and though the money was not substantial, it did give the players a little spending money.

Prior to the draft, Tim went to Houston to work out with B.J. on several occasions. As a result, I became more familiar with some of B.J.'s training techniques. B.J. was not only a world-class person, but also the ultimate basketball player himself. He held himself to the highest standard of a professional athlete. He never drank any alcohol, did no drugs, and always made the game and his teammates his first priority. Accordingly, any player who would listen to him could not help but become a better player, teammate, and person.

B.J. not only worked the players physically but also mentally. He taught them the concepts of team basketball in the NBA, where many players make it about the individual. The individual concept works for many of the superstars who are in the starting rotation, but not so much for the players who are seven through fifteen on the roster. Many times, players make a team because they are not only talented, but because they play team basketball and are "good citizens," so to speak. These players are hard workers, coachable, and the kind of player management wants in the locker room. A team can handle just so many high maintenance superstars. The NBA is not only basketball, but a lifestyle. One danger is that if a player gets caught up too much in the big-time League lifestyle and forgets it is about basketball, he will be saying goodbye to the League prematurely. If a player does not improve, there is always someone eager to take his place on a roster.

Physically, B.J.'s favorite workout involved building up player endurance and speed by making players run up several hills in the city of Houston. His main hill of preference was one near Allen Parkway in Houston. Many players went to work out with B.J. and none ever told me they were not challenged either physically, mentally, or athletically by his workouts. Furthermore, once B.J., had worked with a player, he could give me a close approximation as to whether the player would be able to play at the NBA level. B.J. knew how to improve a player's basketball skills, and could tell them their weaknesses and strengths so they could rise to a higher level of play to grab a spot on an NBA roster.

When Tim went to work out in Houston, he stayed in a hotel across the street from Second Baptist church where many NBA players worked out. Tim could not only train with B.J. but was able to play with numerous NBA players who make their homes in Houston. This included Chris Morris, who was a close friend of B.J's. Tim brought a parachute to work out with when he came to Houston; the chute had been given to him by a trainer at Jacksonville. B.J. described to me Tim working out with the parachute in kind of a comical manner. He did not think the parachute was a good idea for Tim, because it did not make him "quicker." B. J. felt that, as a basketball player, Tim needed to be jumping, running, and doing more basketball-related activities. Tim was a hard worker and in good shape heading into the draft. I knew with B.J.'s help, Tim would be ready to play, whether he went overseas or tried to make an NBA team.

TEN
Rimwrecker is Born in Orlando and Signs the Big Contract

— · • · —

After signing with Orlando, Stanley began to play himself into shape as the 1991–1992 NBA season was starting. He began rounding into shape, and he was playing some productive minutes for the Magic as a backup to center to Greg Kite. His talent and potential began to shine through after he overcame his initial lack of conditioning and lost some weight.

I knew from my observations of the basketball business and players, that most players like to have some type of marketing deals. We were able to obtain a shoe contract, but nothing to brag about. When the season started, he was getting some notoriety, but not the kind that draws endorsement deals. I knew that once he started really playing, he would become popular and some type of marketing nickname might be helpful. Daryl Dawkins had received a great deal of notoriety when he shattered several backboards in 1979. I had seen many of Stanley's monster dunks, and someone (Stanley says it was me) came up with the name, "Rimwrecker," which I patented in hopes of perhaps starting a line of clothing. I began to use the name with the media in Orlando.

On November 4, 1991, Barry Cooper reported in the *Orlando Sentinel* on how Stanley had shattered two glass backboards during a ninety-minute practice. He referred to Stanley as "Rim Wrecker No. 53 a.k.a. rookie Stanley Roberts" when penning the article. Stanley's first backboard shattering dunk was a two-hander, but the second was a one-handed dunk, which demonstrates the power he played with when necessary. He did not try to shatter the backboards, but at that point, the news story really cemented his nickname. It was the first time in Orlando's team history that a player had shattered a backboard. In mid-November, management moved Stanley to the injured reserve list so Orlando would have room to sign its other first round draft pick, Brian Williams.

The New York Times

SPORTS PEOPLE: PRO BASKETBALL; One First-Rounder Left

November 19, 1991

The Orlando Magic and Indiana Pacers signed first-round draft picks yesterday, leaving LUC LONGLEY, who was selected by the Minnesota Timberwolves, as the only first-round selection unsigned.

The Magic signed BRIAN WILLIAMS to a multiyear contract and placed rookie center STANLEY ROBERTS on the injured list with a sprained ankle.

Stanley was only on injured reserve a short time, and moving into 1992, he began to play well. He became a starter just before the All Star game, which took place in Orlando on February 9, when Greg Kite injured his ankle. By February 25,

1992, Stanley was being described as an "impact player" in a news story of that date:

Stanley Roberts

February 25, 1992

Stanley Roberts is quickly becoming an impact player. In his first NBA season, he has set the team record for blocked shots in a game (7 vs. Atlanta 2/6). Roberts has become known as Rim Wrecker No. 53, after shattering two back-boards during a preseason practice. "I knew it would take a while to start playing at the level I'm at now...I just want to keep getting better." he stated.

Around this time, I felt Stanley was ready to be marketed, and I came up with a slogan, "Don't leave the gym without a rim," which we put on a shirt with Stanley's image dragging a rim out of a gym. I had taken some photographs, when Stanley was in Baton Rouge, of him with a rim, and I fashioned the color image out of these photographs. Angela helped with this project, but was to leave the sports team in March or April to marry my client, Mickey Guidry. This was a blow to me and my business, because Angela was a really smart and loyal employee with whom I really enjoyed working. I would never find someone like her again to do the work in my office and help with the sports. She and her husband settled in Baton Rouge, and they have three children. One of her girls is a Dallas Cowboy cheerleader.

We ordered a supply of shirts, and I arranged for them to be sold at the Orlando Magic gift shop by the stadium during one of my many trips to Orlando. I went down to visit Stanley several times just to see how he was doing. He was living the life of an NBA player, and had picked up some bad habits that he was successful, to some degree, in hiding from me. He was dependable generally, but I could never tell when he would get sidetracked by some of his diversions.

He was always successful in getting me my game tickets and after-game pass, but I was always a little nervous when I went to the "will call" window as to whether the ticket and pass would be there. When you are representing players and you are going to a game, you normally go to the "will call" to pick up your tickets and the after-game pass to visit with the player after the game. If it was an away game, generally the player and the team would be leaving after the game to go home or to another away game location on the road trip. If it was a home game, you could visit at the stadium and generally go out to eat with your player afterwards.

I would usually see Stan after the home games, but at times, he would go out after a game with someone else. One time, I cannot remember exactly how, I ended up riding around and hanging out with Stacey Augmon and Rumeal Robinson, who were playing for Atlanta at the time. The Hawks had a night layover after a game in Orlando. Stanley had promised to meet with them and show them Orlando, but he had something else to do so he sent me in his place. It was probably Stan's idea of how to get rid of my supervision and fulfill his promise to Stacey and Rumeal at the same time. I enjoyed spending some time with the two as they were both really down-to-earth, nice guys. I do remember thinking how crazy it was that I was hanging out with these two NBA stars on a spur-of-the-moment situation created by Stanley.

The situation was typical of Big Stan, always trying to take care of and accommodate everyone. I thought it was a lot of fun to meet Stacey and Rumeal and a great idea for Stan to befriend some quality players. However, Big Stan, as a lovable giant, took accommodation to a different level, which worked to his detriment many times, particularly dealing with nonplayers who were attracted by his good nature and took advantage of his resources. Many others and I tried to dissuade him from "helping" these parasitic types many times, but off the basketball court, Stan was a guy who liked to please everyone. Many times, I felt like he was just trying to get them off his back instead of just saying "no." He chose accommodation rather than confrontation, which I'm sure seemed easier to him at the time.

By February and into March, it was beginning to look like Stanley and I had made a really brilliant decision to go with a one-year deal, despite other agents' criticism. Tim Povtak documented it in an article in *Sporting News* on August 17, 1992:

> Although the Magic originally wanted to sign him to a longer deal, Roberts and his agent Oscar Shoenfelt insisted on one season. They were confident he would prove his value quickly. Shoenfelt was criticized by his peers for getting little security for his client.
>
> "Stanley had the confidence in his abilities. I knew what he could do," Shoenfelt said.

My redemption on the length of Stanley's contract continued with other articles beginning in February and the first of March discussing Stanley's impending contract negotiation as a restricted free agent, just as Stanley and I had planned. I was talking with the media to begin building up our negotiating position, even at this point in time, I knew the greater probability was that we would go the restricted free agent route rather than re-sign with Orlando early. You could not officially negotiate with other teams under the CBA until July 1. John Harris published a conversation we had in an article in the *Orlando Sentinel* on February 23, 1992:

> You should be thinking about where all that money will come from.
>
> Let's start with Roberts. He signed a one-year contract worth $550,000 and will be a restricted free agent at the end of the season.

You gambled that Roberts, who reported to training camp weighing more than 300 pounds, would need the entire season to round into shape. You gambled that Roberts' performance would enable you to offer him the standard 25 percent raise—take it or leave it.

You gambled wrong.

Roberts is no David Robinson, but he is superior to Greg Kite who is making $700,000 this season and will earn $905,000 in 1992–93.

You should know that Roberts' agent said the top 20 starting centers in the league average $2 million a year, and that he considers Roberts to be the Magic's starting center (he averaged 17.6 points and 9.3 rebounds during a recent six-game stretch). So draw your own conclusions about Roberts.

Harris, John. *Orlando Sentinel* 23 Feb. 1992. 3c. Print.

Likewise, Dick Scanlon discussed Stanley's pending free agency in an article near the end of February and beginning of March 1992, in the *Orlando Ledger:*

Stanley Roberts will be playing for the Orlando Magic next season. There isn't any question of that.

The question is one of cost. The 7-foot rookie center is playing on a one-year contract, very unusual for a first-round draft choice. After the season, he will be a restricted free agent, which means the Magic has the right to match any offer coming from another NBA club.

"He can't play anywhere else," says Magic President Pat Williams, "unless we decide to let him go."

"He was the 23rd pick in the draft, and now he's a starting center," said Roberts' agent, Oscar Shoenfelt, from Baton Rouge, LA, Friday. "Ability-wise, he's playing at least as well as half the starting centers in the league. And you've got to realize—he's still only 22 years old."

Roberts has averaged 17.3 points, 9.7 rebounds, and 2.9 blocks in just 29 minutes over the last 10 games. Few NBA teams are getting that kind of production from their centers.

If such an offer comes Roberts' way, the Magic will have no choice but to match it, especially in a year in which it will raise ticket prices. Roberts is the most popular player in Orlando right now.

In any case, league rules prevent the Magic from talking contract to Roberts until March 15, leaving 3 ½ months before he officially goes on the market.

Shoenfelt says Roberts likes Orlando, but he definitely wants a long-term contract.

"I'm not really in a hurry to do anything right now," said Shoenfelt, who plans to visit Orlando in April. "I think the main thing now is to concentrate on basketball; the rest will take care of itself, as long as he keeps his play up."

Stanley became a crowd favorite with his laid-back personality and his willingness to sign autographs and make time for the fans. Many times throughout his career, I witnessed him stopping in the middle of a meal to sign an autograph or talk with fans. I don't recall seeing Stanley turn down any fan's request. Actually, I can say this about all the players I represented throughout the years. Stanley was voted Orlando's most popular player by the fans for the 1991–1992 season. David Finnerty wrote about Stanley's popularity in the *Orlando Magic* magazine in April 1992:

Since claiming a spot in the starting lineup, Stanley Roberts has quickly developed into a fan favorite. He has become the inside muscle the Magic have lacked, averaging

17 points, nine rebounds, and a couple of blocks through mid-March since moving into his new role. The 7-foot rookie, who was passed over 22 times in last year's draft before being snagged by the Magic with the 23rd overall pick, is turning a lot of doubters into believers. He is slowly shedding extra pounds and quickly becoming a dominating low-post player and rebounder.

Finnerty, David. "Center Stanley Roberts." *Magic Magazine* April 1992: 24. Print.

Unfortunately, in the middle of Stanley's improving performances, twelve games before the end of the season, he injured his ankle, which effectively ended his season. Stanley ended up playing in fifty-five games and starting thirty-four in the 1991–1992 season, averaging 10.4 points, 6.1 rebounds, and 1.5 blocks. However, after really getting in shape, in his final twenty-four games before suffering the injury, he averaged 15.5 points and 8.1 rebounds a game. Stanley had proven he could play in the NBA and, over the course of the season, demonstrated some awesome dunks and blocked shots. The NBA was now on notice of Stanley's awesome potential to be a dominating NBA center.

At the end of the 1991-1992 season, Stanley was a restricted free agent, and would be able to negotiate with other teams on July 1, 1992. A restricted free agent was defined under the then-CBA as a veteran player who had completed his current contract and had played less than five years in the League. The CBA also contained another rule that any player who was completing his first year would be considered a Restricted Free Agent. The difference between an Unrestricted Free Agent and a Restricted Free Agent is that any team could offer an Unrestricted Free Agent a contract and his prior team could not do anything to retain the player. However, with a restricted free agent, the prior team could match an offer sheet tendered by another team and retain the player's rights. Orlando would still have a fifteen-day window to match the new team's offer under the CBA to retain rights to Stanley, but then Orlando would have to pay what the other team had offered, and this would mean Stanley would presumably receive a drastic raise in salary, as we had hoped at the beginning of the season. If Orlando did not match the other team's offer, then Stanley would have to sign a binding contract with the other team based on their offer.

The key in dealing with other teams would be to attract a very substantial offer which would put Orlando in a bind to find the money to match the offer sheet. There were still some lingering doubts in the League about Stanley's work ethic, his propensity to gain weight, and his habit of playing himself into shape, at the end of the season. However, we felt he had accomplished what we had planned, and we were now in position to garner enough interest to land a substantial offer sheet and then a contract in line with a starting center in the NBA. I had been studying the CBA intently and conferring with the NBPA with questions I had regarding the Restricted Free Agency procedure, and felt like I had my ducks in a row as far as handling what would be the first really large contract in my sports career. Again, based on my negotiations with Orlando, I felt like it would be a great idea to have Steve Thompson help me with any negotiations that might develop as a good guy, bad guy team. Steve had proven very valuable in my first NBA contract, and it really helped to get some feedback from him as we approached the upcoming negotiations.

On Sunday, May 17, 1992, as I continued to prepare for Stanley's upcoming negotiations, a new factor emerged when Orlando was fortunate enough to win the NBA draft lottery. This added a new wrinkle to Stanley's restricted free agency, as there

I arrive at the Madrid Airport spring 1991 with Alvaro to be greeted by Stanley and Carl.

Ervin, Darvin, and me after a Miami Heat game when Ervin and Darivn were with the Bucs.

Shaquille, Chris, and Stanley at LSU (talented group).

Don Sterling's "All White Party" 1992 (left to right) Don Sterling, Stanley, Me, Elgin Baylor, and Andy Rosser.

Willie aka "Top Cat", my brother John, and Me.

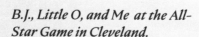

My brother John and Me hanging out in a hotel in Los Angeles, agent style.

B.J., Little O, and Me at the All-Star Game in Cleveland.

2.

1.

4.

3.

1. *Tim Breaux, Me, B.J. and Paul Brown in Houston.*
2.. *George Gervin, unknown, B.J. John Lucas and Ervin in Phoenix.*
3. *Charles Barkley, Little O, and Me.*
4. *Rufus Porter and Me at the office.*

Me, with NBAPA attorneys Hal Biagus on the left and Ron Klempner on the right.

Big Stan and Little O in Houston in Stan's hummer.

Stan and Me in Greece signing a contract.

Ervin, Little O and Me after a game.

Me in Istanbul Turkey working on Stanley's contract in 1999.

Ervin and Me at the Boston Garden January 22, 2003.

VISITING TEAM POST GAME PASS

2002-2003

BOSTON CELTICS

DATE: JANUARY 22, 2003

GAME 22: MILWAUKEE

GOOD ON ABOVE DATE ONLY.
NO LOCKER ROOM ACCESS!
THIS PASS ENTITLES BEARER TO WAIT IN
SECTION 2 IN THE ARENA FOR A PERIOD OF
TIME UP TO 45 MINUTES FOLLOWING
THE ABOVE DESIGNATED GAME.
No AUTOGRAPHS ALLOWED DURING THIS PERIOD.

(NAME)

NO: 131   (AUTHORIZATION)

NON-TRANSFERABLE

Visitors pass for the Boston game. This is your ticket to see your player after a home or away game.

2.

1.

4.

3.

5.

1. *Rufus Porter signing his contract with the Saints .*
2. *Me and Coach Lee Hedges, legendary coach and mentor.*
3. *Bijon (who now plays professional basketball in Australia) B. J.,*
   Little O, Me, and Damon Jones (now a basketball television analyst).
4. *In Toronto 1999 with Dwayne Morgan, Derrell Mitchell, Me, and Willie.*
5. *Little O, Ervin, and Me after a game.*

Coach Brown offered me advice throughout the years including an inspirational (You can do it!) signing of Sports Illustrated with photo on the cover.

My last high school game for Captain Shreve against St. Augustine in New Orleans.

My senior year at Captain Shreve #65.

Little O, Tim Breaux and Me.

Ron Klempner and I visited the Hafbrau House while in Munich.

Shoenfelt Sports Management Brochure.

Stanley signs his contract in Greece 1999.

Staples Center with my brother and some of his friends.

Ervin and Me at the Ritz Carlton Marina Del Rey before an away game in Los Angeles.

B.J., Chance Nicholas, and Me.

Letter from Dale Brown with which he transmitted a Bob Woolf book which had been autographed by Bob. Thanks Coach.

(Above) B.J., my Father, and Me at Portsmouth.

(Left) Tim Burroughs and Me at my Father's house.

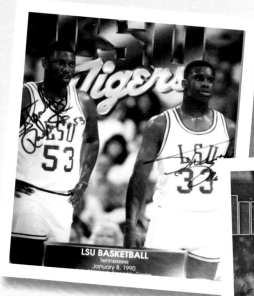

*My favorite photo of
Stanley and Shaq on a
LSU basketball program.*

*Client, Darvin Ham,
made the cover of SI
while at Texas Tech.*

*Sam Cassell, a really funny guy &
great basketball player, and Me.*

*Kevin McHale and Me, Let's take
a hike .*

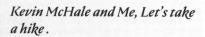

2.

1.

4.

3.

1. *Early recruiting LSU football players, Kenny Davidson, Karl Dunbar, Clint James, Verge Ausberry, Eddie Fuller and Robert Packnett; friends but no clients*
2. *John Lucas and Me. He trained basketball players.*
3. *Mark Davis and Me at Philadelphia.*
4. *My Dad, Stanley, and Me.*

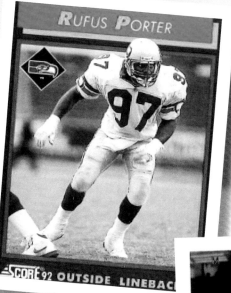

Rufus at Seattle.

Stanley at Orlando.

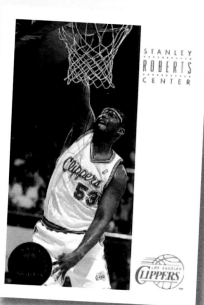

Stanley at The Clippers.

Ervin at The Bucks.

Chris Morris at The Nets.

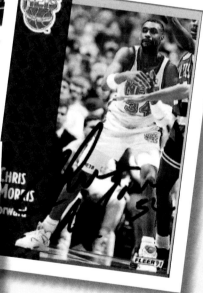

Darvin at Texas Tech.

Stanley, Angela, and Mickey on their wedding day 07.10.1992.

I spend some of my time on TV as an agent.

OSCAR SHOENFELT
Former Sports Agent

REAL MADRID C.F. 90/91

Stanley and Carl on Real Madrid 1990.

Italian agent Luciano "Lucky" Capicchioni at his condo in South Beach. I visited him twice while in Italy.

Ervin meets my nieces and nephews in 2005 after receiving some of his basketball camp shirts.

Michael watches Stanley dunk.

Me, Ervin, and Katie, my daughter in Los Angeles (Western Conference Finals 2004).

1.

2.

3.

4.

1. *NBA Draft Pass, 1991.*
2. *College All Star Desert Classic Pass, 1995.*
3. *NBA Finals Pass, 1996.*
4. *Stanley and Me on our way to the All White Party, 1992.*

was no question that the first pick in the draft would be used to take Stanley's old teammate Shaquille O'Neal.

This was history repeating itself, as Stanley had arrived at LSU before Shaq, but had to sit out one year, so they both started playing for the Tigers during the 1989–1990 season. A great deal was written and discussed about Stanley and Shaq's relationship, whether they got along at LSU and whether Stanley would be happy at Orlando playing with Shaq. My perception is that they were friendly rivals and, as both were very talented big men, they made each other better when they played at LSU. This is not to say that during the heat of play they never said anything negative to each other. I know they are still friends now, and I have never heard Stanley say anything negative about Shaq. Likewise, I have never known of Shaq ever saying anything negative about Stanley, this despite Stanley making some admittedly bad choices during his career.

As to whether Stanley wanted to play with Shaq at Orlando, it probably would not be anyone's first choice to have one of the most heralded college players of all time come to your team to play your position, but if the money was right, Stanley was happy to continue playing in Orlando. Accordingly, after we knew Shaq would be coming to Orlando, Stanley's first choice was to go to a team where he would be the starter and could play without constant comparisons to his friend Shaq. The Magic would be shaping the team around Shaq going forward, as Barry Cooper wrote in the *Sentinel* on May 18, 1992:

> 3 Or 4 Players Could Go Should Magic Add Shaq
>
> By Barry Cooper of the *Sentinel* staff, May 18, 1992
>
> On Sunday, the Orlando Magic won the NBA draft lottery and the right to draft LSU center Shaquille O'Neal. Today, the Magic begin reshaping their team to building around The Shaq. Few details about the Magic's plans are

available, but the Magic concede that next year's club could be very different. Magic General Manager Pat Williams, when asked if three or four players from this year's team might be let go, said: "That could happen." Williams wouldn't name the players. O'Neal, who skipped his senior year at LSU, is regarded as one of the greatest amateur players ever.

Clearly, it was not Stanley's first choice to be a backup to Shaq. My thoughts at the time were printed in an article by Lee Feinswog in the *Baton Rouge Morning Advocate* on May 31, 1992:

Roberts in Limbo with O'Neal Pick

May 31, 1992

So Shoenfelt and Roberts took a chance. They agreed to a one-year contract with the Magic.

"He was being paid what the No. 23 player taken in the draft would get," Shoenfelt said. "Now we're anticipating he'll end up making more than some of the top five. It was a gamble. Stanley and I talked about it. I told him a two-year deal may put less pressure on him, but Stanley said he was going to take care of business and that he wanted a one-year deal. I had no problem with it, because I knew what he could do. And he did it.

"People said we were taking a risk, but now we look like geniuses or something like that."

And what uniform will Roberts wear? "I don't think you can have two starting centers of that quality," Shoenfelt said. "You can sit one on the bench and play one. But I think players of that quality should both be playing. Having them both on the same team wouldn't be the best way to use their talents. I think they're going to bring out the best in each other if they're on opposite teams."

Shoenfelt was asked if that meant he would recommend that Roberts go elsewhere. He said no. But he repeated that he didn't think having them together would work.

"What would you do, play Shaq at four? I think Stanley would have to switch to power forward. But Stanley's a center. That's what he's been playing. I'd like to go down and see Shaq and say hello, but I don't think it's the wisest thing to have them together. Look at what happened that year at LSU. I don't think they both fully developed when they were switching out.

"Plus, Stanley is like my son. I want him to develop his own persona and not be overshadowed by somebody else. That's my personal point of view. But that doesn't figure in to what we're going to do. I like the city of Orlando better than some cities, but it's a matter of taking care of business."

Shoenfelt is a big O'Neal fan. But when it comes to Roberts, he's understandably biased.

"At this point, I would say that Stanley is better offensively than Shaquille," Shoenfelt said.

"Defensively, I think they can play with each other. Shaquille I think may be a little better on defense. Stanley has had a year in the league, and fans in Baton Rouge know this, but Stanley has some offensive moves that Shaquille hasn't developed yet."

"The bottom line is that Stanley's going to come out a winner no matter where he is. I think his maturity is going to come through. He's proven he can play in the NBA. Remember at this time last year there were a lot of people saying he wasn't going to make it," said Shoenfelt, whose support played no small part in Robert's success.

Either way, Shoenfelt didn't seem concerned. "There are very few centers in the league who are going to be able to play with Shaquille and Stanley, so I think that makes Stanley's value go up. He was second-team all-rookie and was voted the most popular player in Orlando (by the fans)," Shoenfelt said. "So he proved what he had to prove this year and did what he had to do. So I think we're in a very good position."

The bottom line was that I was ready and so was Stanley, to move forward, to land a major restricted free-agent deal, regardless of Shaq being picked by Orlando. We knew that Shaq would be headed to a huge contract, and this would put even more pressure on Orlando and make it less likely for Orlando to match any offer sheet which was presented by another team.

In fact, we used Shaq's pick by Orlando in trying to persuade teams to give Stanley an offer sheet. It would be extremely hard under the salary cap in the CBA for Orlando to sign both Shaq and Stanley when Stanley signed an offer sheet, so extending an offer sheet to him would not be a waste of the new team's time and effort. Moreover, it would seem with Orlando picking Shaq, that there would be less incentive for Orlando to match Stanley's offer sheet, though the team would want to obtain some value for a player it picked in the first round of the draft the year prior. If Stanley escaped without Orlando receiving any compensation, it would mean that Orlando essentially wasted one of its first-round picks in 1991.

After the draft, Orlando would have great difficulty in matching an offer sheet for Stanley, because they would have to sign Shaq before they matched any offer to Stanley to stay within the confines of the CBA salary cap. Again, the salary cap is the maximum allowed amount that a team can use to sign players. There are some exceptions to the cap, and one exception was that you could sign one of your own players and exceed the cap. Lee Feinswong explained this in the article he wrote, which was mentioned previously:

> Roberts is what the NBA calls a restricted free agent. After July 1, any team can make Roberts an offer. Orlando has to match it to keep him. Certainly the Magic would have done exactly that had it not won the rights to O'Neal. O'Neal, everyone figures, is THE center of the future. Orlando management says it wants them both and will do what it can to get O'Neal and keep Roberts. And Shoenfelt said matching an offer for Roberts would not count against Orlando's salary cap.
>
> "What they would try to do is sign Shaquille and then sign Stanley for whatever," Shoenfelt said. "It's going to be very interesting."

We anticipated having an offer sheet that Orlando would have to match within fifteen days sometime in proximity to July 1, 1992, when we could begin negotiations with other teams under the CBA. The offer sheet would trigger the fifteen-day clock for Orlando to match sometime in July 1992. History had proven this was significant because the previous two number one picks, Derrick Coleman of New Jersey (1989) and Larry Johnson of Charlotte (1991) had not signed after the draft until November. Therefore, it looked very likely that Orlando would be unable to have an offer sheet for Stanley within the fifteen-day window.

Even before the draft, we were getting some preliminary feelers from teams expressing interest in Stanley, but no "negotiations" which would have been prohibited under the CBA. By now, I really felt like I was getting to be a "real" NBA agent with my experience in the years prior, dealing with Stanley's contract and having players taken in the draft two years in a row. Miami was one of the teams showing some interest, and I was priming the pump when newspapers called me. A story appeared in the Miami *Sun-Sentinel* on June 20, 1992:

Sports

Heat Interest in Roberts? Maybe

By Robes Patton, Staff Writer, June 20, 1992
The agent for restricted-free-agent-to-be Stanley Roberts expects a flurry of attention after July 1, when teams can begin bidding on free agents. "I think realistically, there's going to be a great deal of interest from six or seven teams," said agent Oscar Shoenfelt. Shoenfelt declined to name specific teams that might bid for Roberts, but the Heat fits the criteria of needing a big man and having money under the salary cap to acquire one. "We're here to take care of business," Shoenfelt said.

The 1992 draft took place on June 24, in Portland, Oregon. As expected, Shaquille O'Neal was the number one pick taken by Orlando, the lucky lottery winner. The number two pick was Alonzo Mourning, drafted by Charlotte, and number three was Christian Laettner, drafted by Minnesota. Of course, I was also very interested in the draft to see where and to whom Tim Burroughs would be drafted. Tim was drafted in the second round, number fifty-one by the Minnesota Timberwolves.

As July 1 approached, I was anxiously waiting to begin some real negotiations for Stanley's long anticipated "big" contract. Prior to July 1, Orlando had made a "qualifying offer" of 125 percent of his previous salary to retain the right to match any offer he may receive as a restricted free-agent. I had studied the CBA in detail and was going to try to include anything favorable I could in Stanley's contract. As an attorney, my natural beginning point was to lay a legal foundation for the negotiations.

As with Stanley's first NBA contract and the football contracts I had negotiated, the body of the contract had already been negotiated by the NBA Players Union and was in the CBA. However, there were key portions that I would be negotiating that included the length of contract, amount of compensation, schedule of payment, bonuses, including a signing bonus, and whether the contract was "guaranteed" and under what conditions the contract would be guaranteed. Stanley's first contract had been guaranteed, but now I would be dealing with a long term deal and I wanted to be sure to include every guarantee possible.

There were several categories listed in the CBA for guarantees, such as: lack of skill, personal conduct, death, any type of injury or illness, mental disability, and unfitness to play basketball whether the injury, illness, mental disability, or unfitness to play was insured or uninsured. Lack of skill meant that if the team wanted to cut the player just because it did not feel he was good enough to play, he would still receive any compensation due. Injury, illness, or unfitness to play basketball meant that if he was injured, ill, mentally disabled, or died for any reason and could not play, he would still be paid. Teams could prohibit the players from engaging in some dangerous activities and injuries from those activities would not be guaranteed, for example riding motorcycles and skydiving. The guarantees were an essential part of almost all NBA deals, which was the big advantage of an NBA contract over an NFL contract. The fact that an NBA contract was guaranteed made signing bonuses less important than in the NFL. Back in 1992, guaranteed contracts really did not exist in the NFL, so the signing bonus was the real guaranteed money for a player on a long-term deal. Now in recent times, you do see some NFL contracts that are guaranteed or partially guaranteed.

One item that caught my eye in the CBA which I wanted included in Stanley's contract was a no-trade clause, which is normally prohibited in an NBA contract. However, there was an exception that a no-trade clause could be included in an offer sheet being given to a restricted free-agent. The exception allowing for the no-trade clause was only valid for the first season, but looked like a great provision to put in Stanley's contract. In addition, you were allowed to include in the no-trade clause a provision that if a trade did take place, the player would receive a fifteen percent raise on any monies still owed under the contract. This clause I thought also might make Orlando think twice about trying to match an offer sheet given to Stanley, because he could block any trade the first season of the contract. I also thought that if Orlando did match and try to trade Stanley, which could happen, then he could make over a million dollars without doing anything.

On July 1, 1992, we were officially contacted by the Dallas Mavericks and the Miami Heat with regards to an offer sheet for Stanley. By this time, I had raised my demand to a deal averaging over $3 million dollars a year for around five years. My thought on the increased price was based on the interest we had received and current salary trends. I may have driven a few interested teams off, but I knew I only needed to hook and catch one fish to have a great meal, so to speak. On July 2, 1992, events were documented in the press:

Roberts Contacted by 2 Teams

By Barry Cooper of the *Sentinel* staff, July 2, 1992

Centers Stanley Roberts and Greg Kite remain members of the Orlando Magic. But that may change. The Dallas Mavericks and Miami Heat are the leading candidates to sign Roberts, a restricted free agent, to an offer sheet. And the Magic confirmed Wednesday that they're trying to trade Kite to the Houston Rockets or other teams. Roberts said he is seeking a multi-year contract worth an average of $3 million a season. He said the Mavericks, who have about $5 million available under the $14 million salary cap, may soon sign him. Roberts said his agent, Oscar Shoenfelt, also was contacted by the Heat.

Sun Sentinel

Heat Makes Roberts Offer

July 2, 1992

Robes Patton.

The Heat was one of three teams to submit offers to Stanley Roberts on Wednesday, the day the 7-foot center became a restricted free agent. "The official line is we had offers from Dallas, Miami and Orlando," said Oscar Shoenfelt, Roberts' agent. Heat Managing Partner Lewis Schaffel declined comment when asked if the Heat had contacted Shoenfelt. Should Roberts sign an offer sheet with another team, the Magic would have 15 days to match the offer and retain his rights.

During the next several weeks, I stayed busy discussing potential deals and negotiating with Dallas and Miami, who had shown the most interest in extending a substantial offer sheet to Stanley. Billy Cunningham and Lewis Schaffel of Miami flew into Baton Rouge to discuss a deal. Our firm had just finished building a new twenty thousand square foot office, which I felt was quite impressive. My firm and I were excited and proud to have the owner of the Heat coming to Baton Rouge to sit in my office and discuss a potential deal. We had bought a house that had a swimming pool in the backyard and built the office to incorporate the house. I had the third choice of offices but was fortunate enough to land the office I really wanted and helped design, which opened up to the pool. I had a separate conference room where we met, and we also sat poolside for part of the discussions. I had my negotiating partner, Steve Thompson, sit in on the discussions.

I felt that the fact that the Heat management had flown

to Baton Rouge proved that they were serious. Miami would be a great city for Stanley to play in, and it was in Florida, where he already felt at home. The Heat were very interested in Stanley but at the same time wary of Stanley's conditioning and weight problems. The offer eventually proposed by the Heat contained the same money as the five-year $15 million deal I was demanding, but some of the money was conditioned on Stanley's weight and conditioning, which made it less attractive to me and Stanley. As an agent, your job is to get as much money as possible for your client with as few conditions attached as possible. Any talk by management that your player should earn his money is contrary to your real goal. Performance bonuses for playing time, yards rushed, honors, and such should just be lagniappe and not the basis of the contract. An example of too much conditional money is the contract that Ricky Williams signed with the Saints when he was the fifth overall pick in the 1999 draft. The contract sounded substantial, but was based on too many conditions for the player to be paid, such as playing time, and was considered a flop.

The other team interested in Stanley was the Dallas Mavericks, which was owned by Don Carter and his partner Norm Sonju. They were both strong Christians, which was related to me during the course of my discussions with the Mavericks' negotiating team. Dallas was described as a "family atmosphere," which sounded great to me as a future home for Stanley. Stanley liked the idea of going to Dallas with the team centered around him as the center of the future. He also liked the idea of playing with Jimmy Jackson, who had just been drafted by the Mavericks. Rick Sund was another member of the negotiating team whom I had discussions with in trying to come to an agreement on Stanley's contract. Dallas was very anxious to sign Stanley and began to meet our demands, including compensation, length, guarantees, and bonuses, including a signing bonus. Dallas agreed to the no-trade clause to dissuade Orlando from matching their offer sheet and show they intended for Stanley to stay in Dallas and play. Personally, I liked the idea of Stanley playing in Dallas since it was only an hour and a half direct flight from Baton Rouge to Dallas, and I could see as many games as possible. I was also familiar with Dallas, having gone to college at Abilene Christian, which was a three hour drive due west on I-20.

By the week of July 20, 1992, the Mavericks and I had agreed on all the principal terms of the proposed contract. Both sides were in a hurry to finalize an acceptable offer sheet and have Stanley sign the offer sheet and deliver it to Orlando to begin the clock running on Orlando's fifteen-day match window. I had confirmed the contract details in writing but had not reviewed the actual offer sheet, which Stanley was to sign. We agreed to have Stanley and me fly over on June 23, 1992, to sign the offer sheet. Since I wanted Steve to also review the offer sheet as a precaution, I insisted that Steve arrive on June 22 to review it and make sure there would be no problems after Stanley and I arrived. I did not want to be caught in Dallas unprepared if anything unexpected appeared in the original offer sheet. I had Steve come in my office and listen to a conference call with the Mavericks to go over the terms so he would have complete understanding of the contract.

The double and separate review was a precaution that I would use on very large and complicated settlements on some of the firm's personal injury cases. I would have one of my partners also review the receipt before I presented the executed documents to the opposing counsel. My feeling was that two heads are better than one, especially when I could use one of my partners, who were all exceptional, smart, and excellent attorneys, as a consult. The basketball clubs all had large staffs on call, including attorneys, who would aid in the drafting of player contracts and offer sheets, so I tried to even the odds in my favor to some degree.

As I would later point out to my law students at LSU, being in the actual practice of law is quite different than being in law school. When you attach your name to a letter, a pleading to file in court, or have your client sign a document, you "own" the terms of the document. Any mistakes made are out there for the world to see. You're not just taking a test, you're putting your reputation and your client's well-being on the line. It's important to remember that your client, in all likelihood, will live by the terms of the agreement for the term of the agreement. Moreover, our legal system is an adversarial system, so you need to "assume nothing, trust no one, and try and know everything," a saying one of my friends, Dr. Tommy Priddy, had learned in medical school and shared with me as we backpacked in Montana before I graduated law school. How many times when a mistake is made do people say, "Well, I assumed this" as an excuse? Well, I tried not to assume anything in the practice of law as well as the agent business to ensure as few mistakes as possible.

Steve arrived on June 22, 1992, in Dallas as planned and was taken to a hotel where he checked in. Subsequently, he was taken by Jeep to a nice Dallas restaurant for a private dinner with the negotiating team. Steve recently told me that there were approximately eight people in the room, including Rick Sund and he believes at least one of the Mavericks' owners. During the meal, the "team" again told Steve about the great family atmosphere and presented him with the proposed offer sheet to review. Steve had confirmed again the terms, and the fact that the contract was "fully guaranteed," prior to beginning to read the contract carefully. Things were proceeding smoothly until, during the course of reading the contract, Steve came across a clause in the middle of the contract (that he can't recall at this time) which allowed for Stanley to be cut without receiving the remaining monies due under the contract. In other words, it was not a fully guaranteed contract as I had outlined, and was a precondition for Stanley to sign the offer sheet.

Steve, after reading the clause, stated to the entire group that this was not a fully guaranteed contract as promised. At that moment, the room became silent, and then a member of the group asked Steve if he felt they were being untruthful. Steve basically said that, based on his reading of the contract, a fully guaranteed contract was not being presented as agreed, and that Stanley would not sign the offer sheet in its present form. The clause in question had to be removed or there would be no deal. The Mavericks indicated that the clause was inserted to dissuade the Magic from matching the offer sheet and that, the way they interpreted it, it was a fully guaranteed contract. Steve, after a silent ride home, did not budge, and when he was dropped off at the hotel, he reiterated that it was not fully guaranteed and Stanley would not sign the offer sheet in its present form.

When Steve returned to the hotel, he gave me a call with his results of reading the offer sheet. He read the clause in question to me and I agreed with his interpretation. At that point, I was glad that I had sent Steve in advance, because now the pressure would be on the Mavericks to explain why an offer sheet had not been signed; I'm sure there was a press conference being scheduled for the next day. Stanley and I would catch our flight to Dallas, but not come to the table until the clause was removed.

Fortunately, after Steve got dressed the next day, a member of the Mavericks team, who I'm sure was Rick Sund, knocked on Steve's door. The Mavericks again indicated their position and that the insertion of the clause was done in good faith, but in the interest of moving forward, the clause would be deleted from the offer sheet. Steve then gave me a call, to my relief, and I told him that Stanley and I would head over to sign the "First Refusal Offer Sheet" as provided for under "Exhibit D" to the CBA. We were now on the verge of finally signing Big Stan to a significant contract that would make him set for life, if he followed some rules of reason and did not let others influence him. Stanley, Steve, and I met with the Mavericks, and after Steve and I again reviewed the offer sheet to make sure the deal was what we had agreed on, Stanley signed the offer sheet. The Orlando newspaper reported the signing as follows but had the wrong amount of compensation, which was actually $15 million:

> Roberts Signs Offer Sheet
>
> By Tim Povtak of the *Sentinel* staff, July 24, 1992
>
> The Dallas Mavericks signed restricted free-agent center Stanley Roberts to a 5-year offer sheet Thursday estimated at $12.5 million, giving the Orlando Magic until Aug. 8 to match it or lose him without compensation. The offer sheet contains a no-trade clause in its first year, which would prohibit the Magic from matching with the intention of trading him. Because teams are allowed to exceed the NBA salary cap to sign their own free agents but not their draft picks, the Magic now must sign No. 1 pick Shaquille O'Neal before they can match the offer for Roberts.

I really cannot recall if a press conference followed, because I had to leave shortly after the signing to fly to Orlando to deliver a copy of the offer sheet formally to my old friend Pat Williams. I had noticed that the CBA required that any notice of an offer sheet "shall be either by personal delivery or by prepaid certified, registered or overnight mail" (p. 54) to the principal address of the team, which meant Orlando. The CBA further stated that "An offer sheet shall be deemed given only when actually received by the prior Team" (p. 54).

The CBA required actual receipt of the notice by Orlando, and you could not use fax, only the methods listed in the CBA. Personally, this stood out to me when I saw it and I felt actually delivering the offer sheet was the only sure fire way I could see to start the fifteen-day window for Orlando to match on June 23, 1992, the date we signed. I had brought this to the attention of the Mavericks, and since we both wanted Orlando to fail in its attempt to match the offer and for Stanley to play in Dallas, I volunteered to fly to Orlando and personally deliver the notice to the Orlando Magic office. I had wanted to go to Orlando and spend some time with Stanley after the signing anyway. Dallas, seeing the advantage in getting a jump on the Magic, agreed to pay for the airline ticket for me to fly to Orlando and return. I cannot recall many of the details of the trip other than that I made the flight, made it to the Magic office before it closed, and delivered the notice. I then headed to the hotel feeling extremely tired, but ecstatic, that we had the offer sheet signed and that I had finally negotiated and virtually completed a major NBA contract, after only being a basketball agent for two years. Stanley's other two contracts had been substantial, especially the Real Madrid, but those contracts were only one-year deals.

In Bruce Hunter's book, *Shaq Impaq*, he wrote about an interview with Pat Williams about our contract during which Pat recounted some of the details of our conversation on July 23, 1992: Two days later, Williams took a rare day off to go horseback riding with his daughter. When he got back to his car, the car phone was ringing. His wife, Jill, was on the other end of the line, relaying the expected news that Roberts had been signed. The Dallas Mavericks had extended a five-year, $15 million contract.

That same evening Roberts' agent, Oscar Shoenfelt,

delivered the offer sheet to Williams's office. Williams, surprised that the agent didn't just send it by overnight mail, stopped by Shoenfelt's hotel room that night.

"Why did you waste your money to fly here with the offer?" he asked the agent.

"It wasn't my money," Shoenfelt answered.

"Then, why did you waste Stanley's money?" Williams inquired.

"It wasn't Stanley's money, either," replied the agent.
Williams immediately understood that the Mavericks had sent Shoenfelt as a courier. The Dallas club wanted to establish July 23 as the first day of the 15-day period extended to the Magic to match the offer sheet. That, of course, meant the monumental O'Neal deal had to be closed within two weeks or the Magic would lose the rights to Roberts.

After delivering Stanley's offer sheet to the Magic, I had headed to the hotel for some rest with a feeling of elation that we had the big contract signed, sealed, and delivered. I enjoyed my conversation with Pat Williams after delivering the contract. He was always a witty and entertaining guy to deal with, and I was anxious to see if he could pull off signing Shaq within fifteen days. Either way, I was secure in the fact that Stanley's faith in me had not been in vain and that he had a long term deal upon which he could base his career. This feeling was much superior to the feelings that I had experienced when I negotiated his two one-year deals with Real Madrid and Orlando. However, the two years and time that I had expended in negotiating those deals gave me the experience and knowledge to pull off this deal. Of course, I always kept in mind, if not for Big Stan, none of this excitement would have taken place, and I was grateful to him, my partners, and to God for blessing me with the experience. I was also thankful for my ex-wife, Elizabeth, who allowed me to travel as much as I did while taking care of three children at the time, Katie, Oscar, and Mimi. As a small fish, I had survived and grown enough so as not to have been swallowed by the big sharks who populate the sports agent's world.

After returning to Baton Rouge, Stanley and I watched with interest as Pat Williams and the Magic management got to work to attempt to retain Stanley's rights by signing Shaq within fifteen days. We were anxiously waiting for the approaching Friday, August 8, 1992 date as Stanley really wanted to move to Dallas. However, Stanley and I were really in a great position, no matter what happened, as his contract was done.

To Pat and John Gabriel's credit, they incredibly were able to sign Shaq to a monster deal within the fifteen-day time limit. This feat was considered close to impossible by some, but they pulled it off. Tim Povtak gave an excellent summary of what happened in his August 17, 1992 article in *Sporting News*:

Magic Pull Off Best Trick by Signing O'Neal Early

August 17, 1992

Williams and his management team stunned the rest of the NBA by retaining both centers, a feat most teams and player agents thought impossible only two weeks before it actually happened.

The Magic solved the problem with a furious two weeks of front-office maneuvering, unprecedented cooperation from other players and, most importantly, Sean Higgins convinced Scott Skiles, Greg Kite, Jerry Reynolds, Terry Catledge and Conner to renegotiate their contracts.

"They manipulated the salary cap in unprecedented fashion," says Leonard Armato, O'Neal's agent. "When this first started, I wasn't sure if they would be able to sign him at all. No one believed they could get it done this quickly. But they made a believer out of me."

Despite having a pair of 7-footers, the Magic have no real goal of using a Twin Towers game plan. The likelihood is that Roberts will be traded. Only hours after the deals were announced last week, Williams' phones started ringing.

The Bulls, Clippers, Pistons, Bucks and Celtics—all teams with aging centers—have shown interest in Roberts. So have the Heat, who need more size.

"When you look through the college ranks, there will not be any real centers coming into the league in the next few years," Williams says. "And now we have two of them, good ones, who could become great ones in time." ...

"This is not a risk. This is a good business decision," Magic General Manager Pat Williams says. "We now have possession of two real quality big men. And that's worth a lot." ...

Although Roberts was disappointed he wasn't going to Dallas, there is no disappointment in his contract status. He was the 23rd pick in the 1991 NBA draft and played for $550,000 in his first season.

After signing Shaq, the Magic quickly sent me a "First Refusal Exercise Notice." The exercise notice provided that the Magic would create a binding agreement with Stanley for the Principal terms contained in the Dallas offer sheet. Once we received the exercise notice, we were now obligated to sign the binding contract with Orlando for the minimum of the terms of the Dallas offer.

I was tied up with handling one of my legal cases when the Magic wanted to finalize the contract. Since the terms of the agreement were already set, I asked Steve to go down and review the final contract to make sure that the terms were in line with the Dallas offer sheet. Our plan was also to see if the Magic would come up with some additional money above the Dallas offer as incentive. When Steve went down to Orlando, he was picked up at the airport by Stanley. Local TV stations had received word that Steve was going down to finalize the contract and showed up at the airport. Television cameras followed Steve and Stanley from the time that Steve deplaned up until the time he got in Stanley's car. Until that time, Steve told me that he never appreciated how athletes really give up their right to privacy when they become public figures. I had become aware of this fact after the initial signing of Stanley and the media blitz that had ensued from that point on. Of course, this is even more true these days with the ubiquitous nature of social media.

After arriving in Orlando, Steve met with the Magic and reviewed the contract. In addition, he spent several hours discussing possible "weight incentives" to add to the contract over and above what was in the Dallas offer sheet. After the discussions, Steve told Stanley he could earn a couple of extra hundred thousand dollars if he was willing to "weigh in" periodically and meet certain weight goals. Stanley told Steve not to waste any more time; he was not agreeing to weigh in for the Magic. Thus, Stanley avoided any type of conditioning or weight clauses in his second contract with Orlando. Steve was able to add an extra $160,000 to the contract with various other incentives. Stanley then signed his five-year deal based on the offer sheet presented by Dallas with the $15 million guaranteed and the one-year no-trade clause at Stanley's option. Again, I had insisted on the no-trade clause so if Stanley was traded, he could control the situation and earn an extra fifteen percent on any amount owing on his contract.

After all the time and work I had put into assisting Big Stan, he was happy, and I was ecstatic that we both had some security. I thought now all we had to do was let him grow into his role as a professional athlete and help him with his new financial status. Unfortunately, as with many professional athletes, Big Stan had his own idea as to how he would proceed with his career and the handling of his finances. In any event, the future would not be boring, as Big Stan, though not entirely intentionally, periodically came up with all kinds of ways to stress me out.

With the completion of Stanley's big contract, after four years in the business, I now had finally made a substantial fee which would be paid over the course of the contract. Again, the amount of the fee was controlled by the players union, the NBPA, and through the standard player-agent contract mandated by the NBPA. The NBPA allows a maximum fee of four percent, but Stanley and I had agreed on a lesser amount. The fee has to be paid as the player is paid, and prepayment of the fee is prohibited, which means the agent must collect the fees from the player as he is paid. Collecting your fee is normally not a problem, but you still have to set up a mechanism to collect the fee. Of course, issues could arise about the collection of the fee if, for example, you were fired; however, once you negotiate a contract, you are entitled to the fee even if the player has chosen to terminate your representation.

Stanley's fee at last gave me a financial basis upon which to continue my sports representation. Up until this time, all the time and money I had spent in setting up my sports representation agency certainly was not covered by the few fees I had collected. In fact, the only fees that I had collected were on Stanley's Real Madrid contract and on his initial one-year deal with the Magic. I had put those fees back into the business with my travels to Spain and visits to Orlando. In truth, I don't really remember collecting any fees on all of the other prior contracts, since the other players did not have the financial resources to pay me at the time, and I hated to collect a fee when the players were still struggling financially. The prior contracts were, however, positive in the fact that they had given me credibility as an agent and paved the way for me to sign Stanley.

ELEVEN
King of the Mountain with Leon Douglas

———— · • · ————

During Stanley's contract negotiations, I was still working with B.J. in trying to properly place Tim Burroughs. Tim had been drafted in the second round at number fifty-one by the Minnesota Timberwolves in the 1992 draft. I was happy that Tim was drafted, but the reality was that at fifty-one, he in all likelihood would not be offered a guaranteed contract like the first-round draft picks and even a few of the top second-round picks would sign. Since Tim was married and had children, we had discussed with him prior to the draft that if he did not go high enough in the draft, we would be trying to find him a fully guaranteed contract overseas, which at that time meant Europe. A guaranteed contract would give him some financial stability for his family as he was exiting college. If a player is single and a low draft pick or a free-agent and does not have a family to support, he should have more freedom to go to an NBA summer league team and then preseason camp with an NBA team on a non-guaranteed contract. A non-guaranteed contract meant that the player could be cut at any time with no financial consequence to the team. If a player was cut by the NBA in August, after the European League started, he would be faced with playing in the CBA, the unofficial minor league of the NBA, or trying to get on with a less desirable foreign team that might need a player.

Since the European League begins before the NBA season, and most players going overseas at that time were signed by the beginning of August, I moved forward in seeing what type of contract I could get on the European market. I did have discussions about Tim with Minnesota, and afterwards was not hopeful that the team would offer Tim any type of significant guaranteed contract. Since I already had worked with Arturo Ortega with Stanley, I contacted him and planned on working with his agency in finding Tim a secure, well-paying job. Again, Arturo was one of the people in the business that I always found to be straightforward and honest. He always did what was best for the player and not himself. In this case, I had spent considerable time with Tim signing and training him, so I agreed to split the European agent fee with Arturo.

I was in contact with Tim and Donna on a regular basis, to keep them informed of what was going on with the NBA and the European negotiations. I felt Tim and I had a pretty solid relationship and that things would work out on a good European contract since I knew Arturo would get Tim a fair salary with a reputable team. As August 1992 came with the beginning of the European season, Arturo landed a potential job offer for Tim in the Spanish League. The contract offer was in the $150,000 to $175,000 range, fully guaranteed with a place to live, a car, and some other perks. The team would pay Spanish taxes, which would just about cover all the U.S. taxes that would be due. This is why overseas basketball was a good opportunity for a player to save some money and develop his game at the same time. However, as I had learned when I took Stanley to Spain, some American players have problems adjusting to the cultural differences and the differences in the European game.

While I was working with Arturo for Tim, unbeknownst to me, Tim was talking by telephone with a fellow named Leon Douglas who lived in Italy. Leon was a six-foot ten former NBA player who played center at the University of Alabama, graduating in 1976. He was taken as the fourth overall pick in the 1976 NBA draft by the Detroit Pistons. Leon spent six years in the League and then had gone to play in Europe in 1982. He flourished in the Italian European League and even learned to speak Italian, as I was soon to discover. Apparently, Leon was near the end of his playing career in 1992 and was trying to break into the agent business. He played for a team in Pistoia, Italy, for several years and was working with the general manager of the team to obtain an American basketball player for the upcoming season.

By August, Leon had convinced Tim to come to Pistoia to work out and then negotiate a contract without my knowledge. I was in my office one day when I received a call from Tim; he was on his way to Italy. Tim told me that Douglas was trying to negotiate a contract for him with an Italian team in Pistoia for more money than the Spanish had offered through Arturo. The team in Italy wanted him to come work out there and was paying his way to Italy. I was initially stunned by these sudden developments. However, it came as no surprise to me, based on my past experience with Stanley that someone was trying to represent a player I had signed. Tim still wanted me as his agent, but he now wanted me to work with Leon, whom I did not know by reputation or otherwise. I reminded Tim that I had worked with Arturo and trusted him, and that we still had a deal on the table. However, he was on his way to Italy, and I had no control over the situation. Tim said he wanted me to come to Italy to work on the deal with Leon, and gave me Leon's contact information.

I called Leon and introduced myself, letting him know that I had Tim under contract as an overseas agent and NBA agent.

At that time, there was no real regulation for overseas agents, which are now regulated somewhat by FIBA (the Federated International Basketball Association). Any legal action of breach of contract by Tim and interference by Leon would have to come in some type of court action in the United States, which would be very complicated, time consuming, and potentially expensive. For these reasons, it would not be worthwhile to file a lawsuit. Additionally, I was sure it would not help in attracting new clients to sue old ones. Accordingly, I knew I would have to win the fight to keep Tim, my client, based on my participation in the process and retaining control of the client.

I told Leon that Tim wanted me involved and that we, in fact, had an offer in Spain, and I was working with Arturo on this deal. He knew Arturo, and Arturo's agency was based in San Marino, Italy. Leon said I could come on over and participate in the negotiations; he would arrange a hotel for me in Pistoia. I had looked up Pistoia on a map and found it to be located in the Tuscany area of Italy.

I had traveled to Italy in 1976 between college and law school and loved the country. I remembered Italian people as being some of the friendliest in all my travels. Suddenly, this became a real adventure taking place in a great location. I quickly made plane arrangements for a business trip to fly to Italy and meet Tim and Leon in Pistoia. My objective was to keep the client, and get his contract done so I could make at least a little money on the deal. Fortunately, after having done Stanley's Real Madrid contract, I knew the basics of foreign contracts and was prepared and determined to get a contract done in Spain or Italy. I really preferred to go with Arturo's deal because I knew him well, and knew that if we had any problems, he would be able to help us enforce the contract. Arturo was an attorney besides being an agent, but Leon was an unknown quantity and had no legal background that I was aware of. However, I felt like Leon would know the Italian League and the general manager for whom he had played.

I talked to Tim on a Monday or Tuesday and was on my way to Pistoia by Wednesday. My initial point of arrival was Venice, which I had visited in 1976. I arranged to rent a car at the airport and then drive two-and-a-half-hours to Pistoia. Leon had given me the name of the hotel where he had arranged a room for me. Naturally, I spoke with Arturo about the recent developments, and he was somewhat skeptical about the Italian adventure. He knew who Leon was and that he had previously played for Pistoia. He said he would keep the Spanish deal open as long as he could, but naturally wanted to know if Tim was going to take it as soon as possible.

I had no problem picking up the car at the airport, but was told that it needed a type of gasoline that could be hard to find. This did not seem like a problem, at the time, but would become the source of some stress on my return trip to the airport. I had a flight back to the United States on Sunday, August 16, 1992 and was to fly out of Pisa on the western coast of Italy, which was only about an hour's drive. I needed to get back by Sunday because I had legal work to do the next week. Interestingly, I would be arriving in Italy right at the beginning of Ferragosto, beginning of an Italian holiday season. The holiday revolves around the end of the harvest and enjoying the fruits of labor. It begins on August 15 every year. Ferragosto coincides with the Catholic feast of the Assumption of Mary, and August 15, 1992 was on a Saturday. I would learn from this trip and others in the future that in August, most of Italy shuts down to go on vacation, particularly to the beach.

I looked at my journey by car as a semi-challenge, since I had limited experience driving in Europe. I had driven Stanley's car in Spain a few times, and got lost one night in Madrid for several hours looking for his apartment. I had never driven outside of a city and never in Italy. I spoke some Spanish, but I knew only a few words in Italian.

One of my mottoes as a trial lawyer is "adapt and overcome," and I kept that in mind and headed off in my rental car. I had a map and the name and address of the hotel, as well as the location of the city, and I felt like I could navigate my way there. There were no GPS devices back then, but I was pretty good with a map. I was to meet Leon at the hotel, where he was also staying at the time. The Italian countryside was exquisite, and though I was tired from the journey, I enjoyed driving on the highway and the challenge of adapting to the Italian road signs and signals. Italian drivers are quite fearless and a little crazy, but the real trick, as I had learned in Madrid, was to stay out in front of the traffic; the car in front has a majority of the highway, and is given the right of way by the other drivers trying to avoid a collision. One thing I learned is that Italian motorcycle drivers will not back down to avoid a head-on collision. They must look at passing a car as a badge of honor, so slow down and let them finish passing if you are coming at them on the highway.

Once I began my journey, my prior trip to Italy came flashing back, and I remembered how much I had enjoyed the Italian landscapes, the food, and the people, in 1976. Travel is one of my favorite hobbies. I thought, "what a crazy way to make a living," forgetting that I had made no money, considering all the time and expense I had already spent on Tim. Now I was incurring additional expenses in pursuit of this contract such as an additional $2,000 for my plane ticket to Italy, the rental car, and the hotel where I would be staying. The agent business is not a great business model because of the upfront expense and the risk of no payoff. My sure deal with Arturo, in which I would get a fee to recoup at least some of the expenses, was now uncertain, and I was in a foreign country dealing with a team and another "agent" with whom I was unfamiliar.

I somehow made it to the hotel, which was scenically set in the mountains by a lake. Leon seemed like a nice-enough fellow, but when I asked when we would see Tim, he said it was too late to speak with him that day. It was only early evening, so his response made me a little wary. I was keeping up with the other offer in Spain through Arturo, and it was still open, so I had some leverage with these negotiations. I had dinner and went to bed with the expectation of meeting with Tim the next day. I was tired but still focused on getting a deal done, and setting Tim up with a solid overseas job.

The next morning, Leon drove me up in the mountains to an old gym where the team was working out. It was quite a beautiful setting with the sun caressing the green Tuscan countryside. As I went in the gym, I saw Tim and gave him a wave. The team was working out and running through some drills. After a while, the workout finished, and the players filed into the locker room. As I attempted to go into the locker room to talk to Tim, Leon told me that I could not go in because it was "players only." I stopped; however, Leon proceeded straight into the locker room behind the team. He had full access apparently, since he had played for the team last season, and was obviously buddies with the general manager with whom he was negotiating the "contract."

I felt my temper beginning to rise, but considering I was not on my own turf, in a foreign country, and that Leon was six-foot-ten, and I would estimate 250 pounds and that I was five-foot-nine and 178 pounds, I kept my cool and decided to get to the bottom of what was going on. I had noticed that this older gym had pull-out windows that opened at the top. I ran outside and stood approximately where the locker room was located. All the windows were opened. I moved as close as possible to overhear any pieces of conversation going on inside the locker room. Even to this day, I have excellent hearing, and I could clearly hear Leon talking to Tim and telling him in no uncertain terms that "Oscar did not know what he was doing" and that he needed to fire me.

At this point, any fear of Leon had fallen away with the reality that I had to stick up for myself, or I would lose the client and the contract, and my Italian adventure would end in ruin. I ran around back into the entrance of the gym area to confront Leon on his statements. As he and Tim came out of the gym, I ran over to Leon and confronted him face-to-face saying, "I heard what you were telling Tim in there." Leon seemed a little stunned at first, but soon realized that I really had heard what he had said to Tim about getting me fired. I was sure that Leon had planned on getting rid of me from the beginning, and that he was caught off guard when Tim had insisted that I come to Italy and be a part of the deal. It made sense that he wanted to cut me out and obtain the entire fee. I'm sure that his thought was why should he share the fee with this guy he did not even know.

My next move was to tell Leon that because of his actions, Tim and I would be leaving for Spain for the job that was waiting through Arturo Ortega. This was a risky move of sorts, since I had not really had a chance to speak to Tim in private, and could not really gauge how enamored he was with Leon and the state of their relationship. Leon then looked at Tim and asked the big question, "Tim, are you going with Oscar or staying here?" Tim looked at me and then looked at him and said, "I'm going with Oscar."

Tim's statement was like a lightning bolt aimed at Leon. He was faced with the loss of the one thing an agent must have, the client. To his credit, Leon responded quickly, and announced that he and I would now work together as partners to get this deal done. It was what we had discussed during our conversations before I flew to Italy, but now I had to participate, because Tim and I would be heading to Spain otherwise.

I was anxious to get the deal done, but Leon's "agreement" with the Italian team was not concrete; just conversations he had

had with the general manager. Truthfully, I cannot remember all the details of what transpired the rest of the day, but I do remember him taking me to a nice restaurant and meeting some of the team management. I was impressed with his proficiency in Italian and really wanted to be able to speak a foreign language as well as he did someday. My Spanish was coming along, but was not as good as his Italian. Sometime during this period, we discussed that he had played basketball at Alabama with one of my mother's cousins from Kentucky, Farrah Alford. Though Farrah was my mother's cousin, we were nearly the same age, just like Leon and me. After Tim's declaration of loyalty, Leon and I developed a good rapport, though I never felt like I could put my trust in him, because I really did not know him.

As Thursday arrived and no contract appeared, I began to become uneasy, feeling that the "team," or even Leon, might be trying to drag the negotiations out because the longer we negotiated in Italy, the less likely the Spanish offer would remain viable. Though I did enjoy the Italian food and the atmosphere, I told Tim that the negotiations seemed to be stalled, and that something needed to happen by early Friday.

Friday morning proved to be uneventful, and Friday afternoon I told Tim to pack up because we were going to give the team one last chance or leave for Spain. I wanted to negotiate in a position of power, having another offer, not at the mercy of the team which would know we had no other offer after the Spanish offer expired. Tim and I packed the rental car, and then drove over to a restaurant where Leon was meeting with team officials. When the group saw us in the car, they questioned what we were doing, and I replied we were heading to Spain. The group, including Leon, was startled and surprised because my move had caught them off guard. After I explained to them that we were tired of waiting and that we had decided to take the sure offer in Spain, they suddenly decided that nothing prevented them from moving forward on the contract. I agreed, but let them know that we had to go ahead and sit down and do the contract right then. The restaurant became our place of negotiation, and after several hours, we had a partially handwritten and partially typed contract, which was in line with what Leon had described earlier, and was higher than the Spanish offer. Tim had a great salary, car, housing with bonuses, and the team would pay his taxes. As the afternoon turned into evening, we made copies of the contract by running them through a fax machine.

The issue of agent's fees came up and totaled in the range of close to $20,000, which was to be split between myself and Leon. Unfortunately, I had not really planned the agent-fees -issue out with the ever-evolving situation. Normally, I would have trusted the team and Arturo to make a money transfer at some point as I had with Real Madrid, but this was an entirely different situation. I had a team with which I was unfamiliar, and a "partner" whom I did not really know. The issue was how was I to be paid. I wanted cash or a check I could cash at a bank on Monday. I was willing to delay my flight to get the fee, but then was informed that because of the holiday, all banks would be closed on Monday. Leon would be around to collect his portion of the fee, but what about me? A discussion ensued and the suggestion of "Italian traveler's checks" was offered. These checks would be some type of checks made payable to the bearer of the checks. I agreed to this, as I really could see no alternative. I figured that at least I had something tangible that showed what I was owed, and I could deposit them to my bank when I returned home. The checks were produced, and I accepted those as my part of the fee. The total value of the checks at that time was close to $10,000, which I thought would at least cover the costs of my trip and some of Tim's personal expenses, and expenses incurred in his recruitment and training. The plan was, at this time, for Tim to play a year or so overseas, and then take a shot at the NBA with, hopefully, a guaranteed or partially guaranteed contract.

I slept pretty well Friday night after some more good food, with the knowledge that we had the contract done. I telephoned Arturo and let him know we had taken the Italian deal, and he accepted the outcome, but was still a little wary of the situation. The next day was a holiday and the team was off, so Tim and I decided to do a little sightseeing at the beach. We drove to the beach near Pisa. I figured that the trip would give me a little preview of my trip to the airport the next day. One concern I was now having was my gasoline level in the car; I was now realizing that the type of gas I needed was not highly available and that most of the gas stations were closed. When Italy goes on holiday in August, it really goes on holiday!

The beach was crowded. Tim was surprised that many women had their tops off. Of course, Tim walking the beach drew the attention of many Italians, and they would wave and even throw sand on us in a friendly manner. It was soon explained to us that the throwing of the sand is a custom during Ferragosto, and that there would be some fireworks that evening. Tim and I had a great time on the beach, and then ate another great meal at an Italian restaurant.

We returned to the hotel later that night. I did not mind staying out late, thinking that I could sleep part of the time on the plane trip back, which I've learned is easier said than done at times. Upon my return to the hotel, I confirmed a wake-up call with the front desk and set my alarm for around 7 a.m. so I would be sure to catch my flight back.

My alarm did not go off and the wake-up call never came, so I woke up around 9:30 instead of 7:00. I immediately had an adrenaline rush, realizing that I had missed my flight. Now it was reinforced to me that Italy was on holiday, when I discovered that I could not get any airline on the phone to make another reservation to leave Monday, the next day. Finally, I had to telephone my ex-wife, Elizabeth, at home and ask her to make me an airline reservation home. I still had several crucial legal appointments that I had to make that week. She was successful, but the cost was an additional $2,000. Moreover, I literally had a twenty-four-hour flight time with at least four stops leaving at 7 a.m. out of Pisa. Because of the time difference, I did not learn of the flight time until Sunday night, and I had to get up at 4 a.m. to make the 7 a.m. flight. I still had not found a gas station open to refuel my rental car, and the gas level in the car was nearly empty. This added the additional stress to my return trip of having to worry about running out of gas somewhere during the drive between the hotel and the Pisa airport.

As I went to bed Sunday night, I was tense, knowing I would have to wake up soon and could not really go to sleep. I had said goodbye to Tim earlier, as he was looking for a place to stay and was busy with Leon and the team. I again had asked for a wake-up call and set the alarm, but was tense about the reliability, considering their failures the prior night.

True to form, I only had a few hours sleep Sunday night, and woke up before the alarm and the desk telephone call, which came this time. I hurried and put my suitcases in the car and headed off. I was extremely tired, but energized by the need to get to the airport and get on this flight, as there was no telling when I could leave if I had another miss! During the trip, the gas level in the car showed empty, but I kept going because of the tight time schedule and the fact there were no gas stations open. I made it to the airport about an hour before my departure time. I must have been running on gas fumes, and could not find the rental return. I literally abandoned the car close to the terminal and went inside, where I successfully obtained a ticket and boarded the flight for the first leg of my return trip, which was headed to London.

As soon as I hit my seat, I felt relief and release from the intensity and stress of the trip. I turned on my Walkman and fell asleep almost immediately. I woke sometime later and looked down to a breathtaking view of the Swiss Alps. My thoughts then were, I made it! I came, I negotiated, and I got the deal done for my client. Of course, the rest of the trip was an experience with stops in London, New York, Chicago, and somewhere else, before I finally touched down in Baton Rouge, after twenty-four hours of middle seats and some napping.

I returned to the office the day after my arrival with great stories and my Italian traveler's checks. I delivered the checks over to my banker, and asked him to have the checks redeemed for real money as soon as possible. Naturally, this was something "out of the box" for the bank, so they said they would research it and see what avenue could be opened up to cash the checks. The bank kept the checks, and I waited patiently to recoup some money to at least cover my costs for the trip to Italy.

Approximately ten days later, I was in Costa Rica with my younger brother, John, on a previously scheduled weekend fishing trip. I already had the tickets purchased, and felt like I had to go even though I spent a week going to Italy. We had taken a small plane to the Pacific coast and were staying in a relatively nice resort. I received a telephone call from Tim telling me that he had been fired and was out of a job, even with the guaranteed contract that he had signed with the Pistoia team. The story that Tim relayed to me was that the owner of the team felt like he had been duped into the contract, because Leon and the general manager were working together in some manner of which he was unaware. Regardless, Tim was now out of a job and needed employment as soon as possible. Unbelievable!

I was able to telephone Arturo and advise him of the situation. Arturo was able to confirm what had happened and began to look for an opening for Tim. The previous offer had expired, but he was able to locate another job for Tim, so Tim was able to go straight from Italy to Spain and continue playing. I did not take any fee on this contract, since Arturo really pulled Tim out of a jam, and I felt like he deserved the whole fee, considering the time he had spent previously on Tim, getting nothing in return. Besides, I still had the fee from the botched Italian deal coming in to cover some of Tim's cost. Keep in mind, I still was out all the expenses for his training in Houston, our trip to Portsmouth, my trip to Italy, and other advances to Tim. In any event, by the time I returned to Baton Rouge, Tim was in Spain playing and I turned my attention to practicing law and taking care of my other players, knowing that Tim was in good hands with Arturo.

During the next month and a half, the Italian lira began to depreciate sharply. My nearly $10,000 in traveler's checks had sunk down to a value of around $6,000. I called the bank, but they still were in the process of trying to somehow get them cashed. I mentioned the situation to B.J., and he said he had a friend in Italy, Steffano Lotto, whom he had met when he was working with Sid Blanks, who might be able to help us. B.J. had taken a player who had signed with Sid, Olden Polynice, to Remini, Italy, where he played a year of professional basketball from 1986 to 1987. Polynice had played for the University of Virginia from 1983 to 1986 and was the eighth player taken in the 1987 draft by Chicago. While in Rimini, B.J. had met Steffano, who was a basketball fan. Steffano had also become friends with Jeff Lamp, an American who played in Rimini. Later, Steffano came to Los Angeles for several years when Jeff was playing with the Lakers, and during that time, he kept up his friendship with B.J. Steffano ended up at my house in Baton Rouge with B.J. one night and we have been friends ever since.

Several weeks later, the bank returned the Italian traveler's checks to me uncashed. I was really upset the bank had kept the checks so long while their value plummeted. Finally, with another drop in the lira, I decided to try to use B.J.'s Italian connections, and just fly B.J. to Italy to see if he could at least obtain some value for the checks. I decided the longer I waited, the lower the likelihood that I would be able to cash the checks. B.J. was willing to go see his old friend, so he boarded a plane with the checks and my hope, that he could cash them. That's the way things go in the crazy world of international basketball. B.J. made it to Rimini and, with the help of Steffano's sister who happened to work in a bank, was able to recover about $4,500, which subtracting B.J.'s flight and a few expenses, left me with about $3,000. The $3,000 did not even cover the expense of my trip to Italy to negotiate Tim's contract, so I ended up in the hole for the entire deal. However, knowing that I had closed Stanley's deal did help ease some of the pain for my overall loss on this negotiation.

Unfortunately, Tim never returned to play in the United States, and I lost touch with him for a long while. There were some issues over repayment of some money I had advanced to Tim that led to our disunion, but I took it all in stride. I always do enjoy remembering my trip to the basketball mountain in Italy, and it has always made a great agent story. Tim did touch base with me several years ago, and we met in Atlanta when I was there for a case. He took me out to dinner, and we had some laughs remembering the Italian trip. We are on good terms now, and we talk by telephone periodically and are Facebook friends.

TWELVE
Trade and the End of 1992

I began to hear rumors that Orlando was thinking of trading Big Stan. However, ever since Orlando matched the Dallas offer sheet, Stan and I had been told by Magic management that Orlando wanted to keep Stanley in Orlando, even with Shaq there. At the time, the perception of many was that Stanley may not want to play with Shaq; however, Stanley was more than willing to stay in Orlando and play with Shaq, now that he had his big contract. Stanley and Shaq were always rivals to a degree on the court, but were friends off the court. That is not to say that they hung out together constantly, but they got along. Stan generally got along well with his teammates and was not one to envy the attention received by others, as long as he was treated fairly. Stanley spoke about Shaq near this time in his life in *Shaq Impaq* as follows:

Speaking of Shaq

Stanley Roberts

Former LSU and Orlando Magic center

"Playing against Shaq was like being on a field of war. He was rough. There was some pushing and shoving on the court. But when it was over, it would be all hugs and kisses. Off the court, Shaq was a great person to be around. He likes to have fun, and he's always been a good friend of mine.

"Shaquille and I never had what I'd call a real fight. Sometimes one of us would get the better of the other, and then something might happen. The worst time was when he came after me and I grabbed the trash can. That was definitely the worst time.

"But that's part of being a family. You're always going to have fights and squabbles in a family. We got over them. I accepted the way Shaq was. You've got to remember he was very young at the time, and I'd already been around [at LSU] for a year when he came."

Chapter 12, Pages 176–177

Again, through all the years and all the adventures I have had with Stanley, I have never heard him say anything negative about Shaq. Only recently, Shaq came to Baton Rouge for a celebration of LSU's 1991 SEC Championship Team, and he and Stanley, and the rest of the team, hung out together late into the night at Gino's Italian restaurant.

Based on the assurances from Orlando management, Stanley was prepared to make Orlando his home for the foreseeable future, and excited about it. Stanley and I both liked Orlando as a city and were familiar with the management, the coaches, and the players. Orlando can be hot at times, but it had a lot of upsides, and of course, being familiar with the city made Stanley feel like it was his second home. It was also not far from his family in South Carolina. Personally, I felt like it would be exciting and entertaining to see Stanley and Shaq play together, and through everything, I enjoyed working with John Gabriel and Pat Williams.

Again, based on what management told us, Stanley purchased a house in Orlando. The house was located close to Pat William's house. Stanley really liked his house, and was glad to have a home in Orlando where he would be playing for the upcoming year. A Tim Povtak article of August 16, 1992, seemed to confirm that Stanley would not be traded, and would be in the upcoming fall training camp:

Roberts Good Bet to Be in Magic Camp

By Tim Povtak of The *Sentinel Staff*, August 16, 1992

Many in Central Florida figure Stanley Roberts will be traded soon because there won't be enough playing time for he and Shaquille O'Neal, two of the most promising young centers in the NBA. A good bet, though, is he will be a member of the Orlando Magic when training camp opens in October. One reason is the longer the Magic wait to trade, the better deal they will get. Another reason is that they don't even know what they need. The future of power forward Brian Williams is unclear because doctors remain puzzled over his sudden collapse during a summer-league game last week.

Stanley and I were both relaxed and not worried whether he would be traded, based on what Orlando management kept telling us. Furthermore, we both knew that he would have the ultimate say as to whether he would be traded, because of the no-trade clause contained in his contract. Maybe we were both a little naive about the Magic's intentions, but they did a hard sell on how much they wanted Stanley for the next year. I really did not see the point of them telling us one thing and secretly planning a trade, if we had the ultimate say in where he would play the 1992–1993 season. I thought that getting our input on a potential trade, such as where Stanley wanted to play,

222 | Trade and the End of 1992

made a lot more sense than presenting us with a trade already in place. I should note that players now have a lot more say in where and when they are traded, than back in 1992.

If traded, Stanley would have an additional $2 million added to his present contract, which would sound like a big motivation to most people, but Stanley simply was not a lover of money. Besides a house, Stanley purchased a boat at the urging of one of his teammates, without letting me know ahead of time. This really caught me off guard and alarmed me a little, because he could not swim at the time. Of course, I tried to point this out to him, but he was happy with the purchase and decided to keep the boat.

Apparently, Pat Williams was not as intent on keeping Stanley as he indicated to us. In Bruce Hunter's book, Pat gave an interview discussing the Magic's thoughts on trading Stanley.

Pages 257-258   Pat Williams

Once we signed Shaq and matched on Stanley, we weren't sure what we were going to do. We considered Stanley to be an outstanding asset, and we considered trading him of course. We also thought about playing him with Shaquille and see how that worked out. But we always knew that there would be an option to trade him. Then when that three-way deal came up, we could see it was probably best to move. He had a huge contract. In the worst case, he could get hurt and we'd be stuck with him. There were a lot of bad thoughts going through our minds. There were some good ones, too. We thought we might end up with a better deal later. But we finally decided to grab the chance for two No. 1 draft picks. I guess mainly we were afraid of that big contract and that Stanley might not be happy playing with Shaquille. There was a lot of that fear.

The Magic's "bad thoughts" overrode their assurances to Big Stan that he would be making his home in his new Orlando house the upcoming season. On Friday, August 29, 1992, I was in my office when I received an unexpected call from John Gabriel, the assistant general manager of the Magic. John exchanged some pleasantries and some small talk and asked whether I would be in my office that afternoon. I said I would be in the office in the afternoon, and we concluded our conversation. I thought the whole telephone call a bit odd but was flattered that John took the time to just check in with me.

Later that afternoon, near the end of the day, I received another phone call from John. He said he was on a three way telephone call with Elgin Baylor and Ernie Grunfeld. My gut tightened briefly as I finally realized that something big was up. John quickly informed me that the Magic had agreed to a three-team deal, which involved several players, including some with the Knicks. He said that Stanley would be sent to Los Angeles from the Magic, and Mark Jackson from the Knicks to the Clippers, and the Knicks would receive Charles Smith, Doc Rivers, and Bo Kimble from the Clippers. Orlando would get draft choices as its part of the trade. I really did not get all the details when he initially told me, but he emphasized that numerous NBA big-time pieces were in place, and all the lives of the other players, agents, general managers, and NBA teams were on hold waiting for the approval of the trade by Stanley Roberts, my client. Admittedly, I was in somewhat of a state of shock, not only because of the timing, right at closing time on Friday, but because Orlando was doing just the opposite of what they told us. Truthfully, I also liked that I was really in the big time, with all the names mentioned and the focus of the entire deal now in the hands of Stanley and me, being his agent. There was a bit of selling of the deal, and the opportunity Stanley would have in Los Angeles, and that he would, of course, add to the value of his contract. They made the deal sound like a no-brainer for us to accept, and we were given a short time to approve the trade, or the deal would fall through and Stanley would lose this "opportunity."

There was no question in my mind that the parties were trying to force us into a hurried decision on an important move for Stanley's career. I felt that John's first call had been made to orchestrate the later call Friday afternoon, with the several parties on the line; it wasn't designed to put pressure on us to immediately agree to the trade. I must admit that I was caught off guard initially by the demand to accept or lose the trade. However, the power was in our hands, and particularly in Stanley's hands, and Stanley was not a person you could back into a corner to force a decision. This is a lesson that I had learned with Big Stan early on.

The additional $2 million in salary for simply changing teams did sound good to me, but I was not as up on the basketball implications as I wanted to be with such limited notice. I did know that the Clippers were known as a sort of dysfunctional organization, with Don Sterling as the owner. However, I knew that Stanley had knowledge of the League, and B.J. was available for the inside scoop on any NBA team. Ultimately, I just wanted Stanley to be happy, and find a team where he really could feel like he was an important factor.

After getting off the telephone conference, I immediately telephoned Big Stan and told him what was going on, and advised him of the details of the proposed trade. Stanley was not pleased with the deal, to say the least. Particularly, both he and I were not pleased with how the Magic had not been upfront with us about the trade. Stanley referenced the fact that he was just getting settled in a house that he had purchased, with the assurance from the Magic that he would be in Orlando for the upcoming season. I have to say that I felt the same way, and that it was particularly irritating that John obviously knew about the deal on his initial

Friday call, but did not mention anything to me. After a few more minutes to think about it, I became a little angry with the manner in which the Magic had tried to sandbag us.

Stanley told me in no uncertain terms that he was staying in Orlando in his new house, and that he was exercising his right to veto the trade. Stanley was certainly not intimidated by the number of parties involved, nor motivated by the amount of money he would make. He did not feel that we had been treated fairly by the Magic on the trade, and he was not going along with their plan. I felt that he was entirely justified in his position and backed him. There would be no trade if, as John had indicated to me, we had to let them know our answer that afternoon.

I called John Gabriel back and told him we were not interested in the trade, and it was a no-deal. I think that John was stunned, for he had assumed that we would go along with the trade. I explained to him how Stanley felt, and that we were blindsided by their move to trade him. I mentioned that Stanley had bought a house near Pat. Further, I noted that at any time, they could have discussed a trade in good faith in an up-front manner, rather than giving us a late Friday afternoon call to confirm a trade already in place! After realizing that Stanley really meant that he would not agree to the trade, John then backtracked from having to know "today" to a position that we could have some additional time to think about the trade over the weekend. This confirmed to me that the other parties were confident that Stanley and I would get caught up in the big trade tactics, and agree to the trade immediately. However, this was a definite miscalculation by the Magic and the other teams. Presenting the trade to Big Stan by springing it on him, after the agreement was in place, only made him more resistant. Trying to pressure Big Stan into anything, much less a trade that meant he would have to move across the country, was a mistake. As I had learned on prior occasions, Stanley responded to reasoned talk much better than ultimatums.

The telephone call of Friday, August 29, 1992, began a three -week campaign by the teams involved in the trade, to convince Stanley that he should agree to the trade, especially by Orlando and The Clippers. However, Stanley, at only twenty-two, was not going to be criticized, browbeaten, or intimidated into the trade, and this was my message to the team's management. The press caught wind of the story, and there was even some criticism of Stan, that he had to be convinced to accept the trade, even though an extra $2 million was being added to his contract. Agents have to keep in mind that many times team management and the press do not necessarily have the best interest of their clients in mind, when it really counts.

On Monday, September 1, the *Chicago Tribune* made a reference to Stanley blocking the trade over the preceding weekend:

Chicago Tribune

September 1, 1992

Pro basketball: A proposed three-way deal involving the Knicks, the Los Angeles Clippers and the Orlando Magic has been blocked by center Stanley Roberts of the Magic, who is invoking his contractual right to reject a trade, according to the *New York Times*.

On September 2, 1992, an article in *L.A. Times* by Scott Howard Cooper stated that:

The Clippers are ready. The New York Knicks are ready. The Orlando Magic is ready. But Stanley Roberts is not.

So three teams and four other players, not to mention the destination of three draft choices, await the decision of a 22-year-old with one year of NBA experience to see if a major trade will be completed. As an executive from one of the clubs involved said: 'The kid holds all the cards.'

On Tuesday, September 2, 1992, the Magic asked Stanley to meet with Matt Guokas, the Magic head coach, to discuss the "deal," but Stanley decided not to show up for the meeting, which was recorded in the press:

Sports

Roberts Says He'd Welcome Trade to Heat

By Barry Cooper of the *Sentinel Staff*, September 2, 1992

Orlando center Stanley Roberts, who was a no-show for an 11 a.m. meeting Tuesday with Magic coach Matt Guokas, said he may permit a trade—but only to a team of his choice. Roberts has a clause in his 5-year, $15 million contract that gives him veto power over any trade for one year. He has exercised that right in blocking the Magic from completing a three-team deal that would send him to the Los Angeles Clippers. Guokas planned to ask Roberts to go along with the trade Tuesday, but Roberts skipped their scheduled meeting and spent the morning playing with his baby daughter.

During this time, I was receiving calls from the management of the various teams providing more positive slants on the trade; however, the decision to agree to the trade was Stanley's, and he was dug in about not wanting to go to Los Angeles. He did, however, start thinking about some teams that he would consider as possible trade choices.

The next development in this drama was that Los Angeles unilaterally decided to fly one of its staff, Keith Jones, to Orlando to contact Stanley, and begin the equivalent of a boots-on-the-ground offensive to convince Stanley to agree to the trade. I was not contacted about this move, and when Stanley told me that the Clippers had flown their equipment manager to Orlando to talk to him, I was somewhat disturbed. As an attorney, it would be unethical for me to contact someone else's client, and I felt that this tactic was a personal foul, so to speak. I had nothing personally against Keith, whom I became good friends with subsequently, but it struck me as unprofessional, from a legal point of view, and just sneaky from a business point. However, this is just a side of sports representation that you have to get used to; there can be millions and millions of dollars at stake, but you are dealing with a profession where many contacts are made informally, and seemingly off the cuff. Further, even if a person has a legal background, many times traditional legal ethics and professional standards are not followed or enforced as in other business settings. In any event, Stanley, as usual, was very unconcerned, and, in fact, was enjoying Keith's visit. Accordingly, I never complained, but did mention in a telephone call that I was aware of his presence in Orlando. In the years that followed, I would get to know Keith well, and he and Stanley would become good friends. The trainer on a team is always good to know, and I did get him to hook me up with Clipper gear on several occasions. Keith eventually moved from the Clippers to the Rockets, and was in Houston when Stanley had a short stint with the Rockets. He's still with the Rockets, and I see him on TV when I watch the Rocket's games.

As the next several weeks unfolded, other teams were mentioned as possible alternatives to the Clippers in a trade for Stanley. However, Stanley was taking his time in coming to a decision. It became a big story, and Stanley was taking unfair criticism for "holding up the trade," because it involved several other NBA players. The Magic had put him in this situation, but Stanley was not affected by media reports. For example, on September 9 and 10, Barry Cooper reported in the *Orlando Sentinel*:

Pistons Eyeing Roberts?

By Barry Cooper of the *Sentinel Staff*, September 9, 1992

Unable to persuade center Stanley Roberts to accept a trade to the Los Angeles Clippers, the Orlando Magic may have another option to present to him: a trade to the Detroit Pistons. The Pistons on Tuesday night traded power forward John Salley to the Miami Heat for the rights to rookie forward Isaiah Morris and the Heat's No. 1 draft pick in 1993 unless it's in the top five. The *Detroit News,* in today's editions, said the Pistons were considering offering the No. 1 pick from the Heat and their own first-round pick in '93 for Roberts.

Roberts Content to Stay

By Barry Cooper of the *Sentinel Staff*, September 10, 1992

Orlando Magic center Stanley Roberts has made clear his position on being traded. He doesn't want to be sent to the Los Angeles Clippers, the Detroit Pistons or any other team. But statements he made Wednesday to *The Orlando Sentinel* will keep fans guessing about his status. Roberts, reached at his home in Orlando, said he will appear at a press conference, possibly today, at the Magic's offices. He wouldn't divulge the nature of the press conference, "They (the Magic) told me not to say anything," Roberts said.

Stanley continued to weigh his options, and in the meantime, Keith Jones continued to tell him why he should come to Los Angeles and agree to the trade. However, I had been around Stanley enough to know that unless he really wanted to change his mind, he would not. I was happy to do whatever he decided, and weighed the pros and cons with him several times. As the days, and then even a week passed, he was still considering the offer. On September 11, 1992, a newspaper report by Barry Cooper demonstrated the frustration that some Knick fans were feeling.

Roberts Gets Mugged on New York's Airwaves

By Barry Cooper of the *Sentinel Staff*, September 11, 1992

In New York City, Stanley Roberts' name was mud Thursday. Popular radio talk-show host Christopher Russo made sure of it. Russo, who formerly worked in Orlando for WKIS-AM (now WWNZ-AM) spent much of his afternoon show blasting Roberts, Orlando's back-up center, for blocking a three-team trade that would have strengthened the Knicks. Roberts has refused to waive a 1-year, no-trade clause in his contract, and the Magic, Clippers and Knicks have had to scuttle what would have been one of the biggest trades of the summer.

Suddenly, an invitation was transmitted to me and Stanley to fly out to Los Angeles to meet with the team, team management, and even owner Don Sterling to really get a feel for the city and the team. By this time, Keith Jones had been able to at least convince Stanley to accept the trip offer to come to L.A. Naturally, I cleared my calendar to make the trip to see what the Clippers had to say, and committed to come with Stanley. I felt that if I went, I could get to know the Clippers management with whom I had been speaking, which included Andy Roeser and Elgin Baylor, and get to meet the mysterious Keith Jones. Knowing the team management well would be an advantage if the trade did go through, as I would be dealing with them for some years representing Stanley. It would also give me an opportunity to spend some time with Stanley, and keep a somewhat watchful eye on him while he was in Los Angeles. Although I knew that Stanley was beyond my reach as far as my having any control over him, I felt he did listen and use my advice on occasion, and I was a good sounding board for him. However, Stanley was very much his own man, and it seemed to me he had a cast of questionable characters who attached themselves to him wherever he went, including Baton Rouge, Spain, and Orlando.

The itinerary of the trip sounded great, kind of like something out of a make-a-basketball-fan's wish come true. We were to fly first-class to Los Angeles, stay in Century City, go to an Arsenio Hall show, and attend a party Magic Johnson was hosting. We would then attend the Clipper's "all white party" (meaning you wore all white), at Don Sterling's Malibu home, and have meetings with the team, coach and management mixed in, when there was time. Stanley would be able to chat with his future teammates, and talk with then-head coach Larry Brown. Some of the more prominent players on the Clippers at that time were Danny Manning, Loy Vaught, Ron Harper, Ken Norman, John Williams, Kike VanDeWeghe, and Gary Grant. Mark Jackson would be joining the team if the trade were to go through as arranged. Stanley would be one of the highest paid players on the team, if he joined the club.

When we arrived at LAX, we were picked up by a Town Car, arranged by the team, and taken to Century City. My room at Century City was a small suite with a nice view, and I remember thinking I was living the life of a big-time agent. I had already seen Stanley play outside of Orlando, so I was accustomed to the luxury hotels where players stayed on the road, but this room had a great view, was large, and was, of course, paid for by the team. This just reemphasized what I had already learned; even a minor player-agent, like me, could immediately gain some importance, if the player he represented was valuable and talented enough to be an NBA playing factor. I did have to give myself credit though; after initially signing Stanley, I did do my homework and negotiate two great contracts, which included the language (no-trade clause) in the contract that had brought us here.

After a short time to settle into the rooms, Stanley and I were taken by limo to the Clipper facilities, and then to a lunch with Larry Brown and some of the players. I liked Coach Brown, as did Stanley. After the lunch, we were taken to an early taping of the Arsenio Hall show where Stanley got a shout-out from Arsenio. Stanley remembers having another lunch with Keith Jones and Coach Brown at some other point in time.

During the course of the weekend that followed, Stanley and I were treated like royalty. Not only did we enjoy the great accommodations, we were chauffeured all over Los Angeles, and attended a Magic Johnson party as well as a Clippers party. Of course, I was always introduced as "Stanley's agent, Oscar Shoenfelt."

The Magic Johnson party was a great event. Stanley and I did not go to the charity game, but went to the after party. I did not meet Magic Johnson, but mingled with all kinds of celebrities. Shaq was in the crowd, and so was his ex-teammate assistant, Dennis Tracy. We four sat and talked for approximately an hour. I recalled to Dennis that he had waited on my table at Juban's when Leonard Armato had sent David Spencer to meet with me on his way to Italy. I remember thinking that Shaq had made a great move in trusting a proven friend to come into his world, as compared to Stanley, who with his "friendly" nature would befriend absolute strangers and take them into his confidence. Not to say that Shaq was not friendly—but from my limited experience— he was actually very friendly and very funny, but he had that pride and competitive edge as part of his nature that made him a superstar, and he did not let just anyone penetrate his inner circle, which is a good trait for a celebrity to have. This would be the last time that I would ever get close enough to actually speak to Shaq until more than twenty years later, when he and my client, Ervin Johnson, would be inducted into the Louisiana Sports Hall of Fame in 2013. I would catch a glimpse of him at games throughout the years and wave, but he always had so much attention and security, it was hard to actually reach him.

Stan and I head out while in Los Angeles for the Clippers recruiting trip.

We were told about Don Sterling's vast Beverly Hills real estate holdings and that the site of the Clippers party was his house in Malibu. The party was a Clippers tradition to begin the start of the new season and training camp. Don Sterling invited the entire team and as many celebrities as he could to make it a real event. This had sounded great when Stanley and I were invited to L.A., and were told about it. Of course, I had heard stories about Don Sterling, that he was not really interested in winning a championship, because of the way that he ran the team. The new storyline was that he was assembling a good team for a championship run, and Stanley could be part of that championship team.

I had been told about the "all white" party prior to flying out to Los Angeles, and had brought a white shirt and white pants to wear to the party. I also made sure to bring my new Ray-Ban sunglasses to look really "L.A. cool." Yes, the agent life was going to my head a little by now, but I always had the reality check of knowing that I was only there because I was Stanley's agent. We were picked up in a limo, and when I saw Stanley, I was a little surprised; I had to laugh because he had decided to wear a blue jean outfit with a matching shirt and shorts. Stanley always marched to his own drummer, so his dress was not an absolute shock. I figured that he was the center of attention and he could wear what he wanted. He really didn't care about the all-white theme.

Upon arrival at the party, I noted that, yes, almost everyone except Stanley was dressed in white. I stuck close to him, which was easy, because he was easy to spot. Stanley and I were taken around, and we posed for photos, including a photo with Don Sterling, Elgin Baylor, Andy Roeser, and Coach Brown and his girlfriend. Overall it was a great afternoon. I struck up conversations with most of the players and some of the celebrities.

Don Sterling's "All White Party" 1992 (left to right) Stanley, Larry Brown, and girlfriend, Donald Sterling, me, and Elgin Baylor.

My favorite celebrity was Woody Harrelson. I knew he liked basketball because of his role in *White Men Can't Jump*, and I struck up a conversation about his playing basketball, and my playing basketball. I had not played on a team since the sixth grade, but I did have a goal in my backyard while growing up, and I played with one of my best friends, Richard Hiller, a thousand games, with me winning only a few times. Richard and I had roomed together in law school, and we played during that time at our apartment, and again when he spent the summer with me after our first year in law school. He was about an inch shorter than I am, but he could really shoot from the outside. Woody and I were about the same height, and I thought I might stand a chance to beat him. I challenged him to a game sometime, and he laughingly agreed. However, I never could find a way to follow up with him, so the match never happened. Of course, the party made a great story when I returned to the reality of Baton Rouge, practicing law and being a husband and the father of three children.

After a most interesting and enlightening weekend, I felt that Stanley should have enough information to decide about the trade. I appreciated all the Clippers had done, and came to the conclusion that they really wanted him in Los Angeles. I liked both Elgin Baylor, the general manager, and Andy Roeser, the president of the Clippers, both of whom I would become well -acquainted with as the years passed. I did not have much interaction with Coach Brown, but he seemed like a very reasonable guy and a "player's coach." Stanley was impressed with his conversations with Coach Brown but still a little up in the air. Due to all the interest on September 21, 1992, I issued a press statement that was informative, but still did not say Stanley had reached a decision.

The New York Times

BASKETBALL: Did Knicks Hear Deal? No, but Roberts Talks

By Clifton Brown, Published September 22, 1992

Shoenfelt was returning to Baton Rouge, La., from Los Angeles and could not be reached for comment, but he issued this statement:

"Our visit with the Clippers was an extremely positive one. We were impressed with the owner, general manager, the coaching staff and team personnel. A decision will be made within the next few days."

The proposal has dragged on like a soap opera. And the final decision remains with Roberts, who has the contractual right to veto any trade for one year.

Whether Roberts will change his mind is still unclear. Reached at his home earlier yesterday, Roberts said, "I still don't want to leave Orlando."

When asked if there was any way the Clippers or the Magic could persuade him to accept a trade to Los Angeles, Roberts said, "I don't think so. I don't want to move from Orlando to L.A."

But later in the day, Shoenfelt issued his statement and the guessing game resumed.

Stanley finally made up his mind around September 21, 1992. He really liked Coach Brown and his discussions with him put it over the top. I think he also, by this time, felt like he was not welcome in Orlando anymore, contrary to what we had been told when his Dallas deal was matched by the Magic. On the positive side, Stanley added a little over $2 million to his contract, which would make it worth over $17 million. On the negative side was the city of Los Angeles, which had good distractions, but also a large number of bad distractions where Stanley's weaker side might emerge.

On September 22, 1992, I telephoned the Magic and told them that Stanley agreed to the trade. Stanley made the official announcement by radio. The newspaper ran an account of Stanley's announcement:

Roberts Agrees—Deal Done

By Barry Cooper of the *Sentinel Staff*, September 23, 1992

Stanley Roberts, who vowed he wouldn't be traded, broke his promise Tuesday and pulled on a Los Angeles Clippers jersey. Roberts, 23, one of the most sought-after young centers in the NBA but only a backup for the Orlando Magic, accepted a three-team trade that sends him to the Clippers to be their starting center. He made the announcement on the air at 102 JAMZ radio station in Lake Mary at 5:20 p.m. The 1-year, no-trade clause in Roberts' contract had been holding up the deal for weeks. Roberts waived the clause Tuesday, convinced, he said, that the Magic no longer wanted him. Roberts' announcement was the go-ahead for the Magic, the Clippers, and the New York Knicks to consummate a trade that could alter the balance of power in the Eastern conference.

With Stanley's decision to move to Los Angeles, a new chapter opened in our relationship. My sports business was on the move, and Stanley was no longer a short plane flight away. Even though I wanted to check on him as much as possible, this was no longer possible without a flight to Los Angeles. His big contract was done, so I could take a breath and work with some other sports clients while also keeping up with my law practice.

An October 4, 1992 article about me in the *Morning Advocate* entitled "Sports Agent Shoenfelt Enjoying Life in the Big Time," by Lee Feinswog quoted Brian Schmitz to sum up Stanley's year in Orlando:

> Wrote Brian Schmitz in the *Orlando Sentinel* last week, "Here's a 22-year-old kid who came to the Magic unmotivated and overweight—left unmotivated and overweight. And in between, the NBA made him independently wealthy after one season although he needed half of it to get into semblance of shape."

I actually took the summary as a compliment. My job as Stanley's agent was to get him paid, despite any issues that may have arisen about his conditioning or his attitude, and I did!

THIRTEEN
Sports Business Expansion, 1992

———— • ————

By October 1992, I was thirty-eight and spending at least a third of my time on the sports business. Our law firm was doing well and enjoying the new office we had opened in the spring. We now had four partners and several associates in the firm. On the legal side, I was now almost exclusively working in medical malpractice cases when I was not working on the agent business.

I enjoyed the medical malpractice immensely since I was able to study the medicine, and work the cases up for trial or settlement. Settlement was always preferable, as payment was a sure thing. A large majority of the cases settle, but that's only after you screen your cases and work them up thoroughly to ensure you are in a position to take the case to trial. Medical malpractice cases are difficult to win, expensive and, in almost all cases, take several years to resolve. Since I had joined the firm, "Chick" Moore and I had a couple of big medical malpractice jury trial wins, and I must say I learned a great deal from Chick about trying a jury trial. Our firm had obtained a reputation for medical malpractice, and we had numerous attorneys who referred cases to us.

B.J. and I were working the sports and our friendship continued to grow. By this time, I had taken over the representation of Rufus Porter, an all-pro linebacker and special teams player who played for the Seattle Seahawks. Rufus formally had been represented by Sid Blanks, but became dissatisfied with him, as did several other clients. He and B.J. were close, so when B.J. told him about me, he decided to give me a shot. Rufus was in the middle of his contract with Seattle, so I would not have to do much for him upfront. He was a great pick-up, and finally gave me a legitimate standout football client with whom most sports fans and players were familiar.

Rufus had played his college football at Southern University and was an undrafted free agent in 1988. He made the Pro Bowl as a special team player for two years in 1988 and 1989, and was now starting as linebacker for the Seahawks. Rufus was not only a great player, but turned out to be a great client. Believe me, you can have a great sports player who is not necessarily a great client. Rufus played with great intensity on the field, but was very level -headed off the field. He was mature, listened to what you had to say, always paid his bills, and took care of his personal business. I really enjoyed representing him and watching him play throughout the years.

Willie ("Top Cat" Williams) was still under contract with Phoenix, but had been placed on the Injured Reserve List for the beginning of the 1992 season, where he would remain for the entire season. It was great to have Rufus as an active player whom I could advise and watch play. I was already in the process of becoming more familiar with the NFL Collective Bargaining agreement, with the thought of negotiating his new contract when the present contract expired.

B.J. had also brought with him another player who had

terminated Sid Blanks, Chris Morris. Chris was playing in the NBA at the time, and had been the fourth draft pick in the 1988 NBA draft. Chris was a six-foot, eight-inch small forward who had played at Auburn, and been drafted by the then-New Jersey Nets. He was athletic and talented, and had played extremely well for the Nets since being drafted. His contract was due to expire at the end of the 1991–1992 season, when he became disillusioned with Sid. The disillusionment cameover a house deal Sid had arranged for Chris that did not go well. In addition, Chris and Sid had restructured part of Chris's contract with the Nets with a loan by way of a loan that was to be forgiven as part of his new contracting, beginning in 1992. The loan agreement was a side deal, and not part of Chris's official contract. Unfortunately, before I had a chance to sit down and meet Chris, he had already discharged Sid and hired Bob Woolf as his new NBA agent to negotiate his new contract.

When I met Chris, he retained me to represent him in an agent-player grievance that Sid had filed against him when he stopped paying Sid his agent fees in July 1992, due to his dissatisfaction with Sid. I was excited to work on the grievance at an hourly rate, but it really would have been nice to have picked Chris up as a player-agent client. However, Chris had already committed to Bob Woolf and stuck with him despite me working with him closely on the grievance. I never directly asked Chris to let me be his agent, but felt that, in developing a close relationship with him, this might come up; it never happened.

In order to respond to the grievance, I had to obtain copies of Chris's prior contracts and go through the "business" that had been managed by Sid. Sid had been hired by Chris when he signed as his agent, to manage his "business" for an additional percentage of his salary, a practice that later became prohibited by the NBPA, but was a practice some agents employed in 1988. While in New York, I went to Chris's house in New Jersey and met his wife,

Michelle, and his three boys. I liked his family and it was a very positive experience.

In reviewing his prior contract, I noticed the restructuring of the contract and the fact that he was due to receive forgiveness of the $162,500 loan from the prior year. This was set out in a separate letter and was not part of the contract, which was to my thinking probably contrary to the CBA. I was doing this research in late September, early October, when Woolf's team was negotiating Chris's new contract. When I called them, they had not reviewed the prior contract and were unaware of this provision. I told them of the provision, and they used it in their negotiations for Chris to gain forgiveness for the loan in the form of a signing bonus. I received a thank-you from Bob and Chris but of course no agent fee. Bob did send me an autographed copy of a book he wrote, *Friendly Persuasion*, with the inscription "To Oscar Shoenfelt III, Best wishes to a "Superstar Lawyer" and friend! Sincerely Bob Woolf" June 17, 1993.

Chris signed his new three-year contract negotiated by the Bob Woolf group on October 13, 1992. Since I was working with Chris in preparation for his upcoming grievance hearing, my office began to help him with some of his business management.

After Angela had departed, I had hired another paralegal sports assistant named Libby Reny. I cannot remember exactly how Libby made her way to my office, but she was working for the firm in some capacity before she started helping me. Libby was married and was petite, attractive, organized, a good talker, and had an amazing ability to direct people, particularly men, which included my clients and even me. Libby had begun to work with Chris on some of his personal and business interests, and he really liked the job she was doing.

My thought at the time was that if I could represent Chris on his legal grievance issue and help him with his business, then surely I would be in a position to do his next contract, since he really did not have much contact with his representative at the Woolf group. It seemed like three years would go by quickly, but in agent time, three years is a long time to take care of a client and wait to cash in on a fee. I learned this with Stanley. Once Woolf did the three-year deal, he was entitled to the whole fee, even if he did nothing after that point in time.

B.J. and Chris were good friends, and he kept up with Chris on how he was doing from a player's point of view. Chris, like many players, worked out in Houston in the off-season, so B.J. was in constant contact with him. Libby appeared to be getting an inside track on handling his business matters in total, so it was as if I was his agent, only I was not getting paid. However, the exposure of representing Chris was good for business, as he was a high profile player and I liked him personally, so the relationship continued to grow.

The hearing for the grievance was to be in January 1993, at the NBPA headquarters, and I continued to work up the case; I devised several defenses to payment of the outstanding fees, and even filed a counterclaim for money damages on several grounds. A good offense makes a good defense, and I wanted Sid to have something to lose if we had to actually have a hearing on the grievance.

The grievance system is used under both the NBA and the NFL Collective Bargaining Agreements and the NBPA and the NFLPA player-agent rules. I had already filed a grievance for Stanley against the Magic, but Chris's grievance was the first I really worked up to present to an arbitrator, in this case George Nicolau.

Grievances have few rules of procedure laid out in the agent rules, and the hearings have no real rules of evidence. I filed a written answer to Sid's grievance and a written counterclaim asking for damages against Sid for various actions he did or did not do when representing Chris. I then had to go through documents such as Chris's contract and the documents of the business dealings Sid handled, to work the case up and prepare our evidence for the arbitration. Our evidence consisted of the documents and the testimony of Chris and Michelle. Sid was representing himself, and he was not an attorney, so I felt like I had an advantage in that respect.

During the fall of 1992, I was also overseeing Stanley's move to the West Coast. When Stanley approved the trade, I had thought that this might be an opportunity to somehow get some more positive influences into his life. My younger brother, John, was about Stanley's age, and I thought that he and Stanley might become good friends, if given the opportunity. John had just finished a degree at the University of North Carolina at Asheville in acting, and had no current employment. He was interested in moving to the West Coast. Stanley already had some helpers in Orlando, but he would need someone that he could trust to help him look for a house and get set up in Los Angeles. Libby was working with him but could not be in Los Angeles for an extended period of time. She had been in contact with Clipper personnel to get the lay of the land, so to speak. The Clippers were going to put Stanley up at the LAX Airport Sheraton for a period of time so he could find housing. Libby flew out for a short time to help Stanley begin his potential search for a home. The real estate business in L.A. is cutthroat, but we were soon to learn that when a new NBA player arrives in town, it is like blood in the water for a group of sharks. Suddenly, we had half-a-dozen real estate agents trying to contact Stanley to sell him a house.

I came up with the idea of sending my brother out to act as Big Stan's personal assistant in Los Angeles, and Stanley went along with the idea. When I had seen Shaq working with Dennis Tracy, I had visions of Stanley and John pairing up so as to eliminate the hangers-on that constantly made their way into Stanley's world. In any event, John flew out to Los Angeles and took up residence at the LAX Sheraton to assist Stanley. John is a super nice person, very intelligent, and really gets along with people. However, he is more of an artistic type who moves with deliberation, meaning that he takes his time with things. John and Stanley hit it off fine.

Libby was in Los Angeles when John arrived and was coordinating setting up real estate appointments for Stanley to view potential residences. John commented that Libby had her sunglasses on and seemed to be really at home in the spotlight, dealing with the inner circle of the Clippers. This was a harbinger of things to come. A real estate agent had already worked his way into the picture by way of recommendation of someone at the Clippers. In addition, Keith Jones already had hooked Stanley up with somebody unknown to me who was taking care of Stanley's cars and some of his personal errands.

After a month or so, I discovered that Stanley was just pleasing me when he agreed to John coming out to Los Angeles. After arriving, John began his work setting up appointments to look at houses for Stanley. Though Stanley liked the idea of buying a house, he did not want to spend the time looking at each and every house on the market. John would preview each house to see if it might be suitable for Stanley. If John thought it was a house Stanley might like, he would then arrange a second viewing for him and Stanley. After a month, John moved out of the hotel, flew back to North Carolina, and drove back to Los Angeles to continue to help Stanley out as much as possible.

After Stanley had spent a month or so in Los Angeles and felt more at home, he began failing to show for the appointments John was setting up. I spoke with Stanley and John, and came to the conclusion that Stanley, though viewing John as a friend, did not view him as a potential assistant, because he was my brother and might report back to me if he (Stanley) was up to mischief. Though I was Stanley's agent and very close to him, he generally wanted me in the dark regarding some of his activities, so I would not disapprove and try to intervene. John, while doing his best to find a house for Stanley, primarily ended up meeting many of Stanley's friends and hanging out with him for several months. But in the end, he felt like he was not really accomplishing much in the way of work. Accordingly, John told Stanley he did not feel like he could continue to help him.

It had been suggested that Marina del Rey would be a good spot for Stanley to buy a house since it was close to the airport. He eventually landed a house right on the Marina but soon had caretakers and hangers-on moving in, just like Orlando. Though I would receive reports on Stan's status from Libby and John in Los Angeles, I could not be involved on a day-to-day basis in what was happening with him. I was on call to handle any type of problems that arose with the management and did try to speak with him several times a week.

I began to make trips to Los Angeles every couple of months to check on Stanley and visit my brother. My legal work took me to Los Angeles during this time period, as I had become acquainted with Dr. Ron Wender, head of anesthesiology at Cedars Sinai Hospital in Beverly Hills. I had retained Dr. Wender and some other physicians who worked at Cedars as experts on some of my cases.

Meanwhile, I was continuing to work with B.J. on representing some other clients and looking for new clients. One such client was Chancellor Nichols, a six-foot eight-inch basketball forward who had been represented by Sid Blanks and was a good friend of B.J.'s. Chance and B.J. had met when Chance was at James Madison University in B.J.'s hometown of Harrisonburg, Virginia. Chance had been at Mississippi State from 1987 to 1989, and then transferred to James Madison. He had come out early in the 1991 draft and gone undrafted. He had been working out with B.J. and playing with the many NBA players who come to Houston to live and work out in the summer. When I signed on as Chance's agent, he looked like a good prospect to either make an NBA roster or else go overseas with Arturo's help.

Chance was a very personable guy, and a real smooth talker. I always thought that if he wasn't playing basketball he would have been a great salesperson. He had great potential talent and size, and up to this point in time, those attributes had gotten him a long way. However, he had not been able to land a spot on an NBA roster. He worked hard and was in shape after the summer of 1992, and B.J. was able to persuade the Houston Rockets to take him to preseason camp. I was his agent, but have to give credit to B.J. who literally knew all the Rockets coaching staff and players from his workouts in Houston.

Chance remained on the team for the preseason games, and I was anxious to go over and see him get some playing time in a game situation. It was Saturday, October 17, 1992, and the Rockets had a preseason game with the Pacers. I decided it would be fun to take my eight-year-old daughter, Katie, with me to the game. Katie was a soccer player, but liked sports, and I thought she could see the behind-the-scenes of a basketball game and get to meet some of the players.

B.J., Katie, and I watched the game, and Chance did get some playing time. However, while playing in the third quarter, he collided with Robert Horry trying to get a rebound and went to the floor on his back. We watched as he lay on the floor for several minutes, and became increasingly concerned. We headed down to the floor of the arena as he was being taken out on a stretcher. When we caught up with him, he told us he was unable to move his legs, which was frightening to us all. Katie was not shy and was right there enjoying all the action. The paramedics were loading Chance into the ambulance to take him to the hospital, and asked who wanted to ride with him to the hospital. B.J. thought that I, as the agent representative, should ride, and Katie chimed in that she "wanted to ride in the ambulance." Since only one person could ride in the ambulance, I rode with Chance, and B.J. and Katie met me at the hospital. The ride to the hospital was my first and last in an ambulance to this date. I said several prayers that Chance would be all right, but was also calculating that he should be covered by the Rockets for the medicals and other damages if this turned out to be a long-term injury.

B.J. and Katie made it to the hospital and we stayed with Chance for a while and spent the night in Houston. Katie and I went by to see him as we left town. Chance regained full use of his legs and began some rehabilitation. His medicals were covered, but the injury cost him a chance to make the Rockets. I continued to represent Chance for a number of years, and he played in the CBA and overseas, but never made a roster in the NBA. He now works as a deputy sheriff in Houston, a job at which I'm sure he excels with his flair for public relations.

Throughout the rest of 1992, I worked as an attorney and continued trying to expand my sports business. B.J. and I were in the process of trying to come up with some potential clients for the 1993 NBA draft. I was also working on Chris Morris's grievance, which was set for January, 1993. At the same time, Stanley was getting acclimated to Los Angeles. Unfortunately, he struggled with weight problems, particularly after obtaining the huge guaranteed contract. Stanley's course was not dictated by a lack of people wishing him well and giving him proper advice as to his course of action. Elgin Baylor and the Clippers and some of his teammates worked with him, but Stanley at times had his own agenda. Of course, the team's erratic ownership lead by Don Sterling compounded his problems further in the future.

Stanley did not lack for all kinds of people trying to

advise him in Los Angeles. Again, his gentle nature and his inability to say no to people made him a target for intrusions into his inner circle. Libby helped him in some of his personal interests and became an influence in his decision-making. She was reporting to me, but in time developed her own agenda, of which I was unaware.

Stanley had told me at some point that if we were able to sign a big contract after his first year he might buy me a car to show his appreciation for all the work I had put in on his contract. He was aware that I really had not made any fees for the first couple of years, considering all the time that I willingly put into his career. Sure enough, after the trade and the success of the "no-trade" trade clause, which made him an additional $2 million, he did buy me a new Lexus, which again proves his generosity. I struggled with whether to accept the present, but I did after talking with him and knowing he was truly grateful and did appreciate all the work and stress I had endured. I felt like he was generous to people who did not have his best interest at heart and had not helped him, and this was true appreciation for someone who had actually helped him. I would never forget this in later years when he had some rougher times and still remember it now even today.

A couple of articles from Orlando appeared criticizing Stanley by the end of 1992 for his conditioning as the 1992–1993 season began to get underway:

Sports

Roberts Reportedly Down to 300 But Is Still Out of Shape

By Barry Cooper of the *Sentinel Staff*, November 22, 1992

Bulletin: Stanley Roberts' weight reportedly is down to around 300. Three hundred! Now you know why the Orlando Magic were so eager to send him packing. Roberts, the starting center for the Los Angeles Clippers, is having a miserable time trying to play his way into shape. Won't habitually overweight players learn they can't wait until the start of the season to build stamina? Roberts has been slowed by tendinitis in his right knee, which compounds his problem. Try strapping on 25 extra pounds and jogging on a sore knee.

Sports

Roberts Gets Shot to Prove Magic Wrong

By Tim Povtak of the *Sentinel Staff*, December 3, 1992

This isn't the way Stanley Roberts had hoped to start his career with the Los Angeles Clippers, but it's why the Orlando Magic traded him during the off-season. Roberts, a 7-foot, 300-pound center who played his rookie season with the Magic, will face his old teammates tonight for the first time, hoping to prove them wrong, even though he already has proved them right. Roberts started this season much as he started last season—out of shape, inconsistent and prone to foul trouble.

Stanley did round into shape during the season and ended up playing in seventy-seven games or sixty-five percent of the games that season. He averaged 11.3 points a game and had 141 blocks. Stanley started at center along with Danny Manning, Mark Jackson, Ron Harper, and Ken Norman. Players coming off the bench were Loy Vaught, Gary Grant, Kiki VanDeWeghe, and John Williams, who had played at LSU. The team was inconsistent but did make it into the playoffs with a 41-41 record as a number seven seed and took on the Houston Rockets in the first round of the playoffs, which turned out to be a classic five-game series. (more details later) I made several of the regular season games in Los Angeles when I was there on various trips and caught up with the team several times on the road, including in Houston. Coach Larry Brown turned out to be one of Stanley's favorite coaches of all time.

FOURTEEN

Recruiting and Signing Ervin Johnson

Ervin at Seattle.

During 1992, I was ever mindful that in order to grow my sports business, I had to continually attempt to recruit new clients and establish a sufficient cash flow to justify my continued activity as an agent. Sure, being an agent was great, but if my agent practice did not prove to be a financial success for the firm long term, then there would be no real reason to continue. Stanley's contract was a step in the right direction, but the reality was that his fees only paid a reasonable percentage of overhead and expenses, after which there was only a modest contribution left toward the fees I needed to contribute to the firm. In the practice of law, time is money as in most businesses and I was spending increased time in the sports business.

After our firm built the fabulous new office, we expanded the size of our staff and then had four partners, several associates, and a huge monthly overhead. I was able to work on malpractice cases and generate some big fees as a plaintiff's attorney in the range of $100,000 to $300,000 at a time on a regular basis, so as to pull my financial weight with the firm. This, combined with the patience of my partners, was the reason I was able to stay in the sports business for the initial start-up years, when I made no money as an agent.

The sports fees (in reality, Stanley's fees) were a welcome addition to the fees to help pay the monthly overhead and did warrant moving forward in my sports experiment, so I continued with B.J.'s help, to attempt to build the sports business. I had several "irons in the fire," so to speak, which could lead to some other nice revenue-producing sports clients. If I had been able to sign Chris as a client, that could have been huge, but it did not happen. Still, there was the possibility of him coming around in the next few years so I could do his next contract. If Willie had obtained a big contract, that would have helped, but he had been injured and his contract did not materialize. But I knew he had the potential to play and possibly hit a nice contract in the future. Rufus was a client and a legitimate player now, but any contract for him was several years away. The entire firm enjoyed being in the sports business but, running a very high profile personal injury law firm was our real business.

Though I was interested in the football, my focus switched more to basketball at this point in time because of my success with Stanley; my awesome partner B.J., who had in-depth basketball knowledge, experience, and contacts; and the contacts and experience I had gained in representing Stanley. Furthermore, I felt that basketball, because of the smaller number of players available, was more competitive in the signing of players; however, actually it provided a better shot at a steady fee because you had an opportunity to negotiate a long term contract that was fully guaranteed, as opposed to football, where you would get a payday from the signing bonus and salary, but the salary for the term of the contract was not guaranteed. If you signed a basketball player to a five-year $17 million deal, you were, with overwhelming probability, going to get your three percent of the fee over the next five years, even in the event of termination. With football, if you signed a player to the same deal, you were only guaranteed the three percent on the signing bonus and any salary earned. If the football player was later cut from the team in the second or third year of the contract, he would receive no salary and you no fee. Furthermore, if a basketball player could not make it in the NBA, he probably had the potential to play overseas and make some money.

Though basketball and football both had agents out there illegally paying players (see, again, *Illegal Procedure*), which made it almost impossible to compete honestly, I felt like I had at least a shot with basketball players because of B.J. B.J. was not only a great person to be associated with and great working with players, but he had the ability to assess players and give me a solid indication if the player could make it in the NBA. Throughout my football-agent career, I relied on others to help me evaluate players, and never really had an "in" with any top draft picks. As a result, I was able to sign some potential players, but not high draft picks. This resulted in incurring the time and expense of recruiting with no monetary reward.

In 1992, I read an interesting story about a college basketball player then at the University of New Orleans (UNO) named Ervin Johnson. The story relayed how he walked on to play basketball at UNO after having not played high school basketball, made the team after a redshirt year, and worked himself into position to be a possible first-round draft pick. Ervin's story was incredible and really stuck with me. I just felt that, based on his story, this was a player I might be able to recruit straight up and have a chance to actually sign in an above-the-table manner. Ervin fit my recruiting criteria in that he was from Louisiana, had worked in Baton Rouge, and was playing in proximity to Baton Rouge. I began to do my research on him in order to recruit him as a potential client, and found out as much as I could about him and his family.

Ervin was born in New Orleans, but had grown up in Jonesville, Louisiana, a small town in Catahoula Parish, which is in the middle eastern part of the state. Ervin's mother, Bernice, was born in the country portion of Catahoula Parish in 1942, and was the youngest of fourteen siblings. Several of her siblings had died when the family moved to the town of Jonesville, which even now has a population of less than 3,000 people. Bernice told me that there were ten children living with her parents in a four-room house. Eventually, Bernice's father built his own house, which had five rooms.

Bernice had played basketball in high school at Jonesville Consolidated, a rural high school that had successfully integrated in 1960, without significant problems. After graduating, she got a job cleaning rooms at a Howard Johnson hotel and moved to New Orleans. In New Orleans, Bernice reunited with Ervin's father, Ervin Sr., whom she had met previously in Ferriday while she was playing basketball in high school. Ervin Sr. had been a cheerleader from an opposing school. Bernice and Ervin Sr. had four children in New Orleans: Karen, Venessa, Ervin (1967), and Kevin (1970), and she continued to work at several jobs in the city.

Bernice stayed in New Orleans until 1971, when she caught a bus and, with Venessa, Ervin, and Kevin, returned to her home in Jonesville. Karen stayed in New Orleans with her father's parents until she left home to get married. Bernice moved into her father's old house with her three children. Subsequently, one of Bernice's sisters moved in with three children, so there were six children and two adults in the small five-room house. The family had to double up and sleep on the floor or sofa, if necessary.

Bernice began dating her current husband Steve Curry when she returned to Jonesville. Ervin's second brother, Chuckie, was born to Bernice and Steve in 1974. As Ervin grew up in Jonesville, he frequently had to share a bed with not only Kevin, but also Chuckie. Ervin, as a boy, was taught hard work by his mother who worked numerous jobs. Ervin took care of his chores, stayed out of trouble, and was a friendly young man with several friends, according to his mother. At age fifteen, he built his mother a closet because all of her clothes were hanging on a nail in the wall. One of Ervin's jobs growing up was to cut wood for the wood burning stove that was used initially to heat the house.

Ervin's family had a bicycle rim nailed to a pine tree in the backyard where Ervin played basketball with the neighboring kids. After his ninth-grade year, the family was able to afford an actual goal in the backyard where Ervin continued to play, but there was no court, just the packed dirt of the backyard. Ervin tried out for his high school basketball team, but did not make the cut. Some of the local boys even teased Ervin about not making the team, according to his younger brother, Chuckie. Ervin tried to play football too, but did not make his high school football team.

Bernice's family was very involved in the local Baptist church, and Ervin attended church, Sunday school, and vacation Bible school growing up. Bernice sang in the church choir. Richard Barber (nicknamed "Val"), who had grown up around the corner from Bernice's family in Jonesville, had moved to Baton Rouge after graduating high school. In 1984, Richard began preaching every first Sunday of the month in Jonesville. It was at this time that Richard renewed his relationship with Venessa, Ervin's sister, and they married. Ervin was baptized along with his brother, Kevin, at the urging of his new brother-in-law, Richard, near the time of his high school graduation in 1985.

Richard suggested that Ervin move to Baton Rouge after finishing high school to look for some employment opportunities. Ervin prayed about it, and decided to do it. At the time of his high school graduation, Ervin was obviously not a sought-after basketball recruit, because he measured only six-foot-three inches tall, and had not even played high school basketball. Ervin did have a strong belief that God had a plan for him. He had seen his mother working two to three jobs a day while raising four children, which translated to him that with hard work, you could accomplish anything. Ervin had been taught to pull his weight by doing his chores and helping his mother out, which even included helping with the laundry, if necessary. Ervin and Kevin would bring the clothes to the laundromat on a bicycle with one pumping the bike and the other holding the laundry.

After he arrived in Baton Rouge, Ervin initially lived with his brother-in-law, Richard, and his sister, Venessa, and worked at a fast-food restaurant. He and his younger brother, Kevin, moved into an apartment after six or seven months when Kevin arrived in Baton Rouge. Ervin had no source of transportation at first, so he had to walk several miles each day to and from work. Eventually, he moved up to a bicycle, and after some time obtained a car. During this period in his life, Ervin really matured and learned the value of a dollar, a lesson which some pro athletes never learn. He and Kevin never forgot to show appreciation to their mother back home in Jonesville. With the first of their earnings from their jobs in Baton Rouge, they bought an air conditioner for her living room and bedroom furniture.

Over the next three years, Ervin grew eight inches until he was a legitimate six feet, eleven inches. Richard had helped him obtain employment at the Super Fresh Grocery store, which included bagging groceries. As he grew, customers began to ask

Ervin if he ever played basketball, to which he had to respond "no." Over the course of his growth, Ervin began to feel as if God was calling him to become a basketball player. Ervin was and still is a committed Christian, and one not afraid to act on his beliefs and, as I was to learn, not afraid of what others think. Accordingly, as long as he is true to his beliefs, he has an incredible will to persevere and accomplish goals that would be impossible for almost all people, including even most professional athletes.

After he finished his growth spurt, Ervin was still asked about playing basketball, and was encouraged by store customers and others to give the sport a try. One particularly strong advocate of his playing basketball was the owner of the grocery store, Paul Bologna. After some encouragement, Ervin and Paul began to make inquiries about any university interested in a six foot, eleven inch basketball player. Naturally, being tall does not make you a basketball player, but height is a natural help in playing and, as is commonly said, "you can't teach height." Ervin would be a "project" for any coach, but he did have height and some athletic ability. The real obstacle for a player in his position, assuming he could find a suitable place to begin his career, would be to have the discipline and the mental and emotional strength to start with such deficits in basketball knowledge and skills, and be able to work himself into being able to play at a college level. Simply put, Ervin would need to have enormous "heart" to be able to actually play college basketball when beginning a career at age twenty-one.

Ervin and Paul approached LSU Coach Dale Brown, but they were told that there was no place on the roster for him, as Coach Brown had Stanley on the team and Shaq in the wings. Ervin and Paul turned their attention to nearby New Orleans and the University of New Orleans. Ervin was informed that UNO had a new coach named Tim Floyd, who was looking to add some height to his roster, as the tallest player on the roster was only six foot, five inches. Ervin, urged on by Paul, went down to meet with Coach Floyd and see if there was a possibility of him walking on at UNO. It was November 1988, the last day of the early signing period, and Coach Floyd had a scholarship available.

When Ervin was unexpectedly announced at UNO, Coach Floyd thought that the secretary was joking because Ervin's name sounds like Magic Johnson's, though it is spelled differently. However, when Coach Floyd saw Ervin, he knew that he had the height to play and questioned him on his basketball background. Coach Floyd was surprised to learn that Ervin had never played organized basketball, but gave Ervin the opportunity to show his athletic ability by running in the parking lot. After Ervin ran the parking lot, to his credit, Coach Floyd thought that Ervin had enough athletic ability and the heart to try to make it as a college player, even starting with no developed skills at age twenty-one. He awarded Ervin a scholarship and redshirted him for the rest of the 1988–1989 season so he could develop his basketball skills. This set Ervin on his incredible journey where he would not only have to struggle to learn the game of basketball, but also struggle to make it academically. Ervin would be the first member of his family to go to college and he officially enrolled at UNO in January, 1989.

Ervin's first six months of basketball and college were rough, but he kept plugging away, learning the game and catching up academically. When Ervin first arrived, Coach Floyd, in an interview, stated that Ervin did not even know basic basketball terminology such as a chest pass and a pivot foot. At one point, someone on the UNO coaching staff coined the phrase "Tragic" Johnson to describe Ervin as he threw himself into learning the game. However, Ervin would not be deterred from his goal of attending college and making himself a basketball player. He would get up early and head to the gym to not only work on his basketball skills, but also to lift weights and perform other bodybuilding exercises. At the same time, he worked with tutors to catch up academically and remain eligible to play basketball. Ervin's challenges did not hurt him, rather, they matured him into an individual whom you could always depend on to give you a hundred percent effort on and off the court.

In the spring of 1990, and as the 1989–1990 season drew closer, Coach Floyd approached Ervin about the possibility of transferring to a junior college for at least a season. Ervin looked at Coach Floyd with tears welling in his eyes and asked for just a little more time. Coach Floyd could see that Ervin was giving everything he had to become a player, put his faith in him, and kept him on the team. Ervin would get up early each morning and get some extra coaching to help him improve more quickly. Coach Floyd's faith in Ervin was rewarded, and he began, slowly but surely, to improve to the point where he played 757 minutes during his first season in 1989–1990. Because of his character and heart, Ervin continued to work and improve over the next several seasons, and by the 1992–1993 season, was attracting the national attention that prompted the story that I read in the newspaper.

I was familiar with Jonesville and had represented some smaller hospitals in the area. I felt like this gave me some sort of useful knowledge about Ervin and his family that I could use as an initial starting point. I made telephone calls to some of the local people listed in the article to try to introduce myself and B.J. to his family. I was successful in obtaining the number of Richard Barber, Ervin's brother-in-law, who lived in Baton Rouge. I spoke with Richard, and, being a part-time preacher, he was very honest and gave me an update on Ervin and his "agent" status. I wanted, from the start, to see if I had a chance to recruit Ervin honestly and needed to see if he had already committed to another agent.

Naturally, other agents had been in contact with

Ervin, but he had not committed to anyone and not taken any money or "gifts" from the agents who would have tried to buy their way in. Ervin's incredible story had in fact saved him from the system that entraps most of the great basketball players who develop along the normal course of player development. Most great basketball players, especially big guys, can be spotted by high school because of physical size and ability, and quickly attract a great deal of attention, including agents, AAU coaches, family members and others who want to be involved in the agent process. At times, individuals who want to "help" the player out, and to become involved in the agent process are known as "street agents." The overwhelming theme of most of the persons who attach themselves to the player is obtaining financial support for the player and themselves. Throughout the years, I have had several persons approach me about providing money to a high school or college player in return for representing him later. I declined to accept these offers for obvious reasons. The recent revelations in the FBI-Adidas sting, involving Christian Dawkins, have been present in sports, and particularly basketball, for years.

Just from my conversation with Richard, I could tell that Ervin had made it through bagging groceries for three years with no help and his prior years of college with no help, and he was not about to sell out at this point in time. This meant to B.J. and me that we did have a chance of recruiting him, even at this point in his career, his senior season. B.J. talked to several separate pro scouts, and many thought that Ervin could be a first-round pick. This further confirmed that he would be a great client to pick up for the 1993 draft. B.J. and I decided we would attend as many UNO home games as possible where we would be able to see Ervin play and chat with his family.

B.J. and I met Richard and his wife, Venessa, and provided them with written information to pass on to Ervin, and tried to meet the rest of the family, all of which is within

NCAA guidelines. Through Richard, I met Ervin's brothers, his mother, and his stepdad. The family and I seemed to click at our first meeting. I also set up a meeting with Ervin's father, Ervin Johnson Sr. B.J. and I tried to meet and get to know as much of the family as possible to answer any potential questions that anyone might have. We would never have offered any type of financial inducement to Ervin or anyone else to attempt to represent him, so we had to work to establish trust and a relationship with as much of the family as possible.

By the time Ervin was a senior, he was already twenty-five and his own man, and he would be the person who would make the decision on who would represent him. Ervin was not a person to have someone else make a decision for him, though he would gather input and make a well-thought-out choice. This is another reason that Ervin was different than most players coming out of college; he was mature and could make his own decisions, having overcome so much by this point in his life. Though Ervin would make his own decision, family was very important to him, especially his mother. I felt at this point that Ervin did rely on Richard for some of his decision-making, and we got to know Richard well. Unlike some families, Ervin's family was not concerned with enriching themselves; they wanted the best for Ervin. Accordingly, we were not asked for money to be paid to any family member to influence Ervin's decision, as happens too often in this business. Nor did we have to employ or promise to employ any family member to get Ervin to sign.

During the season, I traveled to New Orleans eight to ten times to watch Ervin play, with B.J. accompanying me on several of the trips. After one of the games, we were introduced to Ervin, so we began to get to know him personally and obtained his contact information. One advantage we had in recruiting Ervin was that we were close to New Orleans and could show him our interest by attending as many games as possible, and could really get to know his family. At each game, we would see Coach Floyd and wave to him as politely as possible, and he would wave back. I really think he must have thought we were alumni, as often as we were attending home games.

By the end of the basketball season, B.J. and I knew Ervin and his family well and had created a potential bond, which could put us in position to actually sign him. We had worked hard and put ourselves in this position without violating any NCAA rules. Our final strategy was to put ourselves into a position to sign Ervin as soon as possible after his NCAA eligibility had been extinguished. The 1992–1993 UNO team, with Ervin leading the way, went 18-0 in Sun Belt Conference play, and was headed to the NCAA Tournament on March 19, 1993 to play Xavier in Indianapolis. UNO was an eighth seed and Xavier was a ninth seed. B.J. and I decided we should fly up to see the game and try to meet with Ervin to potentially sign, after his team lost in the tournament. If his team won both in the first and second round, we would just go to the two games and follow him in the tournament the next week. We telephoned Ervin during our preparations for the trip, and he was agreeable to meeting with us after he played.

Coincidentally, LSU was playing University of California in Chicago on March 18, 1993, in the first round of the tournament. Since Chicago and Indianapolis were only a few hours' drive apart, I thought it would be a lot of fun to try to catch the LSU game and then drive to Indianapolis for the UNO game. Hopefully, both teams would win, and we could see four days of exciting basketball. Jim Childers, who has remained one of my good friends, was still at LSU, and could potentially get us some good seats for the LSU game. I set the wheels in place to make the journey, and flew into Chicago first to catch the LSU and UNO games. Jim came through with some tickets, and we had good seats for what turned out to be an exciting game, but a 66-64 loss after an incredible last-minute shot by Jason Kidd. After I arrived in Chicago and LSU had lost, I suggested to Jim that he and I could drive to Indianapolis together and see the UNO game along with B.J. Jim said he was free since LSU had lost and would check to see if he could change his airplane ticket; he'd let me know in the morning. By the time I was prepared to leave the next day, Jim had found out he could change his ticket with no penalty and decided to go with me so he could watch the UNO game. We would meet B.J., pick up an extra ticket for Jim, watch the game, and then B.J. and I would meet with Ervin after the game. Jim had met Ervin only once when he had come by LSU, did not know him, and would have nothing to do with our recruiting Ervin.

Jim and I met B.J. and went to the UNO vs. Xavier game, as scheduled. We did see Coach Floyd at some point prior to the game and gave him a shout-out, which he acknowledged. Unfortunately, UNO did not play well and lost the game with a disappointing score of 73 to 55. However, UNO did have a great year going 25-4 over the course of the season.

We had telephoned Ervin after he had arrived in town and gotten his room number for the after-game meeting. We called his room and went up to see him, as planned. We brought the player-agent contract for Ervin to review and went over that, along with answering any questions he had at that time. I was told later that Ervin did not particularly like me when we first met, but over the course of the season he had changed his mind and did trust me. After discussing everything with Ervin, he told B.J. and me that he thought he would want to sign with us but wanted first to think and pray about it. B.J. and I respected his wishes and left the meeting without a signed player-agent contract. We felt like we had a good shot at signing Ervin and that he really liked us, but I had already learned that anything can happen if you don't get the player-agent contract signed. Further, even if we had Ervin signed, other agents would still take shots at stealing our client.

Ervin's college eligibility was over now, so there would be many agents trying to sign him as a client. B.J. and I returned to Houston and Baton Rouge, respectively, the next day, hopeful that we were on the verge of signing a first-round draft pick, but definitely not yet celebrating. We knew Ervin had talked to other agents, so we still had work to do in signing and keeping the client.

I called Ervin several days later and asked him how he felt. He said he had prayed about it and he was ready to sign. At this point, I had no hesitation in going to New Orleans and having him sign the player-agent contract. I was dealing with a mature, twenty-five-year-old, self-made man. Ervin understood the contract and what was in store for him in the upcoming draft. I drove to New Orleans and closed the deal with Ervin signing the player-agent contract! I felt ecstatic after Ervin signed and telephoned B.J. We immediately began to lay out a plan for Ervin's upcoming itinerary before the 1993 NBA draft, which was to take place on June 30, in Detroit, Michigan.

B.J. and I decided that he should move to New Orleans to be with Ervin for the next several weeks to help train him and get him ready for any upcoming pre-draft tournaments, which we felt he should attend. This would mean that B.J. would be able to not only help Ervin get ready, but he would be in position to ward off any poaching agents who would likely swoop in and try to dislodge Ervin from his commitment, even though the player-agent contract had been signed and already filed with the NBPA.

One area of concern that we did not really expect was the reaction by Coach Tim Floyd to Ervin's signing with us. Apparently, Coach Floyd had been suggesting an agent to Ervin throughout the season that he wanted Ervin to consider. When Floyd found out that Ervin had signed with me, he was not happy and "encouraged" Ervin to reconsider his decision. Despite all the pressure, Ervin stuck with me, which I appreciate to this day. Floyd's actions made me all the more determined to do a great job for Ervin and not let his trust in me turn out to be misplaced.

I never had to deal with any problems with coaches, in terms of recruiting players, up until this point in time. LSU offensive coordinator Ed Zaunbrecher had actually referred Willie Williams to me. Even though I felt that Coach Dale Brown was not particularly elated at my having signed Stanley, he never threw up any real roadblocks to my representation of him. He, in fact, had given my name to Jamie Ibanez, and never did anything to overtly interfere with my relationship with Stanley. Coach Brown also sent me notes of encouragement throughout my career, for which I am always grateful.

After Ervin signed with me, and B.J. was in New Orleans training him, Ervin was to play in the National Association of Basketball Coaches' (NABC) All Star Game, which would be played during the Final Four weekend in New Orleans on Saturday, April 4, 1993. The coaches were Mike Krzyzewski and Steve Fisher, and some of the players included Bobby Hurley and Thomas Hill, both of Duke, Nick Van Exel from Cincinnati, and Greg Graham from Indiana.

Coincidentally, North Carolina had made it to the Final Four and the game was headed to New Orleans, right in my backyard. My parents, ultimate North Carolina fans, were able to wrangle some lower level Final Four seats from my mother's Uncle Bill, who was a well-connected North Carolina alumnus; therefore, Mom and Dad came down for a visit and to see North Carolina play. In addition, my parents were anxious to meet Ervin and watch him play. I was able to obtain two great tickets to the game, on the floor behind one of the baskets, from a friend who worked for the lieutenant governor's office. B.J. and I used those tickets for the first set of games, which included North Carolina vs. Kansas in the early game and Michigan vs. Kentucky in the second game, which went into overtime.

My father went out with B.J. and me in New Orleans on

Friday night during the Final Four weekend. Of course, as we walked around the French Quarter, we began to run into all kinds of basketball celebrities whom B.J. would introduce to me and my dad. I spent some time with Terry Holland, the ex-Virginia coach, and B.J.'s friend Ralph Sampson, both of whom my father had followed, since he was a North Carolina fan. My parents' seats for the game were near Jimmy Black, an ex-Carolina player, and Dad struck up several conversations with Jimmy during the games. All in all, after the weekend, particularly when North Carolina won it all on Monday, April 5, my father told me it was one of the best few days of his life.

The only downer occurred Saturday morning when my father and I were parking in a hotel to go hear Ervin give a speech before the NABC All Star game. As we got out of cars in the parking lot, I happened to see Coach Tim Floyd getting out of his car near us at the same time. As we started to walk toward him, I did not know how he would respond but threw up a wave hoping he would just wave and move on. Tim did wave initially, but then it seemed to register to him that I was the agent with whom Ervin had signed. He quickly approached me and got in my face, specifically questioning my character and using a very derogatory term to describe B.J. Fortunately, I was moving a little slow that morning, because of the trip to Bourbon Street late the night before, and stood there semi-stunned as he lambasted me in front of my father. Tim then moved on before I started to get really angry, which was again fortunate for both of us, and neither of us took it any further. I explained to my father that Tim was upset about our signing Ervin and left it at that. I could see no real reason or point in trying to retaliate in any way.

When my father and I met B.J. inside, I recounted the event to him and rented what Tim had said. I did not think B.J. would be happy about Tim's words, but I was surprised because, it was the first and probably the last time I saw B.J. angry, which actually scared me somewhat. B.J. did wait for an appropriate time and then approached Tim, who did not know who he was at first. After B.J. identified himself, he told Tim the errors of his accusations. I could barely hear the conversation, as I was some distance away, but the discussions appeared to be quite animated.

Afterwards, B.J., my father, and I just left and enjoyed the rest of the weekend. Ervin played exceptionally well in the NABC game and had sixteen points, fourteen rebounds, two blocked shots, and one steal. He was named the Most Valuable Player for the game in a 104-95 victory for the West.

I did not stay for the championship game Monday night because Jonathan Shaw, my ex-client who was wheelchair bound, wanted to attend. I gave him my ticket and B.J. took him to the game between North Carolina and Michigan. I had to go to Houston on business and watched the game from there.

I did not get into any details with Ervin about our encounter with Tim and just moved forward with getting Ervin ready for the draft and assisting him in becoming a professional basketball player. B.J. did the same, and continued to train Ervin in New Orleans. Ervin was to play in a predraft game in Phoenix.

I never bore any ill will towards Tim, and was glad for the subsequent success in his career. My observations throughout the years are that coaches, first of all, are type A personalities with a huge desire to win. If this was not part of their makeup, they would probably not be very successful in the coaching business. Secondly, in general, most coaches are control freaks who generally live in a world created by themselves and under their own command. This control is what helps allow for their success as they set up their sports program. They attempt to control and motivate their players to perform on a higher level to beat other teams motivated to the same purpose—to WIN! Of course, only one team can win, which sets up a job atmosphere with a high degree of anxiety and lack of job security. Add all this to the intensity and secrecy needed for recruiting, and you come up with a certain amount of paranoia influencing the coach's mental and emotional behavior. Consequently, some coaches, when not successful in exerting influence on their players decisions, can become quite volatile. This is occasionally seen on the sidelines of both basketball and football games when a player makes a mistake and the coach jumps him on the sideline and really gets in his face.

Analyzing Tim's reaction to our signing Ervin thereafter, I knew that he was dealing with an emotional issue, and his great disappointment that Ervin was not taking his advice in choosing his agent really upset him. I know that he really cared about Ervin and felt like he had really helped create Ervin, in a way; he felt like Ervin should have, at least, discussed signing me with him. B.J., Tim, and I over the years moved on from our initial encounter and have become friendly because of our mutual interest in Ervin, a great player and person.

One footnote to recruiting and signing Ervin goes to my good and most honest friend Jim Childers who had decided at the last minute to ride with me from Chicago to Indianapolis to watch the game, and had nothing to do with me recruiting Ervin. A month or more after I signed Ervin, Jim called me and said that he had been contacted by the NCAA compliance people at LSU that an agent had reported him to the NCAA for a violation in him helping me recruit Ervin Johnson. I asked him what the violation was, because there was none, and Jim had nothing to do with me recruiting Ervin, and he could not really get a straight answer.

We both felt he should challenge the report, but Joe Dean, LSU's athletic director at the time, did not want to stir any NCAA waters. Dean told Jim that he would put a reprimand in his file and freeze his salary for a year, and this would satisfy the NCAA. I felt like that was ridiculous, as did Jim, but Dean was insistent on how to handle the matter, and Jim took the hit. I really had problems with many of the things that agents did, but this was a low blow to an innocent bystander and just confirmed to me the true character of this pitiful agent. This is just my opinion of how my friend Jim was treated unfairly by LSU during his tenure there, which all started with putting a highly successful coach in a non-coaching administrative position.

FIFTEEN
Peaks and Valley, 1993

—— • ——

Looking back now, I think the beginning of 1993 was when I began to feel that, at some point in time, I might become a full-time agent. Signing Ervin made me feel like I might have a shot at staying in the business, actually abiding by ethical standards on a level sufficient to satisfy my conscience and the standards mandated by the Louisiana State Bar. I did not want to be an agent if it meant endangering my law license and my ability to practice law. I had been fortunate enough to be able to sign and represent two first-round NBA draft picks within a three-year period. I had a great partner, B.J., now like a brother to me. B.J. really made the business fun and also knew both the sports of basketball and football, giving our clients a great advantage when trying to improve their skills so they could have long and profitable athletic careers. Things were going well, and Ervin's signing just topped things off and made me very optimistic for my future in sports.

On January 25, 1993, I was in New York for the Chris Morris vs. Sid Blanks hearing at the NBPA headquarters. I had briefed the case prior to the hearing, and Simon Gourdine was the arbitrator. The only witnesses to testify were Sid Blanks, Chris, and his wife, Michelle. Subsequently, both sides submitted memorandum and the record was closed on February 16, 1993. The record was reopened, and we responded on March 22, 1993, and Blanks responded April 16, 1993. I really enjoyed the grievance work. The hearing was easy compared to actually trying a lawsuit, and it was stimulating to study past grievances to add to my background in sports litigation. I actually gave a thought to trying to specialize in these cases, but practically it would never happen, because no agent would want to allow another certified agent access to his clients. The decision came down on May 7, 1993, and some of my defenses were accepted by the mediator so that Chris owed a minimal amount, which was a win for us. Chris and I were both happy. Libby had continued to assist him with some of his personal projects, and I continued as his attorney and an advisor of sorts, but not his agent.

B.J. and I did not go to Portsmouth in 1993, as Ervin had been invited to the Phoenix Desert Classic to be held April 20–24. This was a pre-draft camp most of the potential senior draft picks would attend. Our plan for Ervin was for him to play in this camp, and if he played well, he would bypass the Chicago Pre-Draft camp, which was to be held June 8–12, even though he would have to go to Chicago for a pre-draft physical. B.J. would continue to work Ervin out in preparation for June 30, 1993, and to get him ready to play in the fall.

The Phoenix Classic was very enjoyable, and Ervin played decently, so B.J. and I decided that there was no need for him to play in the Chicago camp. Chicago was close to the draft, and generally the best players do not play in that tournament. It is usually for players who feel they can move up in the draft.

Most of the time, sure lottery-pick players do not play in the pre-draft tournaments. The top players rely on individual workouts and meetings with the teams that have the top draft picks. Ervin was slated as a possible first-round pick, and we felt, coming from a smaller conference picked up some momentum by showing what he could do against some quality opponents at Phoenix.

Willie was in Phoenix, and he and Ervin were introduced and spent some time cruising around in Willie's Jeep. Phoenix was a good opportunity for me to get to know Ervin better and build as much trust as possible, as B.J. and I knew that other agents would still be approaching him to get him to change agents. The more I spent time with Ervin, the more I liked him, and I could see he was going to be a great client. Even though no one knew if Ervin would be a long-term success in the NBA, I knew he would work hard and go as far as his hard work and talent would carry him. This assuredness proved to be correct.

As B.J. and I attended the games, we would meet with NBA scouts and general managers. I now felt like I had a place at the NBA sports table with my representing Stanley, Carl, Alvaro, Tim, Chris (as his attorney), and now a possible first-round pick in Ervin. Although I did find some of the games and time sitting around a little boring, I was enjoying the glamour and notoriety of the sports world. I did continue to do some legal work while on the road in order to keep my legal practice progressing.

Meanwhile, back at the office, I had a legal secretary working, and Libby Reny was assisting me with some of my legal work and also working with some of my sports clients and doing other sports-related tasks. Of my sports clients, Libby spent most of her time working with Chris and Stanley. At some point around this time, Chris decided that he wanted to get into the music business. He found some talented young African American men who, he thought, were worth promoting, and decided to help them with their careers. Naturally, B.J. and I advised against this move, but Chris decided to move forward anyway. Chris's move was not all that unusual for a sports figure making what he feels at the time is a large sum of money. Because of their celebrity and the money they are making, there are always plenty of opportunities given players to make questionable business decisions, and the music business is one that has a real appeal. There are always plenty of undiscovered stars who need some financial help to get started, and players who want to get into the entertainment business.

Over the years, since I was an agent and gained a reputation as an "entertainment attorney," I have been contacted on numerous occasions by musicians who need someone to either negotiate or review some type of music deal. Naturally, I would always try to determine how I would be paid for my work. From my experience, musicians do not have funds to pay, wanting me to do the work up front and then pay me when they "make it." I have always declined, because, first of all, I am not that familiar with the music industry, and, secondly, because I know that the music business is extremely competitive and it is extremely difficult to make it, so my odds of getting paid would be remote.

I had enjoyed Stanley's productive season for the Clippers, and though the team ended the season 41-41, they were slated for a first-round playoff game with the Rockets. Overall, I felt like Stanley had really come along as a player and been a plus for the team. However, he did continue to have some conditioning and weight problems. I had an opportunity, while watching games on the road and at L.A. during the season, to observe and meet several of his teammates.

The first games of the Houston series were in Houston beginning on April 29, 1993, and I made it over for at least one game. The Clippers won the second game, and the series turned into quite a classic. My client, Carl Herrera, was playing for the Rockets and Stanley was playing for the Clippers, so I felt involved, like I was really getting into the sports business. The two teams split two games in L.A. and returned to Houston on May 8 for the deciding game. I attended the close, hard-fought game. Ron Harper played well for the Clippers, but Vernon Maxwell threw in a three-pointer late in the game to seal it for the Rockets, who took an 84-80 win. Olajuwon played dominantly for the Rockets, but Stanley went toe-to-toe with him, and I was proud of his play during the game and the series. At this point, I felt so proud of Stanley and so close to him that I never worried about keeping him as a client.

After returning to Phoenix, I began to get ready for the upcoming draft in June and was busy practicing law. B.J. was working with Ervin and even flew to Chicago to work with him, keep an eye out for other clients, and make sure no other agents were trying to poach him right before the draft. All indications were that Ervin would be a low first-round pick; however, you never can tell. We were in contact with the teams and arranged any workouts which were requested. Ervin's draft process was a big contrast to the drama that surrounded Stanley's.

B. J. and I were also working on the basketball end of the business, and we did manage to pick up another player during 1993 who would eventually sign an NBA contract. We did it over a period of time, spending time working with the player and setting him up with the opportunity to make an NBA team. In May 1993, I signed Tim Breaux, a native of Zachary, Louisiana, which is next-door to Baton Rouge, to an NBA contract. Tim was six foot, seven inches, African-American, and played two guard primarily, though he could handle the ball to some degree. He grew up in Zachary and then played his college ball at Wyoming. Tim had worked out with the Lakers after college, but did not make the cut and played in the CBA with the Sioux

Falls Skyforce during the 1992–1993 season, where he earned second-team CBA all-rookie honors.

I do not remember how I first contacted Tim. I believe someone had given him my name or someone introduced us. Since he was from Baton Rouge, it was a natural fit. He had already proven he could play in the CBA, and we could always steer him overseas if he could not make an NBA team.

Ervin was not invited to attend the 1993 NBA draft, so we arranged to watch it in Baton Rouge. The draft was held on June 30, and Ervin was selected by the Seattle Supersonics at number twenty-three, just like Stanley. We were pleased that he had been selected in the first round, though I did wish that he could have gone a little higher than twenty-three, not only for his sake monetarily, but also for my ego. If he had gone higher, it would have broken my personal record and could have enhanced any reputation that I imagined I had at the time. Yes, ego does play a role in one's desire to be an agent, I must admit it. Ervin's draft experience was very different and paled in comparison with the drama surrounding Stanley's pre-draft tour, his weight gain, and his slipping from a lottery-pick down to twenty-three. Ervin had worked hard in his pre-draft tournament and pre-draft workouts and did what we expected in the draft. Both were exciting events, but Ervin's draft experience did not take the mental and emotional toll of Stanley's.

After the draft, I began to speak with the management at Seattle. The primary negotiator for Seattle, Bob Whitsitt, was not as colorful or as fun as Pat Williams. Bob was a straightforward businessman who, compared to Pat, was rather dull to bargain with but not a problem as far as coming to an equitable deal for Ervin. I did explore some European options for Ervin, but Ervin's situation was very different from Stanley's. Ervin did not have the natural talent and size of Stanley, and did not yet have the genuine tools to become a "superstar" like Stanley. Furthermore, he was getting a late start at twenty-five, so he did not have as much room for error when beginning his career.

What Ervin did have was athleticism and size, but his greatest attribute was his great heart and desire to succeed at any cost. B.J. and I believed that all Ervin needed was some time to show his worth to a team, and he would have a long career in the NBA. The three-year guaranteed contract available to first-round NBA draft picks looked like an ideal choice for him. Our thinking was that the guaranteed contract would keep him financially secure for three years while protecting him from injury and getting cut from the team. During those three years, he could build himself into a player that a team would risk a long-term deal on at the end of his first contract. In addition, with the right financial advice, after three years, he would, at the least, have a sufficient financial base to help change his life if anything untoward happened and he did not play beyond his initial contract. Accordingly, my job would be to negotiate a three-year deal with all the correct guarantees and as many bonuses as possible.

The negotiations were fairly straightforward; though I did throw out the possibility of Ervin going to Europe, our real intent was for him to play in the NBA. I was in contact with Bob on a continuous basis, but kept open the possibility of Ervin going to Europe and not being in training camp on time to move the negotiations forward. I flew to Seattle to finish negotiating the contract and to spend some time with Ervin the week before training camp began. On August 2, 1993, the week before camp opened, we came to terms on a three-year, $2.1 million guaranteed deal, which was within the acceptable range based on the previous year's signings and signings by other first-round picks. The deal also included performance bonuses and some additional money for off-season conditioning and playing clauses, which I had not put in Stanley's contract.

Seattle was a solid, veteran team and was headed to the playoffs. We did want Ervin to be there for the beginning of camp so he would be as far along as possible at the beginning of the season. Seattle's team included such stars as Gary Payton, Shawn Kemp, Sam Perkins, Detlef Schrempf, Kendall Gill, Ricky Pierce, and Nate McMillian, so we felt Ervin would get some valuable experience with that group. The coach was George Karl, whom Ervin would end up playing under for a number of seasons. The team would finish with a 63-19 record, a franchise best, and was the number-one-seed in the Western Conference in the playoffs. However, disappointingly, the team would lose in the first round of the playoffs to Denver, which was the eighth seed, after taking a 2-0 lead in the series.

Rookie Ervin Johnson and his new Coach, George Karl, Seattle.

After completing Ervin's contract, I was looking forward to watching him and Stanley compete in the upcoming NBA season, as well as watching Rufus and Willie playing in the NFL. Unfortunately, after spending all of 1992 on the Injured Reserve List, Willie was cut late in training camp. Willie was down, but determined to get back in the League; however we received no offers immediately. Therefore, he decided to go see a former girlfriend in Seattle as the season started.

We assisted Ervin in getting set up in Seattle, which was a straightforward job. B.J. and Libby flew out to settle Ervin in and help him find a place to live so he could be ready for training camp.

B.J. stayed a while to help Ervin settle into the NBA life. Shortly after arriving in Seattle, I received several telephone calls from Ervin after he had been stopped by the police for no apparent reason, other than that he was a black man driving a brand new Ford Explorer. I found this problem worrisome and did call someone at the team, but came up with no immediate plan of action. Fortunately, after three such stops spread over several weeks, they stopped, so it ceased to be a problem.

I was still practicing law, but again the sports by this time were taking up at least a third of my time. As a personal injury firm, we had to constantly settle cases to take care of overhead, and in the end have enough to pay ourselves a salary. I was managing to hold my own but had to work hard to balance both practices. My partners were understanding, and I was now making some regular income from the commissions on Stanley and Ervin, which I received monthly, and this helped. God blessed me with some good cases where I made $100,000 or more at a time to help keep the ship afloat. We had a worrisome lull in 1992, just as we finished the new office with all its expense, but we settled a big case (with most of the credit to Steve) just in time to pull us out of trouble.

*The Seattle trip; Rufus, B.J.
Ervin and me.*

With Ervin and Rufus in Seattle I decided that a visit must be made to the city to see both play. I would also try to swing by Los Angeles to catch Stanley playing for the Clippers. With the growing client list and my law practice, I was depending on Libby to help me more and more with my sports clients. She was getting deeply involved with Chris and his music project. I remember being surprised when I was informed that Libby would be appearing on a TV program called "NBA Inside Stuff "one Saturday morning. Sure enough, the program was doing a feature on Chris's "music company," and Libby turned up on the air with some title like Director of Operations. I can't remember the exact title, but I was surprised to see how far her involvement had become in this project, over which I had no control. Chris was not my sports client, and I was just his legal advisor. As far as Stanley goes, Libby was spending a lot of time helping him with various tasks and I was glad for that. At the time I sensed no threat, since I was assuming Libby was looking out for my best interests with my players.

The fall of 1993 flew by quickly, from a sports point of view. B.J. and I planned a sports client week and traveled to Seattle to watch Ervin play a basketball game and Rufus play a football game. It was great to see two of my clients playing at such a high level. I felt that, as an agent, it was part of the job to be on the scene to keep up a strong bond with each client. Not only did I enjoy it, but I also knew that the competition is always out there looking for a weakness to grab one of your clients. That was one of my weaknesses, because practicing law took up the greater portion of my time, and I could not afford the time to be on the scene as much as I wanted. However, I did have B.J. working with me, and he could fill in some of the face time required.

As the end of 1993 approached, I was still feeling excited and celebratory about the advances I had made in my developing sports career. Again, I was feeling fairly confident after I had managed to sign two first-round NBA picks and negotiate very respectable contracts for both clients.

On December 4, 1993, Stanley went down with a season-ending injury to his right Achilles tendon. This was a big blow to Stan, and we all felt terrible about his injury. As I recall, Libby arranged to go to California to help him with his initial stages of recovery.

It was at this moment that I was about to be blindsided by the greatest disappointment of my career as an agent, and there were more than a few disappointments. The source came from within and I really never saw it coming. On December 7, I received a certified letter from Stanley terminating me as his NBA agent. As I have stated before, the NBPA Agent Player regulations allow a player to terminate his contract at any time by certified mail. Yes, a termination letter from Big Stan, a man I had been through hell and high water with since he signed with me in 1990. The apparent instigator was none other than Libby Reny, one of my own employees! The enemy within was a danger I knew about from watching other agents lose players from employees, but this was the first and last time I would experience this type of betrayal.

Though I knew that Libby had spent a great deal of time away from the office "assisting clients," particularly Chris Morris and Stanley, I had no idea that she was contemplating leaving her husband, moving to the West Coast, and working out there. Worst of all, she had inserted herself into Stanley's management, not acting in my best interests, but those of another "agent." Though I still do not know, and will never know, all the details, Libby had introduced Stanley to an individual by the name of Ken Delpit who lived in Las Vegas. Delpit had never negotiated an NBA contract and was apparently trying to get into the business. I never was able to find out exactly why, but Libby had helped convince Stanley to fire me and sign with him. She was still working with Chris in his "music business," and took that job and Stanley with her and left my firm. My ex-wife always said I was naive when dealing with employees, and I certainly was with Libby.

I was extremely hurt, not by Libby taking another job but by Big Stan throwing me under the bus for another agent. The termination letter was, in fact, dated November 16, 1993. I had noticed several weeks before the termination that he was not communicating with me as he had previously, and Libby seemed to be acting a little strange. However, I wrote this off to Stan just being Stan. I really felt like Stanley and I had grown through all our adventures to become as close as family, and his departure really shook me. It was at this point that I began to doubt that I could stay in the sports business, because of its cutthroat nature. I thought, if Big Stan could leave me, was any relationship ever secure? This thought began to eat at me. Though I would receive several of those certified termination letters in the future, Stan's was the one that really hurt in my gut. On a positive note, after Stan's termination, nothing really surprised or shook me, as far as representing athletes. Stanley's rejection was something new for me, because in forty years of legal practice, I cannot recall a single client terminating me. Of course in the sports business, as I learned, this is an all-too -common occurrence.

Though Stanley had terminated me, hurting my feelings and ego, I really could not help but consider him a friend who had been led astray. After all, he had given me, a novice agent, the initial opportunity to show that I could handle big time negotiations and make something of name for myself as an agent. I knew that Stanley at times could be easily influenced by others and that he was not the kind of person who would intentionally injure another person. I decided to keep the lines of friendship and communication open to him and wait for an opportunity to discuss further why and what had happened between us. I had already negotiated his contract and was entitled to the agent fees on the remaining guaranteed monies from his $17,300,000, which would be paid over the following four years. I could still be his friend, get paid, and wait for Mr. Delpit to show his true colors as far as Stanley was concerned. I knew that four years was a long time for anyone to look out for the best interests of Big Stan, and if Mr. Delpit made a misstep, I would hopefully be there to intervene on Stan's behalf.

SIXTEEN
1994

———— • ————

Losing Big Stan as a client put B.J. and me to work to find other avenues in locating NBA, and even NFL clients. Chris Morris had left with Libby's departure, but I was never his agent and I knew at that point that I would most likely never be his agent. However, me, B.J., and Chris were all friends, and we could keep that line of communication open, just in case he decided to change his mind in the future. We did not have many leads as far as the upcoming draft, so a draft-pick for the 1994 draft seemed unlikely.

One source of potential clients was the basketball players who lived in and around the Houston area. B.J. still worked out at the same gyms where NBA players worked out in Houston. He spent the summer working out with the Rockets in 1988 and had almost made the team. He had a longstanding relationship with the Rockets' management because of his close friend Ralph Sampson, who was drafted in 1983 and played for the Rockets until 1987. B.J. played in the off-season and knew former players such as John Lucas, who played for the Rockets and still lived in the Houston area. John would go on to work with the NBA in its drug-rehab program. He also would begin a business working out young players and preparing them for the NBA. He now works for the Rockets and I can see him sitting behind the bench when the Rockets play on T.V.

B.J. and Jamie had met in Houston, and this had led B.J. to me. Jamie had a relationship with Steve Patterson, which had helped to bring Carl Herrera from Real Madrid to Houston. B.J. was known around the NBA as a great person and someone who could spot and work up NBA talent. During this time, B.J. began to work part-time as an informal scout for the Rockets, primarily scouting the minor league, CBA. B.J.'s connection gave us a way to have professional scouts look at potential clients and get them a shot to be seen by legitimate NBA scouts.

At the beginning of 1994, I was still stinging from Stanley's loss, but I had to move forward with my sports business as well as my legal practice. I was still keeping in touch with Stanley, and he paid my fee on his contract for December 1993 and January 1994. However, in February and March 1994, Stanley did not pay and he told me he had a "cash flow problem." By this time, I had no idea what was going on with him but was already worried that he was being taken advantage of by his "new agent team." How could he make the money he was making and have a cash flow problem? It made no sense, but then again, losing Stan as a client made no sense to me.

Stan made a partial payment in April of 1994 and brought up the possibility of a "buyout" of my fee. I did not know where this was coming from since it seemed contrary to the NBPA rules, which only allowed for a player to be charged for fees on salary that has already been paid under his contract. In any event, I wanted the fee payment to be made current before any discussion of a buyout. Stanley retained an attorney to discuss the buyout, but by the end of April, he had written a letter to me incorrectly stating that I was owed no fees. He subsequently retracted that position and wrote me that he did not feel that it would be necessary for me to file a grievance to get the fees paid, but there was still no payment. There were more delays, and then the attorney failed to return my telephone call to discuss payment of the fees. At this point, I had reached my limit and filed a very nice grievance with the NBPA against Stanley. The last two paragraphs read as follows:

> Although Mr. Roberts and Mr. Shoenfelt are friends, and Mr. Shoenfelt considers Mr. Roberts as a "family member," Mr. Shoenfelt needs to obtain his Agent fees to continue in his business. Moreover, the attorney for Mr. Roberts has failed to return a telephone call to discuss this matter even though the attorney has stated that filing a Grievance probably would not be necessary and Mr. Roberts is out of town for an extended period of time. Accordingly, Mr. Shoenfelt files this Grievance so that an impartial arbitrator can make an award for fees owed and resolve this matter.
>
> Accordingly, Mr. Shoenfelt would ask that Mr. Roberts file an answer in accord with NBPA regulations and that a hearing be held in order to settle this matter as soon as possible.

I really did not blame Stanley for the problems. Knowing him as well as I did, I knew he was just getting the wrong advice, and who knows what influences he had fallen under in Los Angeles. After the grievance was filed, I did begin to receive the payments without a hearing or further problem, although I cannot remember the exact time the payments resumed.

I was to learn later, when I was again representing

Stanley, that his new agent, Ken Delpit, had at some point begun to listen to overtures from the Clippers to "renegotiate" Stanley's contract. Stanley's contract was as he wanted it, clear of any off-season control or conditioning control by the team. Stanley's conditioning had been an issue since he was traded to Los Angeles, and the team clearly wanted a contract with more teeth to force Stanley to stay in shape. Delpit had never negotiated an NBA contract, and, apparently listened to what the Clippers had to say, as the 1994 season approached. Of course, I was unaware of Stanley's dealings with the Clippers during this time and was carrying on with serving my other sports and legal clients.

Stanley was not my client during 1994, but I tried to keep up with what was going on with him and his career. However, I learned most of the facts as to what actually transpired during 1994 later, in 1995. Following his injury in 1993, he apparently had problems with his conditioning and was out of shape during the summer of 1994, reaching about 350 pounds. He reportedly started training camp out of shape and still carrying too much weight. Delpit was talking to, and listening to the team about restructuring his contract to include conditioning provisions and workout provisions. A new contract was to be signed on October 26, 1994, a day when Stanley, during an exhibition game with the Atlanta Hawks, suffered another season-ending injury to not his right, but this time his left Achilles tendon. The contract was reworked and delivered to his home for him to sign the day after his injury, while he was in bed recuperating. Stanley testified in a subsequent hearing that when he executed the contract, he was medicated and was not aware that a Summer Development Program clause had been inserted into the contract with the agreement of Delpit. The contract was executed on October 27, 1994, the same day that Stanley and Delpit executed a standard player-agent contract. Unknown to me at the time, the contract that Delpit had Stanley sign committed Stanley for two more years to the Clippers team with virtually the same guaranteed money, a horrible move, in my opinion. Little did I know at the end of 1994 that I would become heavily involved with Stanley's new contract in at least three different legal disputes that would arise from its execution.

Willie Williams

On a positive note, I was successful in setting up a workout for Willie Williams with the New Orleans Saints on February 9, 1994. The Saints had been watching Willie since his days at LSU when he had played at tight end at six feet, six and a half inches and about 245 pounds. He now weighed in at approximately 300 pounds, playing on the offensive line. The Saints liked his workout and signed him as a free agent along with three other players on March 25, 1994. I was happy that he was getting a second shot after being cut by Phoenix in training camp in 1993, and elated that he was now playing so close to home in New Orleans for my favorite professional team.

Willie and I had become really close, and it was great to get to see him more often. He now had two credited seasons and needed only two more to become vested in the NFL retirement plan, which would be really great for his long-time financial security. Like many low draft picks and free agents, he had been without the opportunity to sign a significant contract up until this point in his career. My hope was that he would come in, and show what he could do for a couple of seasons, and catch a big contract when his contract expired. I knew he was not only huge but also a good athlete and worked hard at his job. Unfortunately, he had been hit with some injury and had gotten on Coach Joe Bugel's bad side at Phoenix. He was still "Top Cat" in some sense, as he always had a little mischief going on.

It was great that he now had a place to work out and prepare for the season. Willie had an outgoing personality and could really tell a story. He soon made many friends in New Orleans and felt very comfortable there, especially with his connection to LSU.

Willie worked hard trying to get back in the League. It was exciting to see him do that and play in the preseason at tackle. He played well and was working as a backup tackle. He made the sixty-man cut, and on August 28, 1994, he made the fifty-three-man cut and was back in the NFL. There was a nice article about him in the *Baton Rouge Morning Advocate* with a huge color photograph of him playing tackle for the Saints in the preseason. I obtained a copy of the photograph and put it up in my office; I still have it hanging there to this day.

Willie played well for the Saints after making the team. On October 2, 1994, in a game against the New York Giants, Willie caught a pass when the team went to two tight ends to help improve the running game. The Saints went on to win the game 27-22, and Willie received another nice write-up in the *Advocate*. It was about this time that Willie decided to go out and purchase a top-of-the-line BMW at Tom Benson's dealership, without telling me. He did not need my permission, but he knew I was available to look over the deal, and failed to ask me. You would think that the Benson dealership would have given him a great deal. The price may have been fair for the value of the car, but it was financed at a very high rate, and I certainly could have gotten him a better interest rate. If he had asked me, I would never have advised him to purchase a top-of-the-line luxury car when he was playing on, essentially, what was a one-year deal for a minimum NFL salary. Again, this is another pitfall of dealing with young players who do not grasp the full economics of their situation while playing the game, despite listening to financial advisers and having them available. Willie told me recently that he remembers this lesson and now does not even use a credit card for fear of paying interest.

Willie ended up playing in all sixteen of the Saints' games in the 1994-1995 season and started in five. He ended up starting at left tackle in the final few games of the season. I remember going down to at least one game, which ended up being a late-nighter. After arriving in New Orleans, Willie, with his outgoing personality, had made friends all over the city; plus, he still had many acquaintances from his LSU playing days. Somehow, he had become friends with the manager of the House of Blues in the New Orleans French Quarter and suggested that we go eat there after one of the home games. While we were eating dinner, he mentioned to me that "some guy named Bob Dylan" would be playing at the House of Blues later that night. I asked him if it was the Bob Dylan, as it was obvious he did not know who Bob Dylan was when he made the comment. He checked with his friend, and yes it was the Bob Dylan. Willie asked me if I wanted to go because his friend could get me into the concert without a ticket. I jumped at the offer and was able to see Bob Dylan in that intimate setting, at the last minute, without paying a cent. The concert ended after midnight, and I had not gotten a hotel room, so I had to make the drive home from New Orleans to Baton Rouge rather late. But it ended up being a good football day punctuated with a once-in-a-lifetime concert with a legendary singer. The sports business did prove to have its fringe benefits, which I had not thought of when I decided to try to become an agent.

Tim Breaux

Tim Breaux at Houston.

B.J. and I did make a great move for Tim Breaux in 1994. Tim had spent some time overseas, but was back in the United States as the 1994 season approached. B.J. thought Tim had the potential to make it in the NBA and brought him to Houston to train and work out, with the thought of him catching the eye of some NBA scouts. B.J. was able to arrange a workout for Tim with the Rockets, the current NBA Champions. The Rockets liked Tim, but there were no open roster spots. However, an injury created a spot on the roster, and Tim was signed as a replacement on Houston's summer team.

Tim took advantage of his opportunity and played well during the summer league. By the time the summer league was over, the Rockets were excited about Tim, as were several other teams. Due to Tim's great summer play, on August 26, 1994, we were able to negotiate a three-year NBA contract for Tim with the Rockets. It was great to have another NBA player under contract playing in the League on the NBA championship team. In addition, I was still the agent of record for Carl Herrera, who was still with the Rockets.

Tim went to training camp, played well, and made the twelve-man roster, after which his contract was fully guaranteed. Tim did not play much at the beginning of the 1994 season, but had his career-high for the season on November 23, against Orlando. He had his first start mid-season on February 14 against the Los Angeles Clippers and again scored twelve points. It was at this time that Portland traded Clyde Drexler to Houston for Otis Thorpe, at Clyde's request. Clyde resided in Houston and was a long time friend of Hakeem Olajuwon and many of the Rockets players. The team went on to win another NBA championship, so Tim received a championship ring in his first season along with $125,000 in bonus money. Tim would play for the Rockets for two years, and then be traded to the Vancouver Grizzlies in 1996, along with Pete Chilcutt. He was cut from the Grizzlies and then played again for Sioux Falls in 1996–1997. At some point after the championship year, he terminated our representation agreement and then rehired me. I signed him to an NBA contract with the Milwaukee Bucks in 1997 when Ervin was playing for the team, but he did not make the team. I still continued to follow his career and what he was doing through B.J., who would keep up with him since he continued to live in Houston.

Rufus Porter

Meanwhile, Rufus Porter was having another good season with the Seahawks. He played in all sixteen games and started fifteen games at linebacker during the 1994 season. Rufus had been undrafted, but made the Pro Bowl his first two seasons on special teams and was All Pro after his second season. I did not know Rufus as well as I did Willie, but I soon could see that he was the ultimate professional. He worked hard, did his job, and was careful with his money. He would be a free agent at the end of the 1994 season, and I was looking forward to doing his contract, and finally representing a football player where I had some leverage to try to obtain a significant NFL deal.

Representing free agents and low-draft picks was stimulating to a degree, but was not the way to make a living as an agent. In fact, it was the opposite, as it amounted to working hard and doing your job and not getting paid. It was nice to get my name in the paper as representing a professional player, but I needed to start turning a profit on the football end of the business.

Speaking of football, it was about this time that I met a fellow by the name of Lee Brecheen. Lee was about fifteen years younger than me and had been raised in Baton Rouge. His father had passed away, but left him with a real love of Louisiana high school football. He had been diligently studying and researching football for several years, particularly Louisiana's high school football scene. Lee ate, slept and lived high school football. He knew all about Louisiana players and their families because he had been watching high school football all over the state on Friday nights for many years. He not only visited the large high schools but the smaller schools as well. At the time we met, he hosted an annual high school football awards program for the state's prep players.

Lee and I hit it off, as we could talk football non-stop. We became friends and are still friends to this day. I have also worked as his attorney on occasion. In 1997 Lee started his own magazine called the *Louisiana Football Magazine*, which still prints an annual issue. After magazines fell out of vogue, he started his own T.V. show which features stories primarily on high school football, but includes some other sports. I have been on the show several times discussing agent-related sports information. While working as agent, Lee was always a reliable source of football information, particularly on Louisiana football players. Again, in the agent business I met all kinds of personalities and people who remained friends for life.

SEVENTEEN
1995

B.J. and I were constantly pursuing potential NBA draft picks from the college ranks. B.J. still had a role as a part-time scout for the Rockets, and this worked out well, for not only keeping constant contact with the game, but also giving him enough to live on since we were still growing our business. Neither of us was making enough to live solely on the fees that were generated from our sports clients. When dealing with sports clients, there are constant expenses generated for which you do not obtain reimbursement. There are yearly requirements to pay fees and attend seminars with the various players associations and state regulatory bodies to stay current as a certified agent, which can add up to a significant amount of not only money but time. In addition, there are many other expenses for which you get no reimbursement. If you fly out to a game to see a client, you can't charge for your flight, room, meals, etc. unless there is some specific reason you are going to see the client, such as attending an arbitration or some specific negotiation. Generally, each client wants you to keep in touch on a regular basis, and to see your face from time to time. Telephone calls are nice, but can't take the place of a personal visit where you can pound the flesh, dialogue with the coach, and spend some time with your client's family. Again, if you are not keeping up with the client, there are numerous agents who will be happy to get to know your client on a personal level; you have to nurture that personal relationship.

Rufus Porter

At the end of the 1994–1995 NFL season, Rufus Porter became an unrestricted free-agent, with the free agency signing period coming near the first of March, 1995. I was naturally excited to finally be on the verge of negotiating and having an NFL player sign a contract with a substantial signing bonus, and a substantial salary. Rufus would be an NFL starter on the team where he went, and it gave me, for the first time, some leverage in the negotiation of the contract. He played at Seattle for seven seasons because of his initial signing as a free agent and subsequent negotiations by his former agent; he did agree to restructure his contract in 1992, just when I had taken over as his agent.

Rufus had made a good living over the previous few years, but this was an opportunity for him to have a big payday near the end of his career. At the beginning of the 1995 NFL season, Rufus would be thirty years old and likely moving into the final stages of his career. I knew that the average NFL career was around four years, and that Rufus played linebacker with such intensity and abandonment that his career could end at any time with an injury. Accordingly, I knew that this negotiation would be really important for his life after football and was determined to do the best job possible.

In preparation for the negotiation, I studied the starting salaries for all the NFL linebackers and contacted the NFLPA.

I again read the entire NFL Collective Bargaining Agreement (CBA), making sure that I was on equal, if not better ground than any general manager I might encounter in negotiations. I sent out communications to all the NFL teams letting them know I was representing Rufus; I reminded them that he was a quality player, and was on the NFL All Rookie team in 1988 and an AFC Pro Bowl selection in 1988 and 1989 for special teams. Of course, the teams that were interested in him would have known all about him, but I thought it could not hurt to remind them.

Rufus had been in Seattle for seven years and was a fan favorite. He would have liked to stay there, if possible, but was looking for a team that would show its affection by making him a really substantial offer out of the gate. Rufus would be a good player for any team, but because of his age would carry the risk of diminishing skills and possible injury; so there would be a limit to what any team would pay for his services. He had torn his right Achilles tendon in 1993 and only played in seven games, but had come on strong in 1994, playing in all sixteen games. My job was to determine the market and get him the best deal with a team where he felt comfortable. Of course, this was different than signing a low-draft pick or a free agent after the draft to a team. Rufus was a veteran, and he himself knew the ins and outs of the League and would be able to give me knowledgeable input on our negotiations.

Seattle had expressed a solid interest in re-signing him and gave me all the sentimental reasons why he should be there, but were tentative with their initial offer. Their plan seemed to be to see what other teams offered and come in at the last minute to match the offer on the table. This strategy did not sit well with Rufus. He felt, as I did, that Seattle should show its appreciation to him for his years of service and come forward with an outstanding offer and challenge any other team to beat it. However, Seattle did not want to get into a bidding war and waited for us to field other offers. Two teams showed some real interest: the New Orleans Saints and the Tampa Bay Buccaneers. New Orleans was changing into a 4-3 defense, and Rufus would fit in well with that system.

I worked New Orleans and Tampa Bay, and ultimately New Orleans came up with the best deal, a three-year deal with a large signing bonus and an adequate first-year salary. The first year, Rufus would be making close to $2 million since no team would cut a player after paying almost a million for a signing bonus. Each of the last two years had a large salary, so if he played out the contract, he would make approximately $3.6 million over a three-year period. I ran the deal by advisors at the NFLPA, and they thought it was in line with what you would expect for a free agent like Rufus. In addition to the money, Rufus was happy that he could return to his home state of Louisiana. He had grown up in Baton Rouge and played his high school ball at Capitol High School and college ball at Southern. Of course, I was happy that Rufus would be playing so close to Baton Rouge and on the same team as Willie.

I had been asking Seattle for an offer, and as we were closing out the negotiations with New Orleans, Seattle realized they had waited too long and made an offer very close to the offer of New Orleans. However, the goodwill that Seattle had with Rufus at the beginning of free agency was gone at this point. Rufus had enjoyed his time in Seattle and loved the fans there, but the course of the negotiations and our discussions with New Orleans now negated his previous feelings. We were closing out negotiations with New Orleans and had verbal commitments, so even though Seattle came close, Rufus wanted to go with New Orleans, and I concurred.

Rufus came to my office on March 15, 1995, and signed his three-year deal. His deal would be the biggest one

I negotiated as an NFL agent, and the only one I would make any real money on, though I did at least fifteen deals total. The remaining deals were free-agents and sixth-or seventh-round draft picks who had small signing bonuses and never made the money to get financially set I generally never collected a fee or ended up spending more than I made. I have to add that Rufus was not only a great player, but the type of individual who took care of business and wanted to pay what he owed.

Mark Davis

Mark Davis, Paul Brown and Me in Philadelphia.

In the fall of 1994, during the course of my sports and legal business, I made the acquaintance of a most pleasant practicing attorney by the name of Paul Brown. Paul, who is white and stands about five feet, six inches, is always well groomed with a short haircut on the sides that peaks into a wave of hair on the top, which he combs over. He usually wears at least a jacket, if not a tie, most of the time and looks like an attorney. Paul was one of the plain nicest guys I met during my agent career. When I met him, he struck me more as a character out of a Charles Dickens novel than a basketball "gym rat," that is, someone who loves the game of basketball and spends a great deal of time in any kind of gym watching basketball. Of course, as I came to learn, there are no rules as to who can turn out to be a huge basketball fan.

Paul lives in Houma, Louisiana, which is about sixty miles southwest of Baton Rouge. Paul has been a huge basketball fan for many, many years. His brother, Corky, who was a Baton Rouge dentist, played basketball for four years at Southeastern Louisiana University, which is located forty miles from Baton Rouge. Corky is still the fourth leading scorer in Southeastern history. Paul, over the years, became involved with some of the area players who needed some support to develop their skills while growing up without the advantages that many kids were afforded. He has legally adopted five young black men, and has helped nearly a hundred more along the way. Unlike many in basketball, Paul's actions were motivated by true altruism rather than trying to cash in on the player when he reached the college or professional level.

Toward the end of 1994, Paul reached out to Dale Brown to see if there were any local sports agents with NBA experience who might be interested in representing one of the young men he had mentored over the years. Dale gave Paul my name and told him that I had been representing Stanley for several years and to give me a call. Thanks again to Coach Brown for all the help over the years.

Paul and I spoke, and he said he was close to a player from South Louisiana who was playing college basketball and would probably need an agent when he graduated from college. Paul did not want any money or reward for introducing me to the player; this is where he differed from many who befriend young players and later seek to profit off their relationship to the player.

Paul and I went to Houston, and I introduced B.J. to him. The two hit it off from the beginning, since both were "basketball sports nuts" and, as I said, "gym rats." I had told Paul about how B.J. had been instrumental in helping Tim Breaux land a contract with the Rockets, and about his ability to work with players to help them reach the NBA level. We were able to watch Tim at a

Rockets practice and get tickets for a Rockets game. Paul was impressed with B.J. and, I believe, with me, and really liked the fact that we were headquartered in Baton Rouge. Paul told us that he felt like we were the kind of people he would want to handle the representation of players he might know. We were equally impressed with his sincere concern for any young man whom he might want us to look at for potential representation, and with the fact that he had ethical standards and was a truly good person. The fact that he was a practicing attorney who graduated at the top of his class also meant that we were dealing with a sophisticated and intelligent person who would give any player good advice and help us in our efforts to do what was best for the player. Having gotten to know Paul, B.J. and I felt very comfortable in dealing with any player recommended by him.

The player Paul wanted us to meet and potentially represent was Mark Davis, who was playing at Texas Tech. Mark was from Thibodaux, Louisiana, a small town with Cajun flavor about forty-five miles southwest of Baton Rouge and about fifteen miles from Houma, Louisiana. I was very familiar with Thibodaux since I had actively campaigned for U.S. Congressman Billy Tauzin for the Louisiana Governor's race in 1987. Billy was originally from Chackbay, Louisiana, but lived in Thibodaux in 1987. Thibodaux was part of Billy's home base and we had several events in the area, and Billy had taken me fishing several times during and after the campaign. Unfortunately, Billy did not win. However, I have remained good friends with him and members of his family, especially his sons Tommy and Bill, to this day.

Mark is African American, six foot, seven inches, athletic, and was around 210 pounds when he became eligible for the NBA draft. He played high school basketball at Thibodaux High and had known Paul for several years. Paul acted as an informal mentor and advisor to Mark as he grew up, and spent time with Mark for years watching him play. He knew Mark and his family quite well. After high school, Mark signed to play at Washington State, but he eventually decided it was too far from home and opted to play at Howard Junior College in Big Spring, Texas. As a sophomore, Mark was the Western Junior College Athletic Conference player of the year. He then signed to play at Texas Tech.

His first year at Texas Tech, Mark virtually played every position on the floor and was named Southwest Conference newcomer of the year. His senior season, he averaged 17.3 points, 8.5 rebounds, and 4.7 assists per game, and was named to the All–Southwest Conference team and the all-defensive team. He recorded eleven double-doubles, one triple-double (sixteen points, eleven rebounds, and a school-record thirteen assists) and had a school-record forty-one dunks.

B.J. thought he would be a good prospect and had the tools to potentially play in the NBA. Paul introduced us to Mark, and B.J. and I went down to meet his mother and his family in Thibodaux. By this time, my reputation as an agent had grown, and with B.J. working with me, we now had the credibility to approach the player and his family with confidence and the knowledge that we could do as good a job as any in the business and a better job than many. Mark was a quiet young man, but we soon got to know him and his family, and we began to feel comfortable with each other. I particularly liked his mother and sisters, who were a lot of fun and naturally thought the world of Mark. After some time, Mark indicated that he was leaning toward signing with us after his college career had ended. He was a good potential prospect but not a sure first round pick; however, we were willing to spend the time necessary to help him prepare so he would have his shot in the NBA and/or professional basketball, depending on how things worked out.

We kept in touch with Mark up until he played his last game when Texas Tech lost to Washington State in the first round of the National Invitational Tournament on March 15, 1995. After ending his college career, Mark did sign with us, despite a last minute push by an agent recommended by his coach, James Dickey. We had already come up with a game plan for Mark, which was that he would play in as many pre-draft camps as possible so that he could potentially move up in the draft order. He had been invited to play at the pre-draft camp at Portsmouth, and B.J. accompanied him. Mark played well at Portsmouth, where his team made it to the finals. Consequentially, he was invited to the camp at Phoenix, which we took as a very good sign, since a number of first-round players typically play at Phoenix, as had Ervin. B.J. went to Phoenix and Mark received an invitation to play in the final pre-draft camp in June in Chicago. We decided that the more teams saw him, the more they would want him, and he played at Chicago and put on another good showing with B.J. in attendance. Other positive signs were that three teams, Chicago, Indiana, and Portland, brought him in for personal visits prior to the draft.

By the end of June, just prior to the draft on June 28, 1995, in Toronto, we were hopeful that Mark had moved to a potential mid-to-low-first-round draft pick. Several teams had shown interest, particularly Portland, which had intimated that they would probably take him in the first round at number eighteen. Of course, teams can say anything to get a player to come in and work out, which they do many times; and one cannot forget those players who are invited to appear on TV for the draft, based on predictions, and then sit there embarrassed when they are not drafted as predicted. However, because of the many conversations we had with NBA teams, particularly B.J. and Mark at the camps and visits, we were still hopeful that Mark might go in the first-round.

On draft day, we arranged a party at Mark's mother's place so the whole family could attend. Her apartment was packed for the party with Mark's family and friends, including myself, B.J., and Paul. Unfortunately, the draft did not go as planned and Portland did not take Mark at number eighteen as we had hoped. After the number eighteen pick was announced, we had to sit and wait until he was drafted at number forty-eight by the Minnesota Timberwolves. Naturally, the draft was disappointing for Mark after all the hard work he had put in, but such is the way of professional sports. With the amount of talent and competition in all sports, you can work very hard and still not be evaluated and drafted at the preferred spot.

Mark did all he could have done from our point of view, and we were still proud of his accomplishment in being drafted. Of course, we knew that anything can happen in the draft, but it was hard to put a pessimistic reality check on Mark with the visits he made and the comments from the teams. After the draft, Mark was upset, but he still believed in himself, and that he was good enough to make an NBA team. B.J. and I felt the same although Europe was still an option. We knew, because of his draft position, it would be unlikely that we would be able to negotiate a contract for guaranteed money; however, Mark would be invited to Rookie and Veterans camp with Minnesota.

Mark decided not to go to Europe, making the choice instead to go to camp with Minnesota on a one-year deal that did not become guaranteed until December 1, 1995. This decision took a lot of courage and determination on his part, as it is quite difficult to make a team as a second-round draft pick. Mark put his head down, worked hard and made the team, which was quite an accomplishment, and B.J., Paul, and I were all very proud of him. Just making the roster of an NBA team is a great accomplishment in itself, as it is a very select club with worldwide competition. I managed to go to a few of Mark's games and kept up with him as time would allow, but it was difficult to gauge our relationship since he was a quiet individual.

I had "negotiated" Mark's contract with Minnesota with Kevin McHale, who was a super nice guy and did not come off as a regular business person; that had its good points and bad. I had been a Celtics fan over the years, as Robert Parish, Kevin's Celtics teammate, was from Shreveport, was my age, and had played for Woodlawn High School against my school, Captain Shreve. I enjoyed the games we had against Woodlawn, though we did not win, and followed Robert's career to some degree as he went to Centenary College in Shreveport and then on to the NBA. It was really cool being on the telephone and actually speaking with Kevin as an equal. It also made good beer-drinking conversation when I mentioned to friends that "I had been on the line with Kevin McHale today." I would deal with Kevin several times over the upcoming years and kept up a good relationship with him, though we had a couple of issues with communication. There was not much negotiation in Mark's first contract since he was a second-round draft pick. I was able to get the contract guaranteed if he made the roster for a period of time and built in some bonuses. We discussed playing-time bonuses, and I had to write him a letter after I actually saw the numbers, as they did not comport with my memory of the discussions. However, we were able to work it out.

Willie Williams

The Saints training camp opened in July 1995 with my only two players in the NFL, Willie and Rufus, on the team, but the two were in entirely different positions. Willie was playing out the second year of his free-agent contract and was in a position to make some money if he was able to make the team. His odds were good to make the team, since he had played the year before and ended the season as a starter. However, a player in Willie's position was vulnerable since his contract was not guaranteed. Rufus, on the other hand, had just been paid a significant bonus, was a seven-year veteran, and slated as a starter, so he was, in reality, assured to make the team and collect his substantial salary for the 1995-1996 season.

Willie was doing well in training camp until he had a disciplinary problem. The issue blew over, but then, in the second week of camp, Willie developed a knee problem that was giving him a great deal of pain. His knee began to swell when he practiced, and it was drained several times; but he was unable to perform during the exhibition season.

Willie was examined by the Saints orthopedic physician, and diagnostic studies failed to show any objective evidence of injury. Willie began treating the knee, and the swelling went down when he was not playing, but he was still having the pain. I had a serious discussion with him to verify that he was indeed in pain, and that he felt he could not play. A player injured while under contract obligates the team to pay for his medical recovery and his salary until he is recovered. If a player is announced physically fit by the team physician and gets back on the field to play, then the team could at that time try to cut him to avoid paying medical and salary. Willie and I both knew that a player in his situation is caught in a vice in the sense that the minute an injured player gets back on the field, the team could treat him as non-injured, and he could be cut with an open issue on his injury protection; however, the longer he remains on the sidelines, the less likely it will be that he makes the team. Since the team physician was saying he saw no "objective reason" for Willie's complaints, the coaches and management were encouraging him to play and get back on the field, and their frustration grew when Willie would not get back on the field. He had tried a few times and the swelling kept returning.

Fortunately, I knew from my legal personal injury experience that tears to knee cartilage and ligament strains can occur and not show up in diagnostic studies. I also knew that, at times, team physicians were pressured to not act in the player's best interest by coaches and management. This happens in personal injury automobile litigation when the defense demands what is termed an "IME," an independent medical evaluation. In automobile cases, your client may have sustained soft tissue injuries, that cannot be picked up in diagnostics, and are causing your client pain and discomfort. Though it is called an IME, the defense attorney can pick a physician that he uses regularly and that he knows will, in all probability, say there is nothing wrong with the patient. To be fair, there are a few clients who may exaggerate an injury following an automobile accident to collect some kind of money damages. In addition, there are some plaintiff's attorneys who send clients to physicians who always find something wrong, and will send out the same report on almost every patient. As an attorney, I believed my clients and sent them to physicians that, I knew would give them good care. If a client was not hurt, I would tell them that I could not handle the case or we should settle, based on the actual injury, though my job was to get as much for the actual injury as possible. This is why I did not settle my cases quickly just to make fee, but worked the case to get a maximum recovery.

With my personal injury background, I was not shy about advocating for my clients when they were treated unfairly or injured, or about filing grievances under the CBA, if necessary. I had studied the NFL CBA and already knew the procedure for an injury grievance, and there was also an allowance for an injury grievance in the player contract. I had already handled several NBA arbitrations, and with my litigation experience, trying an injury arbitration would not be a problem.

In Willie's case, I knew he was injured because he told me. I talked with management and then demanded that Willie be given an independent medical examination as allowed under the CBA. By this time, management, including coaching, was not pleased with the situation, and any future Willie might have with the Saints looked grim. The most important thing was that he was hurt and could not play for any team until he received treatment. The upcoming year was very important to Willie, as he already had three credited seasons and only needed one more to "vest" in the Bert Bell Retirement Plan under the CBA. This, of course, meant that he would be eligible for pension benefits later in life when it would be really important.

The first thing I did was ask for a second medical opinion, which was allowed under the CBA. The second physician did find swelling, which in my opinion was an objective finding of injury. I knew the only way to really determine the cause of the problem now was to perform a scope of the knee to see what was causing the problem. Surgery would, of course, mean a few weeks of not being able to play or even worse. By now the final Saints' football team cuts were underway, and Willie was cut by the Saints prior to the beginning of the season. I immediately filed an injury grievance to protect Willie's rights.

Willie had the scope, and a small tear in his cartilage was found and repaired. He needed several weeks of rest and rehabilitation. Afterwards, the swelling did not reappear, and he was ready to play again. I negotiated the injury grievance, and obtained a payout and an agreement that he would be credited for another season under the Bert Bell Retirement Plan and be eligible for his pension. Unfortunately, we were not able to get another team interested in picking him since the season was well underway by the time he recovered. However, he was drafted in the second round of the World League of American Football (WLAF) by the Amsterdam Admirals before the 1996 season and decided to attempt to get back in the League through this avenue.

Stanley Roberts

During this year, I periodically kept up with Stanley since he was still paying me fees from the contract I had negotiated. In speaking with Stanley one day, it came to my attention that he and Delpit had hit an impasse regarding fees that Delpit alleged Stanley owed him for the "contract" he had renegotiated with the Clippers in October of 1994. The agent was alleging that he was due fees on the entire amount of the contract being paid, even though the new "contract" was, in reality, guaranteed money I had negotiated in the contract with Orlando prior to his trade to L.A. If Stanley paid the fees as demanded and mine, he would, in effect, be paying twice the fees for the same money, which in our opinion would be unfair and inappropriate. Consequently, Stanley had stopped paying the Delpit fee in August, 1991. I agreed with Stanley, and after talking he again retained me as his personal attorney, on an hourly basis, to represent him in the pending legal struggle against his now former agent. Here again I was back in litigation springing from my sports agent business. I had really missed Stanley and was glad to be again working for his best interests. Because of our friendship, I would keep the bill as reasonable as possible.

I began to work on Stanley's situation in September 1995, and this is when I studied in more detail the actual October, 1994, contract with the Clippers. Basically, Delpit had extended the contract with just about the same guaranteed money, and the Clippers had added summer workout and conditioning clauses and some deferred compensation. This confirmed to me that Stanley owed no fees on the monies he was being paid at the present time. Per the NBPA regulations, he should only owe fees on any additional money he might make, which would not be until 1997 and 1998.

By September 28, 1995, Delpit had filed a grievance with the NBPA against Stanley, demanding fees. I moved aggressively and initially filed defenses to the claim noting that Delpit had not served Stanley properly with the grievance, according to the NBPA regulations. The NBPA regulations require that the agent serve the player with the grievance either in person or by certified mail within thirty days of the "grievance," which in this case would be nonpayment of fees. I did not know how far these defenses would go, but came out firing as a matter of strategy. I telephoned the NBPA and conferred with attorney Ron Klempner, with whom I had spoken previously on other matters. I prepared and filed an Answer to the grievance, and then filed a counterclaim against Delpit as I had on the Chris Morris grievance.

My Answer noted the fact that Stanley did not sign a player-agent contract with Delpit until October 27, the day the renegotiated contract with the Clippers was signed. At that time, Stanley was severely injured with a second Achilles tendon tear and was on powerful pain medications. Based on the date of the player-agent contract, I raised the question of how Delpit could have negotiated the contract if he was not acting as Stanley's agent at the time. Furthermore, I contended that if he did negotiate the contract, he would have been doing so in violation of the player-agent regulations because he did not have a player-agent contract. In the counterclaim, I asked Delpit to return any monies he had obtained from Stanley, fees or otherwise, including any loans he had obtained from Stanley.

Around the same time, I became involved with the Clippers on issues arising out of Stanley's renegotiated contract. Andy Roeser had touched on this issue during a prior telephone conversation we had on or around October 12, 1995. The Clippers had added a weight provision into the conditioning portion of the contract, and were now contending that Stanley had reported for training camp "overweight and out of shape." On

October 12, 1995, Andy and I discussed by telephone that the Clippers might move to suspend Stanley under his new contract because of his conditioning. I was prepared to counter this move by filing a grievance against the Clippers under the injury clause of his contract, since Stanley was coming off his second Achilles tendon injury having developed bone spurs, and was playing in pain.

I did draft the grievance but did not need to file it. Stanley was held out of the exhibition games, but was placed on the roster for the opening game of the season on November 3, 1995. I then could move in preparing for the Ken Delpit hearing. On November 27, 1995, I had a telephone conference call with George Nicolau, the NBPA arbitrator, and Ken Delpit, and a hearing date was set for February 16, 1996, in Los Angeles. I was headed back to some more interesting sports litigation.

EIGHTEEN
1996

———— • ————

During January, 1996, I continued to prepare for the Delpit hearing, which had been scheduled for February 16, 1996. I drafted letters and spoke to potential witnesses, including Andy Roeser, the general manager of the Clippers, who would testify about the contract and the "renegotiation" of Stanley's deal in October, 1994. I also asked Ron Klempner and David Mondress, both of the NBPA, to be available to testify. I finished preparing the witness list, prepared exhibit notebooks, and organized the documents I would submit to the arbitrator.

I even prepared a cross-examination of Delpit, which compared to preparing the cross-examination of a physician defendant in a medical malpractice lawsuit. It was a simple task and because of the circumstances, very enjoyable. Ken Delpit was not an attorney nor a big-time agent with lots of clients and friends in the business. In fact, if memory serves me correctly, Delpit had no clients other than Stanley, and it still remains a question to me why Stanley would have wanted to hire him. Stanley never really gave me more of an explanation other than Libby had somehow influenced his move. Of course, back in those days, other decisions of Stanley's defy logic except to say he was at times easily influenced by others and really living in the moment.

It was obvious to me that Delpit knew little of the procedural policies of the NPBA just from his initial filing of the Grievance against Stanley. Based on the contract he had "renegotiated" for Stanley, I felt that he knew nothing about the CBA and did not know how to negotiate an NBA contract. To a knowledgeable agent, there was no reason to renegotiate Stan's deal, because the new deal was for a longer period of time (two years) and offered very little guaranteed money over the remaining guaranteed money on the original contract. At the time of the renegotiation, Stanley had three years left on his contract, all with guaranteed money. The final year of the contract was to pay almost $5 million a year, an excellent salary at that time in the NBA. Since I had negotiated the contract, I should have been entitled to an agent's fee on all the remaining guaranteed money in Stan's contract. Below is a chart of Stan's contract.

Stanley Roberts: Original Contract Negotiated by OLS

Year	Protection Guarantee	Compensation
1994-95	Full	$3,496,000.00
1995-96	Full	$4,151,500.00
1996-97	Full	$4,761,000.00

Analysis of Contract:
Guaranteed Money: $12,408,500.00

Term: Three years

Below is the renegotiated contract that Stanley signed while under narcotics after his first Achilles injury on October 27, 1994. As can be seen, the contract has less guaranteed money over a period of two years and had conditioning, weight, and workout clauses, which would lead to several confrontations with management and will be detailed shortly.

Renegotiated Contract

Year	Protection Guarantee	Compensation
1994-95	Full	$2,850,000.00 with $646,000.00 deferred until 1999
1995-96	Full	$3,000,000.00
1996-97	Full	$3,250,000.00
1997–98	At team's option—team must pay $2.1 M if not exercised	$3,500,000.00 Deferred $250,000.00
1998–99	At team's option with $600,000 buyout(?) (not guaranteed for ruptured Achilles tend on injury)	$3,750,000.00 Deferred $750,000.00; Payable in 3 equal installments beginning June 15, 1999

Analysis of Contract:
Guaranteed Money: $2,850,000; $3,000,000.00; $3,250,000; and $2,100,000, equaling $11,200,000.00

Deferred Compensation (Guaranteed): (Included in
Guaranteed Money): $604,600.00

Term: Five years

The party that had really benefited from the renegotiation
was the Clippers, who extended the contract but, at the same
time, were able to guarantee the same money and gain far more
control over Stan as far as his weight, conditioning, and his
off-season activities. I had been successful in keeping the
original contract devoid of any specific weight requirements,
workout requirements, and off-season requirements for
workouts and training per Stan's explicit instructions. After
Stan fired me and I was replaced by Ken Delpit, the Clippers
began to talk renegotiation, which I'm sure sounded good to
Delpit so he could get my name off the contract and take
credit for Stan's big "new" contract. In my opinion, Delpit really
did not gain any new money or advantages for Stanley in the
"renegotiation" of the contract that I had negotiated for
Stanley. Accordingly, my argument to the arbitrator was that
Delpit did not deserve any fee until the very end of the contract,
when any "new money" not previously guaranteed in my
contract would be paid.

I decided to just cross-examine Delpit on the facts of his
employment and his renegotiation to prove that Stanley should
not be charged for any work that did not produce an added benefit
under the contract that I had already negotiated. I was relishing,
to a degree, the prospect of meeting face-to-face with the man
who had gone behind my back and convinced Stanley to fire me
and hire him. This kind of opportunity did not present itself too
often, particularly in the shadowy underworld of sports agency.
Having Stanley back as a client was a sweet moment, which came
with the added cherry, so to speak, of defending Delpit's grievance,

being hired to file the counter grievance and knowing that I would face him in my own backyard, in a sort of legal proceeding. Even though this payback would be sweet in a sense, I wanted to keep the grievance hearing very professional and operated the preparation on a cordial and friendly basis. My strategy was not to create a dramatic intense scene but to keep the arbitration on a friendly level, if at all possible. I really did not know Ken personally and did not have any personal animosity toward him, only the fact that he had interfered in my business. At this point his own actions were the ones that had brought on this grievance.

On February 13, 1996, I traveled to Los Angeles where Ken Delpit had agreed to hold the arbitration by telephone. I spent five to six hours preparing for the hearing on February 14 and 15 while in Los Angeles. I prepared Stanley to testify and spoke with witnesses. I do not remember, with exact detail, the events of those days, but do remember spending some time with Andy Roeser. Andy and I were well-acquainted, as he was the go-to guy for the Clippers if there were any problems with Stanley. Andy had a good sense of humor and professionalism, and I always enjoyed working with him, much like Pat Williams. Although I knew he had pulled one over on Ken Delpit with the new contract, he was only doing his job, and we remained professionally on good terms throughout Stanley's tenure at the Clippers, even when things became a bit dicey at times. Andy would be called as a witness regarding the events of the renegotiation. The NBPA witnesses, either Ron or Dave, would be called to demonstrate that there was no need to renegotiate the contract I had negotiated, and that Ken Delpit should not be entitled to any agent fees until the end of the contract.

I know that I spent about eight and a half hours on February 16, working on the arbitration because I still have a copy of the bill I sent to Stanley. However, neither Stanley nor I can remember any real details of what occurred. My meeting of

Ken Delpit appears to have been anticlimactic, as I really can't remember the man's face. The arbitration must have gone as planned, since subsequently we were able to reach a settlement and have the matter dismissed. I was now again Stanley's agent in terms of basketball matters and contractual matters, but had nothing to do with his finances, which he had turned over to other people since his arrival in Los Angeles. Beginning 1996, I felt great that Stanley was back on board and that my client list was still growing. I now had Stanley, Ervin, Tim Breaux, and Mark Davis as NBA clients, which, looking back at it, was a minor miracle considering the volatility and unscrupulous nature of the business. Carl Herrera and I were still friends, but Jamie was working with him and I really had stopped handling anything for him.

Darvin Ham

By this time, I had learned that I had been extremely fortunate in signing two first-round NBA picks in Stanley and Ervin. I had been in the right time and right place to sign them, but it looked unlikely that I could compete consistently with the top agents; their connections to the AAU coaches, college coaches and shoe companies helped them in recruiting the top college and even high school players coming out each year. I refused to begin paying anyone off to influence a player to sign with me, which put me at a distinct disadvantage in recruiting the large majority of players. Moreover, I had been in the sports-agent business long enough to know that I really did not want to be in the business full-time, due to the issues of recruiting andservicing clients. I enjoyed the business, but really loved my legal work where there were ethical and legal rules that other attorneys and the courts enforced, clients were not high maintenance, and they really appreciated what you did for them. This is not to say that the practice of law was restful; to the contrary, it was much more stressful, but you were on somewhat of a level playing field when competing, and I did love to compete.

B.J. and I, realizing that first-round picks with those guaranteed first-year contracts would be few and far between, instead focused on players who, though not high-draft picks, might make it in the NBA. This decision was all on B.J., since he was tremendously talented in working with and evaluating players. Darvin Ham from Texas Tech was one such player whom we signed in 1996.

B.J. and I had met Darvin through Mark Davis, his Texas Tech teammate. Darvin and Mark were good friends and we had opportunities to spend some time with Darvin during Mark's workouts and his being drafted. Darvin was a great guy, intelligent, and a good communicator. B.J. and I both thought a lot of him as an individual, not just as a client. Darvin was not slated as a high-draft pick or even a draft pick, but we knew he was smart and a hard worker, and if he followed B.J.'s training and advice, he had a shot at making an NBA team.

Darvin was from Michigan and came to Texas Tech in 1993. He was six feet, seven inches, 230 pounds, muscular, and very athletic, and as B.J. says, "he could jump out of the gym." Darvin gained instant national recognition after shattering a backboard in the 1996 NCAA Tournament, while playing against North Carolina. His photo, while shattering the backboard, appeared on the cover of *Sports Illustrated*. I still have the autographed cover in my office to this day.

Darvin was not a huge scorer, averaging 9.1 points per game his senior season at Tech, but could defend well and played with incredible energy. He was selected second-team All South West Conference by the AP and started all eighty-nine games of his Tech career, scoring in double digits numerous times. After his last season, he was the all-time Tech career record holder for dunks with 115 in three years.

After Darvin finished his season, he was anxious to get to work and signed a player-agent contract with me on April 1, 1996, which I promptly mailed to the NBPA in accordance with the agent rules. Darvin was not slated to play in any of the pre-draft camps such as Portsmouth and Phoenix, so he moved to Houston and began working out with B.J. Importantly, Darvin was willing to listen to our advice and do what was necessary to get the attention of NBA personnel.

B.J. and I decided that a stint in a minor professional league, the U.S. Basketball League, would help Darvin's development and exposure. Darvin was willing to play in this league, which had a late-spring to early-summer schedule and only offered a salary of around $350 per week. Initially, I signed Darvin with the Jacksonville Barracudas in the USBL. Tim Bourroughs, with whom I had lost contact years before, was also playing there at the time. Subsequently, Darvin moved to another USBL team, the Florida Sharks, coached by Eric Musselman. Darvin played hard and proved he was a pro player in the USBL. He won the League championship with Florida.

After his stint in the USBL, Darvin then went back to Houston to work out. At that time, Houston was a hub of pros working out in the off-season. Working out in Fonde Rec were the likes of Sam Cassell and Mario Elie from the Rockets. I continued to contact NBA teams and advise of Darvin's availability prior to the 1996 NBA draft, which was held on June 26, 1996. Darvin went undrafted, but still did not let this affect his goal of reaching the NBA. After the draft, he attended a Miami rookie free-agent camp.

B.J. was still working part-time for the Rockets, helping the team prepare for the summer league, the Rocky Mountain Review, in which several NBA teams would participate with free agents, draft picks, and younger players. Just before the team was to leave for the Review, one of the Rocket's players was injured and could not go with the team. The team was left looking for a last-minute replacement. B.J. told Larry Smith, the coach of the team, that Darvin was the perfect guy to replace the injured player. Larry was familiar with Darvin and agreed. B.J. left and went over to the gym where Darvin was playing, and literally pulled him out of the gym in his workout clothes to go practice with the Houston team preparing for the Rocky Mountain Review.

Darvin now had his opportunity to show what he could do and he took full advantage of it. He had played with pros in the USBL and was working out with pros in Houston, so the summer league almost seemed like a step down. Darvin played really well at the Rocky Mountain Review and caught the eye of Bernie Bickerstaff, who was the head coach for the Denver Nuggets. As a result, Darvin was signed to attend training camp with Denver.

The Nuggets had Antonio McDyess on the roster, a previous first-round draft pick. However, McDyess was injured during the preseason and Darvin ended up getting his playing time. As a free agent trying to make the team, this was again a great break for Darvin, of which he took full advantage. For example, the Nuggets went to Hawaii to play a two-game stint with the Lakers. At the time, Shaq was the center and Kobe had just been drafted. Darvin played both games against the Lakers and had eighteen points in one game. As a result of his great preseason play, on October 1, 1996, Darvin signed a free-agent contract with Denver, which became guaranteed in January. Through his hard work and great attitude, Darvin made the NBA as an undrafted free agent his first year, which is no small feat. He subsequently was traded to Indiana in February, 1997. There he was coached by Larry Brown, Stanley's favorite coach, but did not get much playing time.

Ervin Johnson

Throughout 1994 and 1995, I had been in contact with Ervin by telephone and attended as many basketball games of his as I could fit into my schedule. I ended up seeing mainly away games because of the distance and difficulty in reaching Seattle, and because Ervin had a girlfriend, Renee, who became his wife, so he had plenty to do socially in Seattle. I really did get spoiled, as the team would always provide me with a discounted room in whatever luxury hotel the team had booked for the players. The simplest venues were Houston, Dallas, and Atlanta since they were a direct flight away. Miami became one of my favorite venues because it was a beautiful and exciting city. At times, I would add some legal work in conjunction with a game. Once I saw Ervin play in Boston on an incredibly cold night in conjunction with a deposition of one of my physician experts. Between Ervin and Stanley and my other clients, I ended up seeing games in almost every NBA city. The one city that I had wanted to visit, but did not, was Vancouver when the Grizzlies played there. I had heard what an interesting city Vancouver was, but the length of the trip always deterred me from making it until it was too late and Ervin retired in 2006.

When I had negotiated Ervin's original contract, it was the safe guaranteed three-year deal, with the thinking being that at the end of that deal, he would be in a position to get his career-making deal that would hopefully set him for life. Of course, this plan was premised on the expectation that Ervin would work hard, take care of business, and continue to develop as a player. In some cases when players reach the pinnacle of signing an NBA contract, they take their foot off the accelerator and do not develop as expected because of lack of work. Others can be derailed by the temptations of the League, such as women and drugs. Still others are derailed by things out of their control such as injury or even the fact that they are just not talented enough to play in the League.

Because of Ervin's character, he continued to work hard and stuck to the business of developing himself. He did not fall for any of the temptations of the League and remained a humble, hardworking player. Ervin married Renee in 1995, and his focus was on his family and his career. As a result, and with God's help, he did not suffer any serious injuries as he continued to develop. Ervin was a low-maintenance client in the sense that I always knew he would do what was right and best for his development. He was older and more mature and had a solid set of principles he lived by. He could be stubborn at times, but this trait had served him before and would now, in that he would not give up on any goal he set for himself.

Ervin would work outside of practice to continue to develop his basketball skills. He was always in shape and at six feet, eleven inches could run the floor, block shots, and score if needed. He was more known as a good defensive player who could guard and shut down penetration to the basket. The real question was whether he could develop into a starter in the NBA. During his first season, he ended up starting three games and averaged 2.6 points and .5 blocks per game. During his second season, 1994–1995, he started thirty games and averaged 3.1 points and one block per game. During the 1995–1996 season, he started sixty games and averaged 5.5 points and 1.6 blocks per game.

By the end of the 1995–1996 season, Ervin had certainly proven that he could play in the NBA. However, there was still some question among League personnel whether he was an all-around "starting center." Defensively, he could hold his own with anyone and he could dunk the ball, easily given the right pass, but he could not really create his own shot down low like Stanley. Our position for purposes of his upcoming contract would be that we felt he had proven that he should be a starter, and he certainly was the kind of player who improved team chemistry with his hard work and low maintenance. Ervin and Darvin were two of my hardest-working basketball clients. They both made the most of the talent God had given them. The fact that Ervin started sixty games during the 1995–1996 season for the Sonics gave me ammunition for my argument that he deserved to be paid like an NBA starting center for his new contract.

In 1995, the NBA and the NBPA had agreed to a new CBA. Under the new CBA, Ervin would become a free agent on July 1, 1996, so I was eagerly awaiting the negotiation of his new contract. The 1995–1996 season, which would be Ervin's last season under his original three-year contract, was really exciting in that the then Seattle Supersonics, who relocated to Oklahoma City after the 2007–2008 season, played in the NBA championship against the Michael Jordan–led Chicago Bulls. The Sonics had a deep roster that year that included Shawn Kemp, whom the team had drafted in 1989, and Gary Payton, drafted in 1990. Other members of the team besides Ervin were forward Deltef Schrempf, forward Sam Perkins, guard Hersey Hawkins, and guard Nate McMillian, now the head coach of the Indiana Pacers. Coach George Karl, who was the Sonics Coach from 1992–1998, had done a masterful job with the team that went 64-18 and made the Finals.

I met Coach Karl several times and he was always very cordial, but my conversations were always brief. He ended up coaching the Milwaukee Bucks from 1998 to 2003. Ervin played for Milwaukee from 1997 to 2003, so Coach Karl coached Ervin for most of his career. Over the years, I had the opportunity to observe him on many occasions, both on and off the court, and felt he was an excellent coach, but not as laid-back as some I had met such as Kevin McHale, Larry Brown, or Rudy Tomjanovich. He coached an angry, intense style which seemed to follow him off the court as well. Ervin always respected and liked Coach Karl. He feels like he is a very good coach and that he was lucky to have him as coach when he first entered the League.

I knew Coach Karl must have liked and trusted Ervin to keep him on his team for that many years, but he was not one to give out any compliments on his play. In his recent book, *Furious George*, Coach Karl particularly described Ervin as Michael Cage's backup: "His backup Ervin Johnson, blocked shots and defended the perimeter amazingly well for a big guy, but he had no offense to speak of" (p. 105). He further wrote in assessing the team after the disastrous playoff loss to Denver in the 1994 playoffs: "Ervin Johnson: big heart, good character...but is he talented enough to be the center on a championship team?" (p. 116). Describing the 1995–1996 season, he wrote, "I started Ervin Johnson, a 6' 11" kid who played great D all over the court but couldn't score" (p. 122). He then went on to explain how he would replace Ervin with Sam Perkins and that Ervin would play thirteen or fourteen minutes a game and that Perkins would average "twice that." Coach Karl did not think enough of Ervin's play prior to July 1, 1996, to try to keep him on the team following the expiration of his contract on July 1, 1996.

I was following Ervin's play with great interest during the 1995–1996 season and watched him on TV if possible. As the playoffs began, I was hoping the team would do well, especially since they had lost in the first round the previous two seasons. The Sonics beat eighth seeded Sacramento 3 to 1, and then swept Houston, the defending NBA champion, 4 to 0. The team won the Western Conference in a dramatic seventh game against Utah 4 to 3, to set up the showdown with the Chicago Bulls who had the advantage of resting while Seattle played.

I was naturally excited about the chance of Ervin getting a ring with only three years in the League. Furthermore, I was not about to miss a chance to see at least a couple of games of an

NBA championship series, particularly a series featuring Michael Jordan and one of my clients. B.J. and I immediately decided to attend some games to see Ervin and make the scene for public relations purposes. Since school was out, I decided that this would also be a once-in-a-lifetime chance for my son, Little O, to see Michael Jordan and attend some big games. He had already been to Houston and, courtesy of B.J., had visited the Rockets locker room and met Charles Barkley, Akeem Olajuwon, and Clyde Drexler. Charles was impressively friendly and took some time to chat with Oscar about how he was doing in school.

The first games of the finals were scheduled to take place in Chicago on June 5 and 7, 1996, and I arranged flights for B.J., Little O, and myself so we could spend some quality time with Ervin and his wife, Renee, and of course see some good basketball. Playoff basketball in almost all circumstances is the best in terms of intensity and entertainment. During the Rockets' run to the championship in 1994–1995, B.J. and I had attended several of the games between the Rockets and the Spurs in the Western Conference Finals. Those games, along with the Clippers vs. Rockets 1993 series when Stanley played, still stick in my mind as some of the best NBA games I personally attended.

In addition to the basketball, B.J. and I would use the finals to network and talk with team's scouts and player personnel about our clients. Ervin was our primary focus, as he would hopefully be a sought-after free agent. We could also be on the lookout for opportunities for Darvin, who had not signed with Denver at this time, and Mark Davis, who was a free agent. Our other clients, Stanley and Tim Breaux, were still in their contracts with the Clippers and Rockets; however, I should note that Tim would be traded to Vancouver on June 19, 1996, and was waived by Vancouver in October, 1996, becoming a free agent on November 4, 1996, and playing in the CBA the remainder of the 1996–1997 season. He would play briefly with the Milwaukee Bucks from

August 6, 1997 to November 18, 1997.

We had an excellent time attending the games and talked to numerous teams during our stay. The first game on June 5, 1996, ended with a Bulls victory and a score of 107-90. Our seats were not as good as for a regular NBA game, but were good enough to see the action. The game was not as competitive as we had hoped, but it was still a great experience. Between B.J. and myself, we now knew numerous NBA management personnel and we had good discussions and talks. B.J. was always super friendly, and any encounter would normally turn into a fifteen minute discussion at a minimum. The second game, on June 7, 1996, was more competitive, but the Bulls won again 92-88. Naturally, the losses did not create the warmest atmosphere, but we left the day after the game with the feeling of a great sports experience and looking forward to seeing Ervin play many more years in the League.

The Sonics went on to lose the third game, at home, in a blowout. The team had lost Nate McMillan, who was injured and could not play in this game. It was after this game that Coach Karl wrote in his book that he made a list of free agents "that we'd let go when the time came. Four names: Vince, Brick, Ervin, and Gary" (p. 131). Coach Karl would change his mind about releasing Gary Payton after he made a defensive change and Seattle won the next two games, but not about Ervin. The Sonics had pulled to one game behind the Bulls at 3 to 2, but lost the next game with cold shooting.

B.J. and I, knowing the way the agent business runs, were keenly aware that other agents might try to contact Ervin since he was fast approaching his new contract negotiation; this would be an opportunity for another agent to swoop in and pick up a huge payday with very little work. The NBPA agent regulations have no explicit prohibitions against contacting a player under contract, so my experience was that it was not uncommon for this to occur.

I'm sure that some other agents had at least made a run at Ervin about his upcoming free agency. However, Ervin held true to his word, and stuck with me as his agent, at this time and throughout his entire career.

After returning from Chicago, I continued my preparation for the upcoming negotiations for Ervin by reviewing financial information on the salaries of the top centers in the NBA and analyzing the centers that would be available. I had obtained from David Mondress, director of finance for the NBPA, the financial information on the top twenty centers in the League. I also had my practical experience, having negotiated Stanley's contract in 1992, and being privy to the subsequent "renegotiation" in 1994.

There had been labor tension in the past few summers as owners became increasingly worried with the escalating player salaries, starting with Shaq's $41 million deal over seven years (with an option to get out of the contract in four years). After expiration of the CBA at the end of the 1993–1994 season, the owners and players had entered into a no-strike, no-lockout agreement in October, 1994, with a moratorium on signing or restructuring player contracts. The moratorium expired on June 15, 1995, which was one day after the NBA Finals. The first lockout in NBA history was then declared by the owners, which allowed the expansion draft and the regular draft to take place, but all other League business was suspended from July 1 until September 12, 1995. No games were missed in this first lockout, and again a new CBA was negotiated before the start of the 1995–1996 season. Among the key issues at stake in the negotiations for the CBA were the usual important top priorities for the NBPA: salary cap, free agency, a rookie salary cap, and revenue sharing.

The July 1, 1996, free-agency period was looming as one of the most anticipated events in the NBA. It was being billed as a time when the most talented group of free agents in League history would be on the market. There would be 140 free agents and another twenty-six players that could opt out of contracts including Shaquille O'Neal, Horace Grant, Alonzo Mourning, Juan Howard, Dale Davis, and Alan Houston. Among the free agents were Michael Jordan, Reggie Miller, Gary Payton, Dennis Rodman, and the top center Dikembe Mutombo.

The star players were going into the 1996 free-agent period with significant salary increases in sight. For example, a *Sports Illustrated* article of July 1, 1996, quoted Alan Houston who made $1.2 million in 1995–1996, as wanting an average of $7.3 million, in line with Grant Hill's contract. The same article stated that center Jim McIlvaine's agent was demanding $3 million a year. Shaq, of course, was going for a huge contract, as were the other star players. I would be going into the free-agency period with Ervin Johnson and Mark Davis, neither a "star player," and each were in different stages in their career. My position with Ervin was that he was a potential starting center.

My position for Mark was that he showed that he could play in the League and would develop into a star. Of course, the real test was what NBA personnel thought about my players at this point in their careers. Ervin had played in the NBA for three years, and team managements had formed opinions on him that, realistically, I could not change with some sales pitch. It was the same for Mark, who had played a year in the League. I was extremely excited getting ready for the free agency, and my excitement, and B.J.'s, built as July 1, 1996, approached. Unfortunately, I did not have any teams contacting me aggressively about Ervin or Mark as I had with Stanley. Kevin McHale had told me, however, that Minnesota was interested in re-signing Mark. I knew that each NBA team would have a strategy it would follow to obtain the players they needed. Obviously, the more teams interested in one player the better leverage you have in negotiations; just as I had when both Dallas and Miami wanted to make substantial offers for Stanley.

Under the new CBA, teams could sign their own qualifying veterans for any amount beyond the cap; however, Seattle did not express interest in Ervin. Instead, the Sonics would sign Jim McIlvaine, a backup center, to a $35 million seven-year deal, which is considered by some to be one of the worst deals in basketball history. McIlvaine was bigger at seven feet, one inch and 265 pounds and was considered a defensive center like Ervin. Karl was quoted as saying that "Ervin didn't play a physical game" and that "With Jim, you'll see more of a body-to-body game" justifying McIlvaine's contract. McIlvaine's contract caused quite a stir in the League and the team. His arrival to the team at his outrageous salary angered more than six other players on the team including Sean Kemp. Kemp did not show up for the first three weeks of training camp in protest of McIlvaine's contract, and his dissatisfaction eventually led to his trade to Cleveland in September, 1997.

Since Seattle had not shown an interest in re-signing Ervin, I had contacted all the teams in the NBA regarding Ervin and really did not get back much response. I knew this should be the chance for Ervin to get set for life and it was a crucial time in his career, as he was older (twenty-eight) than most players coming out of his initial NBA deal. He was in his prime, and once he reached thirty or so, most teams would begin to argue that he was older and not want to do long-term deals that would give him the money he wanted. The fear of a major injury in the future is always a concern for an athlete, and a long-term contract would alleviate the potential for this ruining his career. I knew Ervin would not waste his money, as some would, so all he needed was the right deal and he would be set. The figures that he and I had in mind were in the $2-to-$3-million-a-year-starting-range over a five year period, but I would naturally wait for an offer and go from there.

I would wait as long as possible to see where the market was headed. There would be a type of domino effect with the most wanted players going first and the rest signing later for less money. The key would be to not miss the opportunity to be in their line of dominos, and consequently miss out on a deal that would not be there later when the teams had spent their money and filled the needs. I would contact the NBPA for information on signings and follow news accounts, though I knew from previous experience that the NBPA did not demand the information from its agents like the NFLPA, even though the agent-rules stated that the contract should be provided to the NBPA within forty-eight hours. My observation was that the NBPA, with fewer members and fewer agents controlling most of their players, does not have the motivation or ability to enforce its regulations as well as the NFLPA.

In 1996, there was still labor unrest, and there were interpretation issues with the 1995 CBA between the owners and the NBPA. July 1, 1996, came and went without the teams beginning to sign players. There was a disagreement between the owners and the NBPA over $50 million in profit-sharing from the television revenue. On July 10, 1996, the owners declared a lockout, but this particular issue was resolved in a few hours. After talks between the parties, the League agreed to allocate an additional $14 million per season in revenue toward the salary cap during the last four years of the then-current CBA, which was supposed to be a six-year agreement.

I had been waiting since July 1, 1996, for the "action to begin," so to speak, putting everything on hold, including my family vacation to Destin, Florida. I purposely did not set the time for vacation until mid-July, thinking that I would have negotiated Ervin's contract by then, if there was nearly the interest in him as there had been in Stanley. I also knew that I could negotiate from Florida if necessary, and even took a separate car to return home if needed. The drive is only about six hours. I now had four children, Katie, Little O, Mimi, and Sally, my youngest, and we were all set for our annual vacation to Florida to begin on July 16, 1996.

Despite the July 1, 1996, deadline, teams still had the right to sign the players whose contracts were expiring for any amount over the salary cap, unless they renounced those rights so they could add other players to their rosters. After the team renounced the rights, the player's salary no longer counted against the cap. I had been talking to Minnesota about Mark, and his rights had been renounced on July 11, 1996, but Seattle still had Ervin's rights, and though I had a few teams express some interest, no team was making a strong run at him. Seattle did not want to sign him to a long-term deal, but had not let him go, which probably meant it was negotiating with his replacement. In the meantime, I was sitting around with not much happening and unable to really work with all my players on my mind.

On July 16, 1996, I got in my car and headed to the beach as planned, figuring that I would continue the negotiations for Mark, and hopefully have some teams that were really interested in offering Ervin a substantial contract finally give me a call. Sure enough, on July 16, the Sonics finally renounced the rights to Ervin, and while in my car headed to the beach, I received a call from the Denver Nuggets. The initial call was that they viewed Ervin as a "starter," not just a role player, and wanted to do a long-term deal. I knew immediately from the conversation that this was a legitimate effort by Denver to sign Ervin and listened to the proposed terms. While listening to the offer, I decided that since I was only an hour or two from Baton Rouge, I would return to the city. I wanted immediate access to my office staff, the fax machine, and my negotiating team attorneys, Steve Thompson and Abboud Thomas. I telephoned my wife and told her I was heading back to the office, as I had prepared her for this possibility when I decided to make the trip to Florida. We transferred some children, and I turned my car around and headed back to Baton Rouge. Of course, I called Ervin and B.J. as soon as possible and told them we had a real offer from Denver on the table and I was heading to the office. When I returned to the office, I found out that the Hawks had signed Dikembe Mutombo that same day. The dominoes were falling, and I was ready to do my best to get Ervin the contract that he deserved.

Over the course of July 16, 17, and 18, I negotiated with Denver and fought for a market-bearable contract that would give Ervin the financial and career security we sought using the financial figures we had discussed. There were now a number of players being released and players were signing, so teams were focusing on the players they really wanted. I contacted the NBPA to get any information available. Importantly, I had no other teams contact me that were interested in signing Ervin, so he obviously was not the top priority for any team, save Denver. I was seeking a higher yearly average with an opt-out clause after three to four years, and Denver wanted a longer term deal with no opt-out clause. I pushed Denver for higher numbers, which maxed out with a seven-year deal for around $18 million and averaged about $2.5 million a year, which was in the range of the goals we had set, all fully guaranteed. I really fought for the opt-out clause, as I knew that Ervin would be thirty-five when the deal expired, and if he developed any further he might be underpaid. However, Denver would not budge on the length of the deal. I did negotiate the fifteen percent increase in salary clause to be placed in the contract if Ervin was traded.

I was in constant contact with Ervin and B.J. during the negotiations, and we discussed the contract offer thoroughly. Denver would not keep the offer on the table long and would move on if we would not accept. Given all the factors, particularly that we had no other teams showing an interest at this point, we decided to take the deal and were happy that Ervin was set in the League for at least another seven years. The trade clause would prove very beneficial because, after starting for one year at Denver, Ervin was traded to Milwaukee, which bumped up the contract to around $20 million total, right in line with the upper limit of our goals. I believe the contract held up to the test of time, as it secured Ervin a very steady income flow for seven years; and even though you always want more money, I never felt like he was really underpaid at any time. Of course, other players received bigger contracts, including Shaq, who signed a seven-year $120 million deal, but he was obviously a very special superstar. After the end of his seven year contract, Ervin would play three more years. He never really developed a great offensive game and was never a "superstar," but was a very good defensive presence and a player with a great attitude. His attitude and work ethic were qualities any team would welcome. He was a dedicated family man and made his permanent home in Denver, despite only playing one year there. He and his wife, Renee, have two daughters, Ezekia, who was born on August 10, 1998, and Erin, born on July 31, 2000. He has been really dedicated to them and his wife Renee.

Mark Davis

My negotiations for Mark Davis did not turn out as I had hoped, and emphasized how uneven the hand of fate can be to different players. Mark had played well-enough for the Timberwolves to re-sign him to a longer term contract, and I was in the process of nailing down a three-year deal with Minnesota when NBA player J.R. Ryder intervened. Ryder was an extremely talented but apparently troubled player who was the Timberwolves' fifth overall pick in the 1993 draft. J.R. was with Minnesota when Kevin McHale came on board as general manager in 1995, so Ryder was not a player whom McHale necessarily wanted on the team. J.R. had a reputation for being "high maintenance." He had troubles with his team, which included being late for practice and missing buses and airplanes when traveling. Beyond that, he had several run-ins with the law. In 1994, he was convicted of kicking a woman during a dispute in a shopping mall. After the end of the 1996 season, he was detained for questioning in connection with an alleged sexual assault against a woman in an Oakland, California hotel. On June 28, he was again arrested, along with a companion, in Oakland; in their possession was a small amount of marijuana and four illegal cell phones."According to the Associated Press, there were trade talks in the works between Portland and Minnesota, moving J.R. to Portland. J.R. was then arrested again on July 17, 1996 in Oakland on a misdemeanor charge of gambling; right in the middle of my negotiations with Mark, with an offer on the table that I accepted on July 22, 1998, Minnesota reneged on the offer because, after July 17, its top priority was getting J.R. out of town.

I talked to several teams about signing Mark after his rights were renounced by Minnesota, but the Timberwolves had the best offer with a three-year deal, and Mark and I were intending to sign there. I tried some soft negotiations to bump the numbers up to some degree, but always made sure that the initial Minnesota offer was on the table. This was what I considered a standard negotiation technique. I sensed from the signals I sent, that we were at the point in all negotiations when both sides were so close that everyone felt the deal would get done, and it was just a matter of time. It was similar to negotiating a settlement on a lawsuit when you are so close to settlement that you stop preparing for the upcoming trial.

I knew that I was not negotiating from a position of power so was careful not to outright reject the outstanding offer, and I indicated that we wanted to wrap it up quickly; however, I could never get Kevin to return my phone calls or respond to my faxes. In the legal community, under most circumstances, it is considered unprofessional not to return telephone calls. However, there are times during negotiations when you may send a signal that you are in the position of power by not responding promptly. If Kevin was sending this signal, I already had the message; I just wanted to confirm he was not changing his position as I was agreeing to take his offer, but the line of communication was very difficult. Kevin is a nice guy, but I was totally frustrated with his negotiation style during this year and the year prior. Someone had described him to me as a "tree hugger" so many times that I had a picture of him hiking in the woods wearing shorts, boots, wool socks, and a floppy hat, carrying a walking stick as I waited for him to return my calls, which rarely happened. He probably had a lot to deal with in trying to move J.R., and I got the impression that ownership wanted that done immediately. This was a stressful process; even though the size of the contract was not huge, it was still very important to Mark, and I wanted to nail him down a three-year deal very badly.

After making a counter offer and being unable to get in touch with Kevin, I faxed an acceptance to the original Minnesota offer on July 22, 1996, which was still on the table. However, I then received a letter from Kevin saying for the first time that Minnesota was in a "holding pattern," because of the J.R. Ryder change. In my mind, Minnesota had reneged on its oral offer, which I had confirmed in writing and accepted in writing, but had no written confirmation on from Minnesota, and there was no written contract signed by the parties.

I considered our options and discussed them with the NBPA attorneys, a client, and B.J. I certainly had not been shy about enforcing my client's rights (Stanley's) under the CBA, but felt like it would not be a winning situation to file any type of grievance, in this case if that was even an option. After all,

Minnesota was not saying they would not extend the same offer later, only that it was in a "holding pattern" and we were still free to negotiate with other teams. Our conclusion was that it was much better for Mark to be playing as opposed to litigating this issue. On July 23, 1996, J.R. was traded to Portland. I eventually was able to secure a one-year guaranteed deal for Mark with Philadelphia, which he signed on September 11, 1996. It was admittedly disappointing in light of the previous Minnesota offer.

Sometime at the beginning of the 1996 season, a newspaper article written in Minnesota stated that Mark had "walked away" from a three-year Minnesota deal, which was completely inaccurate. Minnesota had told Mark this story also, which hurt my credibility with Mark, but I had the written documents to prove it was incorrect. Though it was a minor story, it really made me and Mark angry. I got his permission to write a letter to the reporter in Minnesota relating what really happened complete with written documentation to back up our version. I tried to find the source of the article, which included telephoning Minnesota and speaking with Ron Babcock, but with no success. I did consider some sort of libel lawsuit, as I felt my reputation had been damaged. Ultimately, Steve Thompson, B.J., and I felt like we would garner more negative public exposure filing the lawsuit than had been done by the article.

My correspondence to the reporter is reproduced below along with the documented facts. I do not have most of the original documents that were attached, since the paper file was destroyed:

Mr. Ray Richardson

Pioneer Press

345 Cedar Street

Minneapolis, MN 55101

Dear Mr. Richardson:

I have been informed that you are the author of an article which appeared in your newspaper on September 12, 1996 regarding Mark Davis signing with the Philadelphia 76ers, a copy of which is attached. The information contained in this article is incorrect and Mr. Davis and I would like a retraction and correction of the article. Specifically, your statements that Mr. Davis "turned down a three year offer from the Timberwolves totaling almost $1.2 million in July" and that the "Timberwolves management broke off negotiations" with Mr. Davis in July are incorrect. We feel that these statements are damaging to me, as Mr. Davis' agent, and to Mr. Davis.

The true facts of our negotiations with the Timberwolves were that an offer was made by the Timberwolves and we made subsequent counter offers to that initial offer. Subsequently, after approximately one week, we accepted the initial offer made by the Timberwolves. The Timberwolves at that time indicated that they were not "in a position to sign Mark" at that time. The signing of a center and a possible trade were given as the reasons. The Timberwolves indicated they were in a "holding pattern" regarding Mark, however, we continued to talk for several months, up until the time he signed with Philadelphia. The Wolves, however, did refuse to make a new offer or even offer a minimum guaranteed contract to Mr. Davis.

Mr. Davis' contract negotiations were not only extended, but I had to deal with several different teams and changing situations throughout the NBA in a new free agency period. Neither Mark nor I regret any decisions we made during this time period and Mark is very excited about playing in Philadelphia next season. I did find these negotiations extended, and difficult in the sense that there were various teams involved and actions which we could not control were affecting our negotiations on several fronts. I take great pride in my work and I did spend a great deal of time representing Mark. I find it extremely disturbing that you printed an apparently uncorroborated story which portrays our negotiations in a bad light. I feel that this does damage me as an agent and will be used by potential competitors in the agent business against me in a negative manner.

Ron Babcock has informed me that the Timberwolves did not provide you with the inaccurate information in your article. Your reporting of this matter in my opinion was inaccurate because you failed, first of all, to have a source for your information (if what Mr. Babcock tells me is true); and second, you did not contact me or Mark for a comment or to see if this story was true.

We request that you set this matter right. If you have sources for your information, please reveal those sources to us so we may direct our comments as well as any actions we feel appropriate toward them.

Documented Facts:

Prior to July 1, 1996, Kevin McHale indicated an interest in resigning Mr. Davis and was to make an offer after the free agent period started. On July 11, 1996, the Timberwolves formally renounced rights to Mark Davis. On or about that same day, July 11, 1996, I had a conversation with Mr. McHale wherein I requested an offer from him and he requested an offer from me. In response to our conversation on July 12, 1996, I faxed a contract recommendation to Mr. McHale on behalf of Mr. Davis. In this fax, I indicated that Mr. Davis would like to sign with Minnesota, all things being equal. (correspondence and fax of July 12, 1996,

Exhibit A)

In response to my fax of July 12, 1996, Mr. McHale telephoned me indicating that the Wolves were interested in signing Mr. Davis to a three year contract beginning at $400,000 the first year, $480,000 payable the second year, and $560,000 payable the third year. On the same day I received this offer, I conferred with Mr. Davis and responded to Mr. McHale by fax with a counter offer. (See correspondence of July 12, 1996, Exhibit C) In my second correspondence, I asked that Mr. McHale expedite negotiations by telephoning me at home over the weekend. However, Mr. McHale did not get in touch with me. Thereafter, I spoke with Mr. McHale either on the afternoon of July 15 or the morning of July 16 and he indicated the Wolves could not raise their previous offer at that time. We indicated we would both continue to discuss signing Mr. Davis. I telephoned Mr. McHale as I was leaving for Florida on July 16, 1996, and asked him to telephone me. I did not go to Florida until July 19, 1996, and continued to telephone Mr. McHale. Mr. McHale telephoned me on Friday, July 19, 1996, and indicated some unexpected developments had occurred (Isaiah Ryder's arrest) with the Timberwolves, making negotiations difficult at that time. However, Kevin told me the initial three year deal was still open. I told Mr. McHale I would discuss all of the events taking place with Mr. Davis and the Timberwolves position on not offering any additional money.

I discussed the situation with my client and because I could feel something was going on with the Timberwolves, Mr. Davis decided to accept the three year deal. On July 22, 1998, I forwarded an acceptance of the initial three year deal to Mr. McHale by fax. (Correspondence of July

22, 1996, Exhibit D.) After accepting the offer, Kevin McHale telephoned me and indicated the team was having problems due to the trade of J.R.Ryder and other unforeseen events. Mr. McHale also faxed me correspondence on July 22, 1996, after we had accepted the offer. It is evident from Mr. McHale's correspondence, the Timberwolves had changed their position and would not sign Mark at that time but were in a "holding pattern" and that a deal was still possible.

On July 23, the Timberwolves traded J.R. Ryder to Portland for James Robinson, a reserve guard; Bill Curley, a forward who had been injured for a good part of his career and a first round draft pick in 1997 or 1998.

Despite being disappointed in the actions of the Timberwolves, we continued to discuss Mark's signing with the Timberwolves for a three year deal for approximately six more weeks. I forwarded the attached correspondence to Mr. McHale (Exhibit F) along with several other clubs with whom I was discussing Mark's situation. Mr. McHale did not respond to calls to his office. Ron Babcock returned one call made by my partner, in my absence, and indicated that Minnesota's position was unchanged, but that they were still interested in Mark. Finally, near the first of September, I spoke with Ron Babcock, of player personnel, and indicated at that time that Mark was willing to accept a minimum guaranteed contract. We never received any response from the Timberwolves.

I discussed signing Mark with the Philadelphia 76ers beginning on or about July 15 or 16, immediately after the free agent period began. I also had numerous conversations with other NBA teams and we did pass on one offer of a minimum guaranteed contract from one team, which we felt would be very good for Mark because we hoped to get a three year deal.

I never heard back from the reporter and there was never any clarification published. I did feel a little better after letting off some steam with the letter. I sent a copy of the letter to both Kevin McHale and Ron Babcock with Minnesota but never discussed it with them at any time later. I felt like I had spent a lot of time negotiating Mark's contract and had been successful in keeping him in the League for another year where he could continue to prove himself. I felt like I had properly applied negotiating tactics to his potential Minnesota contract but had been hit with a fluke incident of bad luck with J. R. being arrested and traded. This was somewhat similar to when, as an attorney, you try a great case but lose the case on some unexplained whim of the jury or a judge. You can look back and think what you could have done differently and really can't think of anything. Yes, I could have immediately accepted the three year deal, but I did not ever turn it down and Minnesota never withdrew it until after I had accepted.

Big Stan

Now that I was back representing Big Stan, I was actively involved in dealing with the Clippers and the consequences of Stan's new contract signed in October, 1994. We had several disagreements about the new clauses, which called for a summer development program in 1996, including a suspension by the team, and Stan's attendance for physical therapy. All these disagreements culminated in fines and monies withheld from his contract totaling $167,000. I filed three separate grievances against the team for its actions, attempting to recover up to $164,500, which resulted in an arbitration hearing at the NBA headquarters in New York on September 22, 1997.

NINETEEN
NBA All Star Game and B.J.'s Departure, 1997

I had never attended an All-Star game and decided to go to the NBA All Star game in 1997. The League was celebrating its fiftieth anniversary, and it would be a great show with many of the fifty greatest players appearing at half time. Little O was now eleven and really into watching and playing basketball, so bringing him to the game was one of my chief motivating factors in wanting to attend. Michael Jordan would be playing in the game, which was also an attraction.

In late 1996, B.J. had started working full time for the Houston Rockets. The scout with whom B.J. had been working died unexpectedly, and he was asked to come onboard with the team full-time, based on his previous scouting for the team and the friendships he had built up within the Rockets' organization. This was the opportunity B.J. had wanted since his retirement as a player, to work full-time in basketball with a regular salary and benefits. Working with me had been fantastic, and we had built up a friendship that would last a lifetime, but I knew in my heart that it would be better for him to get on board with a solid corporate employer that would be in the business on a permanent basis.

Both he and I knew that the agent business was fraught with all kinds of problems, and that job security could change overnight. I knew by now that I would never be willing to go full -time in the business. Though I liked being an agent, I did not love it in the way I loved being an attorney, a field where I knew I could make more money while adhering to legal and ethical considerations. Considering the total circumstances, we both felt that he needed to take the full-time job. Of course, I was saddened that I would not be spending as much time with him, but happy that we had experienced some great times and some success in the business. B.J.'s leaving did mean ultimately that I would not be able to sustain my continued growth in the basketball side of the agency business. I simply did not have enough time to recruit, manage, and maintain a close relationship with my players, as the job demanded, while practicing law.

I contacted B.J. and he wanted to attend the All Star game too, so we made plans to attend along with Little O. Little O and I flew to Cleveland, checked into the hotel, and met up with B.J. The NBA All Star game was played at Gund Arena in Cleveland, Ohio, with the East defeating the West 132-120. Glen Rice of the Charlotte Hornets was named the game's MVP, and Minnesota's Kevin Garnett became the youngest player to perform in the All Star game. The fifty greatest players were introduced at halftime. It was a great experience.

One of the high points of the trip was a chance encounter with David Robinson at our hotel. We were walking in the hall of our hotel when a door opened and David Robinson came out right in front of us. Of course, B.J. knew him and started greeting him. B.J. introduced both myself and Little O to the Admiral and we had a short conversation. David was very gracious in greeting Little O, just as Charles Barkley had been. It was a real treat to see my son get to meet this NBA All Star on a personal level, and neither he nor I have forgotten it.

Stanley Roberts

I really had no guidelines as to how to handle contesting the monies withheld from Stanley other than the CBA and some other grievance decisions. I did get some guidance from the NBPA attorneys Ron Klempner and Hal Biagas. However, the procedure in the CBA was pretty straightforward and my real job was as a professional litigator, so I had no problem following the procedures, and if one did not exist, I pretended I was in a real court. I really enjoyed the preparation and litigating of the grievances I filed throughout my career. I was not afraid to litigate on behalf of my clients, and this ended up helping the few who needed my litigation skills. Of course, most grievances were filed for Stanley.

Stanley and the Clippers had a somewhat tumultuous relationship in 1996–1997. Stanley had already suffered Achilles tendon injuries to both his feet, had ankle and heel problems, and begun developing a back problem in the summer of 1996. The back problem was diagnosed as a herniated disc in December of 1996, eventually leading to back surgery on March 21, 1997. Stanley really had to watch the effect of impact exercises on his body after this point in time, and I can remember him exercising on an exercise bike most of the time after this point.

During the middle of 1996 and into 1997, I stayed busy directing and defending Stanley on the various issues that arose pursuant to the summer conditioning and development clauses in his contract; this included his suspension and the fines assessed for missing his physical therapy sessions after surgery. Stanley's arbitration was set for September 22, 1997, at the NBA offices in New York, and I was preparing for the arbitration by speaking with witnesses and preparing defenses. At some point, the Clippers referred me to their attorneys, two of whom were Robert Platt and Eric Sherman, and I was told I could not speak any further to Clipper employees. In the course of my preparation, I made several attempts to obtain copies of Stanley's records from his back surgeon, Dr. Daly; however, I was met with some resistance even though I sent a valid request for records with Stanley's signature on it to his office. The following is a paragraph out of a letter sent to Eric Sherman shortly before the arbitration:

> I propounded a Request for Production of Documents to Mr. Platt on June 18, 1997, and requested a copy of any and all medical records of Stanley Roberts. Subsequently, Mr. Platt wrote me on July 1, 1997, indicating that the Collective Bargaining Agreement did not call for a propounding of discovery in connection with an arbitration. I then had to draft additional correspondence to Mr. Platt dated July 30, 1997, wherein I had to point out to Mr. Platt that the Collective Bargaining Agreement does allow a player to obtain his medical records during an arbitration. I again requested a copy of the medical records in my correspondence of July 30, 1997. Mr. Platt's only reply to my correspondence was on August 8, 1997, when he wrote and told me that the Clippers would fully comply with the provisions of the Collective Bargaining Agreement. I then had to subsequently telephone Mr. Platt and again request the records. He indicated to me that he would provide me with Stanley's medical records within one week of August 20, 1997. I left for Europe on August 21, 1997. During that time, Mr. Platt forwarded me a portion of the medical records which he, or someone, felt were "relevant" according to the transmittal correspondence. I did not return to my office until September 3, 1997.

When I returned to my office and reviewed the records it did not seem as if all the records had been produced, so I requested that all the records be faxed to the NBA offices on the day of the hearing. The buildup to the arbitration and the arbitration itself were held in a friendly atmosphere. The Clippers staff liked Stanley but had become frustrated in dealing with his injuries and his conditioning and other issues. As I noted previously, Andy Roeser, whom I dealt with over many issues concerning Stanley over the years, and I had become pretty good friends. We even had a friendly wager over whether we would be successful in recouping any significant money by pursuing the arbitration. The winner of the wager would take the other to dinner. Elgin Baylor is a prince of a gentleman and was always easy to deal with. I know he had spent a lot of time talking with Stanley and trying to help him without great success, but Stanley and I were always grateful for all of the time he spent with him.

On June 25, 1997, during the 1997 NBA draft, Stanley was traded by the Clippers to the Minnesota Timberwolves for center Stojko Vrankovic. The reason for the trade, as stated by the Clippers, was that they would take a center with less talent for one who would be healthy and in condition to play each night. In his five seasons with the Clippers, Stanley played in sixty-five percent of the games only once, in the 1992–1993 season, when he had come over in the three-way trade. He missed most of 1993–1994 with his right Achilles tendon injury and all of 1994–1995 with his left Achilles tendon injury. He played in fifty-one games in 1995–1996 because of heel and ankle injuries and lost sixty-one games of play because of his back injury in 1996–1997. On his departure, Coach Bill Fitch was quoted in the *L.A. Times* as saying, "this guy has as much ability or more" than any of the past big men he had coached, which says a lot since he had coached Kevin McHale, Robert Parish, and Hakeem Olajuwon, among others. The same article, written by Scott Howard-Cooper on June 27, 1997, quotes Elgin Baylor as follows:

> I've had a lot of talks with Stanley...I spent a lifetime talking to Stanley since he got here. Through a lot of injuries, through moments when he showed brilliance. I'm sure it was all very frustrating to Stanley. It was frustrating to me. Each year. To get injured three years in a row...A lot of the injuries were not his fault. They were injuries that could happen to any player. But having the extra weight brought on other aches and pains that only compounded the problems.

When Stanley was traded, he only had one more year on his contract with another year at the team's option. At Minnesota, I would once again be dealing with my old friend Kevin McHale. In June, I confirmed in writing with Kevin that Stanley could fulfill the thirty days of his summer development program by coming to Minnesota on or about September 1, 1997, and working out with the team prior to training camp. I also confirmed in writing with Kevin that Stanley would have to be in New York for September 21 and 22 for the pending arbitration. Before his trade, I called Kevin for a brief chat and did inform him that Stanley would have to be available in New York for his arbitration on September 22, 1997.

I was excited and looked forward to the arbitration. An arbitration, unlike a jury trial, does not have the built-in stress of dealing with a judge, then having a jury decide the case with the potential for significant economic loss accompanying an adverse decision. Of course, a jury trial verdict in your favor is one of the most satisfying victories you can achieve as an attorney, but a win in the upcoming arbitration for Stanley would also be sweet. The arbitrator appointed pursuant to the CBA was John D. Feerick. In preparation and in order to lay a base for legal precedent of how earlier arbitrations had been decided, I read as many prior arbitration decisions as I could find. I decided the only witnesses we would need to bring were Stanley and his personal trainer, Mr. James Cross. The Clippers were going to have present Andy Roeser the Vice President, Elgin Baylor the General Manager, Bill Fitch the Head Coach, and Johnny Doyle, the Clippers Strength and Conditioning Coach, all of whom I could call under cross-examination if necessary.

The arbitration was held at the offices of the NBA on September 22, 1997. I remember thinking at the time how crazy it was that I was in New York and would soon be questioning basketball legends like Elgin Baylor and Bill Fitch. Formal rules of evidence were not enforced, so it was a very relaxed atmosphere, and felt like we were all there to explain to the arbitrator the facts of the case. The witnesses all stayed in the room while the others testified. I had prepared with Stanley as much as he would allow, and we put on our case first. We basically explained the reasons for Stanley's failure to attend some of the summer training, the facts surrounding the suspension, and why he had missed the physical therapy sessions. Stanley was a good witness and told his side of the story, which centered on the fact that he was dealing with injuries. He at one point testified that he considered GM Elgin Baylor "like a father to him," which set a good tone for the meeting. The Clippers called their witnesses, and I was allowed to cross-examine them. The hearing lasted three or four hours at most. After the hearing, I submitted a post-hearing brief on behalf of Stanley and the Clippers, and the NBA also submitted briefs. On November 13, 1997, Arbitrator John Feerick handed down his decision as follows:

Award of the Arbitrator

The Undersigned Arbitrator, having been designated in accordance with the Collective Bargaining Agreement entered into by the NBA and the NBPA, hereby renders the following:

Award

    1. The $100,000 deduction from Stanley Roberts' 1996–97 compensation was unreasonable and will be limited to $22,222.22.

    2. The length of Roberts' 10 day suspension in October 1996 was reasonable and will be upheld. The fine of $32,000 will be reduced to $30,500 in accordance with the fine structure specified in the Collective Bargaining Agreement, Article VI, Section 1.

    3. The $35,000 fine imposed on Roberts for missing physical therapy sessions in March and April 1997, was excessive and will be reduced to $7,500 in accordance with the provisions of the Clippers' Team Rules and the overall structure of the Collective Bargaining Agreement.

Dated: November 13, 1997   John D. Feerick
New York, NY   Grievance Arbitrator

Stanley and I were extremely pleased, as the Arbitrator's decision refunded around $107,000 and Stanley felt like he had been vindicated to some degree for the punishment he felt like he did not deserve.

After Stanley's training in Minnesota in September, I confirmed in writing with Kevin that Stanley had fulfilled the summer development portion of his contract. Stanley spent the 1997–1998 season with the Timberwolves, where Kevin Garnett and Stephon Marbury were the main stars. Stanley was still hampered by lingering injuries and then hurt his back near the end of the season. He was also dealing with a lung condition that made it difficult for him to breathe. However, he ended up playing in seventy-four games and starting in forty-four but only averaged 17.9 minutes per game, 4.9 rebounds, per game, and 6.2 points per game. The Timberwolves made the playoffs with a 45 win and 37 loss record but lost to the Seattle

Supersonics in the first round of the playoffs.

I had telephone conversations with Kevin throughout the season. It was during one of these telephone conversations that Kevin made a comment that the baggage Stanley came with was the size of a moving van. Therefore, it came as no surprise when on June 9, 1998, Kevin McHale and the Timberwolves did not pick up the option on Stanley's contract for the next season. The Timberwolves' failure to pick up Stanley's option for the 1998–1999 season triggered a provision in his contract wherein he was to be paid $600,000. This was a provision placed in Stanley's 1994 renegotiated contract. The actual provision read as follows in Section 1.3 "Option": "In the event Club does not exercise its option by June 15, 1997, as provided herein and provided that this agreement was not terminated prior to June 15, 1997, then Club agrees to pay Player a fee of $600,000 on June 30, 1998."

I had personally made Andy Roeser and Kevin aware of this provision, which said to me that if the contract was in effect on June 15, 1997, then Stanley was owed $600,000. Andy had told me that the June 15, 1997, date should have been June 15, 1998, but I disagreed. We never had to decide the issue, as the June 30, 1998, date had not occurred, and the issue was premature. To avoid any problems, I sent a letter to Kevin on March 25, 1998, asking for the Timberwolves' position on this issue. The Clippers' position was that the Timberwolves had assumed all liabilities for the contract with the trade. I talked to Kevin at one point, and he acknowledged the debt; however, he changed his position on or about June 22, 1998. This led to me filing a grievance against the Timberwolves and the Clippers alternatively for the $600,000. I also alleged that Stanley was due a bonus under the contract. The Grievance read as follows:

Grievance

Now comes Stanley Roberts, a person of full age of majority, who files the following grievance against the Minnesota Timberwolves, and alternatively, against the Los Angeles Clippers, by providing this written notice of grievance in accord with the provisions of the NBA Collective Bargaining Agreement.

1. On or about November 28, 1994, the NBA player contract, attached hereto and made a part hereof as Exhibit 1, was executed by Stanley Roberts and the Los Angeles Basketball Club, Inc. and approved by the NBA.

2. Roberts' player contract contains Paragraph 1.3 entitled "Option," which provides for a "fee of $600,000" payable on June 30, 1998, in the event the team does not exercise its option for the 1998–99 season. Mr. Roberts played for the Los Angeles Clippers until the summer of 1997, when he was traded to the Minnesota Timberwolves. Thereafter, Mr. Roberts played for the Minnesota Timberwolves for the 1997–98 season pursuant to Exhibit 1. On or about June 9, 1998, the Timberwolves informed Mr. Roberts that it was not exercising its option for the 1998–99 season. (See correspondence; Exhibit 2) The Minnesota Timberwolves through their executives, particularly Kevin McHale and Roger Griffith, acknowledged the debt of the $600,000 and that the fee would be paid. The Timberwolves were specifically made aware of and acknowledged the debt at the time of Roberts' trade, according to Clipper executives. Despite the assurances by the Timberwolves that the monies would be paid and the clear language of the contract, the Timberwolves have refused to pay Mr. Roberts his $600,000 fee. The Timberwolves alleged for the first time on June 22, 1998 that the Los Angeles Clippers Club was

liable for the $600,000 fee. (See correspondence; Exhibit 3)

3. Alternatively, and only because of the Timberwolves' accusations and because Mr. Roberts does not know the agreement between the Timberwolves and the Clippers, Mr. Roberts pleads that if there is an agreement between the Timberwolves and the Clippers that the Clippers Club was to pay the $600,000, then, in that event, Mr. Roberts pleads that the Clippers Club should pay the $600,000 fee.

4. The contract attached hereto as Exhibit 1 also contains Paragraph 1.2 entitled "Bonuses." This paragraph provides that in the event the player plays in 70 or more regular season games, which Mr. Roberts did during the 1997–98 season, and the team wins at least three more regular season games during that season than in the prior season, which occurred during the 1997–98 season, then the team is obligated to pay Mr. Roberts another $100,000 on June 30, 1998. Despite amicable demand, this bonus has not been paid timely, just as the $600,000 fee owed by the Minnesota Timberwolves.

5. Mr. Roberts requests that the grievance be processed and pushed forward to hearing. Mr. Roberts requests interest from June 30, 1998, penalties, attorney's fees and any applicable consequential damages arising from the untimely payment(s) of Mr. Roberts' monies.

Submitted by:
Oscar L. Shoenfelt, III
6513 Perkins Road
Baton Rouge, LA 70808
Telephone: (504) 766-8730
Attorney for Stanley Roberts

Kevin had again gone silent on Minnesota's position on paying the $600,000 to Stanley, necessitating the drafting of the grievance. Minnesota eventually paid the monies because it was part of the contract. I really hated to be involved in so many litigation-sided issues, and there was no question that representing Stanley played a part. I had noted from my previous dealings with Kevin that he did not become part of the Timberwolves management due to his legal or business background, but because of his great basketball career, which I admired greatly. However, I had thought if he had just let the attorney for the team handle these kinds of problems, he might be better off. I had already had communications problems with him before when dealing with Mark.

Later, in 2000, I learned that Kevin had made a secret deal with Joe Smith's agent to circumvent the salary cap before the 1998–99 season by signing three one-year deals way below market value. I felt like Kevin, with no legal background, probably did not get the correct legal advice and was carrying on a practice used by others in the business. As an attorney, I would never rely on an informal agreement, not part of the NBA contract, to protect my client's rights. These types of agreements are prohibited under the CBA and would scare me to death as to my potential liability if the deal did not occur. However, I had already discovered that some general managers did cut these deals with agents when I discovered the side agreement made between Willis Reed and Chris Morris's old agent, Sid Blanks, during the mediation between Morris and Blanks. Fortunately, I had discovered the agreement during my research and saved Chris this money by telling Bob Wolf.

As a result of Kevin's secret agreement, the Timberwolves lost three of their five next first-round draft picks and were fined $3.5 million. Joe Smith was declared a free agent with all three of his contracts being voided, which meant he did not have his "Bird" rights with Minnesota, severely affecting what Minnesota could pay him. Timberwolves owner Glen Taylor was suspended through August 31, 2001, and Kevin took a leave of absence through July 31.

Interestingly, according to a *U.S.A Today* article of January 9, 2014, by Sean Highkin, the whole deal was exposed during a lawsuit between two agents who had represented Joe Smith. The lawsuit led to the production of documents, including those detailing the secret agreement. In the article, Kevin denied any knowledge of the secret agreement and was quoted as saying in his defense that, "I haven't read a contract in four or five years." When I read this statement, I thought that perhaps Kevin was unaware of the $600,000 provision in Stanley's contract when the trade with the Clippers was made.

During my representation of my clients in the NBA, I never had any type of side deal suggested by any representative of a team and would think these would be a rarity despite Kevin's defense of his secret agreement. However, during my tenure as a professor teaching sports law at LSU, I came across a case entitled Mandwich v. Watters, 970 F. 2d 462 (8th Cir. 1992), which involved a lawsuit by a player against his agent who had made a side deal, not in the player's contract, with a general manager while negotiating the player's contract without the knowledge of the player. The side agreement did not work out well for the player and he ended up suing his agent. This was an obvious breach of the agent's fiduciary duty to his client involved in the case. There was testimony by both the agent and the management representative that in 1985, side deals were common in the NHL, so maybe these deals were more prevalent in the NBA than I imagined.

NBA Lockout, 1998

On October 1, 1997, the Minnesota Timberwolves and Kevin Garnett agreed to a six-year contract extension that was valued at an unparalleled $126 million. Garnett's contract, which some considered a huge risk, scared the NBA owners to death and led to the third NBA lockout from July 1, 1998, to January 20, 1999. Garnett's contract had been preceded by the previously described contracts of Shaq's $123 million 7-year deal with the Lakers, Hakeem's 5-year $55 million extension, Mutombo's 5-year $50 million deal with the Hawks, and Michael Jordan was making $30 million a year in 1997.

Under the terms of the previously negotiated 1995 CBA, the owners could reopen negotiations after three years if the percentage of basketball-related income devoted to players' salaries exceeded 51.8 percent. During the 1997–1998 season, the players had received about 57 percent of the $1.7 billion in revenue. (See Paul D. Staudohar's April 1999 article "Labor Relations in Basketball: The Lockout of 1998–99.") On March 23, 1998, the owners voted 27 to 2 to reopen negotiations on the 1995 agreement at the conclusion of the season. The League contended that nearly half of the twenty-nine teams were losing money. The League was determined to put in place a hard salary cap that would eliminate exceptions that had allowed salaries to increase fifty percent over the previous five years. On June 22, 1998, the last sessions of negotiations ended with the players saying no to a hard cap, and on July 1, 1998, a lockout was announced by the League.

Agents had started to become very active in these labor negotiations in 1995, when the CBA was negotiated. There was a move to decertify the NBPA when a petition was filed with the National Labor Relations Board (NLRB) by some players under the direction of some of the agents. This was a move with which I was familiar, as it followed the strategy of the NFLPA, which had successfully decertified at one point to pursue a case under antitrust law. I was not active in the moves being made by the basketball players and their agents, as I really did not have sufficient players or interest to spend the time necessary to become that active. I did watch and keep up with what was going on, and the NBPA gave us regular updates. In any event, after a threatened delay in starting the 1995–1996 season and some additional negotiations on free agency, the players voted against decertification. As a result of the rift in the NBPA from this episode, Simon Gourdine was replaced by Billy Hunter as the head of the Union.

My personal view at the beginning of the 1998 lockout was that the present CBA was creating inequality in distribution of the players' money. It seemed most of it was going to the superstars, leaving a lot of players behind. Of course, the most powerful agents were pushing for their clients to get the larger share of the players' money. During the 1997–1998 season, the highest paid nine players received fifteen percent of the players' revenue and twenty percent of the players were making the League minimum salary.

Once the lockout began, the agents were updated on a regular basis by the NBPA. The powerful agents expressed various opinions and were influencing their clients in different directions. I sensed that most players were somewhat prepared for a short work stoppage but would not be prepared for the loss of a whole season. I felt Billy Hunter did a pretty good job of holding it all together against David Stern and the owners.

By October, the owners had dropped their demand for a hard cap with no exceptions. On December 19, the players staged an exhibition game in Atlantic City with the initial thought being that the proceeds would go to help players with financial difficulties. This turned out to be a public relations nightmare and the proceeds went to charity. On December 23, David Stern announced that if there was no agreement in place by January 7, 1999, then the season would be canceled. David Stern and the NBPA both sent out outlines of the position of the parties as the cancellation deadline neared. Kevin Willis called for a secret ballot vote and the NBPA agreed to allow the players to vote on January 6, 1999, on a proposal the players' nineteen-person committee had recommended **opposing**. Just before the vote, Hunter and Stern met in a marathon bargaining session, reaching a compromise that the players voted on and accepted on January 6, 1999, which ended the lockout. The tentative agreement was ratified by the players 179-5 and the owners 29-0. The first games of the season were scheduled to begin on February 5, 1999, and the NBA played a fifty-game shortened season.

My personal feeling was that most players wanted to play, and that the move to reject the agreement was led by the wealthiest big-time players who had the most to gain under a new agreement. Obviously, the end of the lockout was good news to fans, owners, and the players. Billy Hunter took some criticism, which would eventually lead to his ouster, which I felt was unjustified, but I really had no dog in that hunt.

Darvin Ham

Darvin finished up the 1996–1997 season with Indiana and went to summer camp with the team; however, Indiana did not want to re-sign him to a guaranteed contract. I was successful in signing Darvin with the newly-named Washington Wizards for the 1997–1998 season, where Bernie Bickerstaff was the new coach, on a contract which became guaranteed in January, 1998. Bernie was familiar with Darvin from his time at Denver and really liked him as a player. Darvin, though not necessarily a starter, was a player you wanted on your team for his versatility and, importantly, good work ethic and attitude. In his book, George Karl commented on Darvin's "snarly attitude," in describing his 2000–2001 Milwaukee team: "What I hated about the 2000–2001 was its happiness. A couple of guys had the snarly attitude I like—Scott Williams, Jason Caffey, Darvin Ham—" (p. 150). Moreover, besides a "snarly attitude," Darvin was a player who motivated other players to play harder and was the kind of guy you wanted in your locker room.

Darvin played the 1997–1998 season with Washington. The 1998–1999 season was shortened to fifty games, and the season's All Star game had to be canceled. Unfortunately, Darvin fired me in November, 1998, during the lockout. I was to find out later that the reason had to do with another player I had signed who had roomed with him the summer of 1997, in Houston. That player was a bust all the way around, but such is the business.

Darvin and I remain friends to this day. I kept up with his career and saw him on several occasions when he was with Milwaukee and a teammate of Ervin's. Darvin retired from playing basketball after 2008, and went into coaching. He coached in the developmental league for several years and became an assistant coach with the Lakers in 2011, where he stayed until 2013, when he became first assistant coach with the Hawks. He was an assistant with the Hawks from 2013, to just recently. I have followed his coaching career and he has provided me with tickets to meet up with him at games. He has proven to be an excellent NBA coach, and I am certain he will be a head coach at some time in the future. B.J. continued to mentor Darvin throughout the years, and I was sure that Darvin planned to hire B.J. as an assistant coach when he became a head coach.

Mark Davis

Mark played the 1996–1997 season in Philadelphia. He did not have a breakout season, but had a productive season for the team. He played in seventy-five games and started in seventeen, averaging 22.7 minutes a game and 8.52 points per game. Paul Brown and I took a trip up to Philadelphia to watch him play a couple of games and had a great trip. That's when I met Allen Iverson's posse.

Mark was kind of quiet and I never could get a good read on how he was feeling toward me. I know that he was disappointed, as was I, in the Minnesota negotiation. In any event, as I prepared to negotiate a new contract for him just before the free agency period of July 1, 1997, I received a letter terminating me as his agent. Of course, I was extremely disappointed but really understood that this was an inherent part of the business. There were no hard feelings. Mark signed with an agent with whom I was on friendly terms. He continued on in his basketball career for several years, has become a successful high school coach and basketball mentor. He's on my Facebook and goes by Coach Davis. I am so glad he was able to continue working in the career he loves, just as B.J. had taught him.

Ervin Johnson

In basketball, Ervin was my steady-as-a-rock client. Ervin played in Denver for the 1996–1997 season. In 1996–1997, Ervin started eighty-two games for the Nuggets, averaging 31.7 minutes per game and 7.1 points per game. During the 1996–1997 season, he led the League in defensive rebounds with 682 and led the team with 2.77 blocks per game and 11.1 rebounds per game. In the final game of the season, Ervin had twenty-six rebounds and scored twenty-one points. However, the team finished with the fourth-worst-record in the League (21-61). As part of a roster overhaul for Denver, he was traded to the Milwaukee Bucks after the end of the 1996–1997 season, which bumped his contract up another fifteen percent in accord with the clause I had inserted in the negotiations with Denver. During the 1997–1998 season, Ervin started eighty-one of the games and was a consistent defensive presence for the Bucks.

The lockout by the owners in the summer of 1998, naturally affected the players, because they did not get their paychecks with the beginning of the 1998 season. It also affected the agents because their pay was determined by payment from their clients after they received their paychecks. Under the NBPA regulations, normally a player is not allowed to prepay their fees, so all fees are normally paid after the player receives his paycheck. In the years prior to the lockout, there had been warnings to the players about the need to have cash reserves in the event of a lockout so it would not leave them hurting financially when the paychecks stopped. I had preached to all my players about budgets and savings and the need for sound economic decisions, particularly on the purchase of luxury items. Some players listened and some did not. I'm sure that, as a whole, the NBA players were not prepared for a work stoppage of any duration. In one article, a player interviewed said something to the effect that he was preparing for a lockout by cutting back from seven cars to six and that this would save him money on insurance and expenses for the seventh car.

Ervin was a player who had done well with his money, so though the lockout concerned him, he was prepared financially when the lockout was implemented. I was not really affected by the freeze on fees, since I was not collecting a large amount of fees from a large number of players, and I still was in my law practice.

Damon Jones

In 1998, B.J. was still working for the Rockets full time, and did recommend me as a potential agent to Damon Jones, who had played his college basketball at the University of Houston from 1994–1997. While at Houston, Damon played with the older local players and the pros that worked out in Houston at the time. He had known B.J. for years working out at the gyms in Houston. He declared for the draft in 1997 but went undrafted. Damon had played for minor league teams, the Black Hill Posse (IBA) from 1997–1998, and then for the Jacksonville Barracudas (USBL) in 1998.

While in Houston, Damon ran into B.J. and said he was looking for a new agent. B.J. recommended me and he signed with me as his agent in June 1998, just about the time the Jacksonville Barracudas season was winding down. In 1998, I signed Damon to play with the Idaho Stampede of the CBA. After the lockout, Damon played for Orlando in training camp, then went back to Idaho, where he became the leading scorer in the League. He was picked up by New Jersey and played in eleven games but was released. After New Jersey, Damon was picked up by the Boston Celtics for the remainder of the 1998–1999 season, playing in thirteen games.

I really liked Damon and he was a fun guy to be around. He was relaxed and always had a smile on his face. I took Little O to Houston and Damon was in town, so we went to the game. I snapped a photograph with B.J. and his young son, Bijan, at the Rockets basketball complex with me, Little O, and Damon. I really tried to work for Damon and help him establish himself in the League, and by the end of the 1998–1999 season, I felt we were in a good position to hopefully get a full year guaranteed contract for the 1999–2000 season. I spent as much time as I could spare keeping up with his game and staying in touch with him, and felt we established a good relationship.

I Leave the Firm

In 1998, I left my old law firm of Moore, Walters, Shoenfelt, and Thompson to practice law and sports agency on my own. Our firm had added several attorneys along with paralegals and support staff, so our overhead had grown to a significant number for each month. I had been able to handle my legal cases and take care of the sports side of things but as a result had to spend a lot of time out of the office. My partners were great attorneys and I considered them all friends, but I had become frustrated with the organization of the firm and what seemed to me, an inconsistent income flow that led to pressure situations. We had four partners and it seemed like all we did was have meetings, and then afterwards all we did was go back and do what we had done before. I began to express my frustration too often, and eventually it was felt that we would be better off if I were not practicing with the firm. It was a friendly breakup and not a case of me going in at night and taking all of my files so no one would know. We came to an agreement on which files I would take, and I agreed to sell my portion of the building in accordance with the partnership agreement. I was given a five-year lease in my same office, which I loved, at a reasonable rate. I was able to take all the sports clients, which meant I would receive the fees that were due under Ervin's and Stanley's contracts. This would be helpful initially, because I would be receiving some regular income without necessarily settling a case. Now that I was a solo practitioner, I could not rely on my income coming in from other members of the firm when I would have a drought between settling cases. Again, as a plaintiff attorney, I had no regular paycheck unless a case was settled from which I could draw a fee.

I was a bit nervous for about a week, but then my competitive nature took over and I knew I would survive. I said a prayer and then just decided to do my best and let God take me where he wanted. With the breakup, I knew that I would be fully in charge of my cases, and my skill as a trial attorney would have to develop to another level, since I would now be trying the cases by myself. I had thirteen years, 1985–1998, of working with my partners, particularly Charles Moore, who was a great trial attorney. Both Charles (Chick) and Ed Walters had taught me a great deal about trying a lawsuit and practicing law, for which I am still and always will be grateful. I also spent six years on the defense side and had that experience to rely on as well.

The first months of my solo practice went well, and I was off to a good start as I picked up several serious medical malpractice cases that I was able to settle without as much work as usual. One was a case that came when the client fired another attorney. The client came to me based on my reputation. When I reviewed the case, I could see that the other attorney was wasting time and not developing the case where the actual improper care occurred. I worked out a deal with the previous attorney as to any fee he would recover for his previous work and took over the case. When I had a chance to speak with the opposing attorney, he told me he was hoping that I would not get the case and then conceded it was a bad case and one we should settle. I had another case come in that had been refused by another attorney. I had a medical review made of the case, and my expert advised me not to take the case. I thought about it and really liked the clients, so I decided to go ahead and file the complaint and see what facts I could develop before the case would be reviewed by a Medical Review Panel, which was required under Louisiana law. Within a few months of filing the complaint, the other attorney, whom I knew, called me and said his client wanted to settle. I was surprised but happy for my clients and myself that we could resolve these cases quickly. Settlements like these were rare, and I can't remember any other cases that settled so quickly.

Most medical malpractice cases lasted at least through the Panel, which normally takes several years. After the Panel, you are allowed to file a lawsuit, and it normally takes another couple of years to get to trial. My strategy was to try to win the Medical Review Panels. The Panels are formed after you file a complaint. The plaintiff's attorney would choose a doctor, then the defendant's counsel would choose a doctor, and then both of the doctors already chosen would choose a doctor. The Panel would be directed by an attorney, agreed to by both sides, called an attorney chairman. The Panel decisions were heavily in favor of the doctors and hospitals at a rate of 90% to 10%. However, I was able to win over half my Panels because I screened my cases well, worked the cases up, usually taking depositions to present to the Panel, and I really feel I have a special skill dealing with medical cases that many attorneys do not have. Part of this skill is based on the fact that I have both defended medical providers and patients in medical malpractice lawsuits over many years.

Leaving the firm did put more pressure on me alone to produce a living for my family, which meant I had to focus more on my legal career and gave me less room for error, so to speak, when it came to representing athletes. Continuing to rent my old office was a help, and I usually had a secretary, paralegal, and sometimes an extra helper who was usually a college student. One person who worked for me for twelve years during two different periods was my paralegal/secretary Tiffanie, who was a trusted, dedicated, and really intelligent worker. She was a real help in representing my clients, both personal injury and sports.

Willie Williams and Football

After playing overseas for the Amsterdam Admirals in the WLAF in 1996, Willie signed a contract with the Oakland Raiders, but did not make the team. However, Willie did catch on with the Toronto Argonauts in the CFL for the 1997 and 1998 seasons. Toronto contacted us and Willie signed on in 1997 to play left tackle and protect Doug Flutie the quarterback. There was not much negotiation with his contract. The season was successful, and the team went 15-3 and won the CFL version of the Super Bowl, the Grey Cup. Willie received a nice ring and gave me a football autographed by the entire team as my fee. The next year without Flutie as quarterback, the team went 9-9 and lost in the first round of the playoffs.

I was able to make two trips to Toronto to see Willie. Due to the football schedule, I was never able to see an actual game but did get a great tour of the city. Toronto is a very cosmopolitan city and had some great restaurants, and I enjoyed seeing Willie. I also made an excursion down to Niagara Falls. Willie was one of the few clients who actually recommended me to his teammates and other athletes as an agent. The purpose of my second visit was to spend time with and attempt to sign some of Willie's teammates who had expressed some interest in meeting and signing with me. I was successful in signing all three of his teammates and was able to get them free-agent contracts in the NFL in the 1999 season. However, all three failed to make the NFL team after getting into training camp. I enjoyed meeting and representing the guys, but as I already knew, signing NFL players trying to make a team as a free agent is not the way to make a profit in the sports agency business.

Willie came back to Baton Rouge after the 1998 season and tried to start a couple of businesses. He took a shot at starting a night club and gave it his all, making a good run at it, but ultimately the club failed. He would later use the practical knowledge he gained from this experience in becoming a highly successful bartender at the Ritz Carlton in Dallas, Texas, for many years. For a brief time, he helped me with the agent business. With his life and NFL experience, Willie could relate to the younger players graduating and coming out in the draft. Now with my years of experience in the agent business and former clients to legitimize me as an agent, we were able to sign some free agents but really could not get in the mode of operation necessary to sign high-potential draft picks. I could not really compete with the full-time football agents as a solo attorney practicing law and trying to stay within the proper legal and ethical parameters.

From 1998 until 2002, I signed several free agents and a couple of low-draft-picks but failed to sign any high profile players or high-draft-picks that warranted keeping the football end of my business going.

Rufus Porter

Rufus played two seasons with New Orleans Saints, 1995 and 1996. I enjoyed having him close by and went to several of his games. He finished his career at thirty-two with the Tampa Bay Buccaneers after signing a two-year deal, but decided to retire in 1998, after a long (ten-year) and successful career. He made the Pro Bowl in his first two seasons on special teams and was All Pro following his second season with Seattle. Rufus was a class act and a great client who always did his job, and took care of his personal and professional business. I am still in contact with him and talk with him every couple of months. His son, Rufus Porter Jr., followed in his dad's footsteps and went on to be an outstanding linebacker at Louisiana Tech. I followed his football career with interest even though he was unaware of it.

If I had been able to sign more players like Rufus, I would have continued with my representation of football players. However, I was only able to sign low-draft-picks and undrafted players who for one reason or another could not sustain a long NFL career. In football, unless you are able to sign high-draft picks, you don't make any money on the player unless they are successful and sign another large contract down the line. What Rufus did, go from being an undrafted free agent in 1988, to being a starter with real value able to obtain real dollars on his subsequent contracts, is extremely difficult, which is a great tribute to him.

TWENTY
Stanley and I Go Greek

Stan and me in Greece signing a contract.

During the lockout, I made contingency plans for any players who wanted to go overseas, with Stanley primarily in mind. I had several agents inquiring whether Stanley wanted to go overseas, and he was considering the move. Since he had played for Real Madrid, he was known overseas. At the end of November 1998, I entered into a written Sub-Agency Agreement with a European agent regarding the procurement of a contract for Stanley to play in Greece, France, Israel, or Turkey. The agent was named Andy Bountogianis, and he told me he had great contacts in those countries, particularly Greece. I provided Andy and his company with my exclusive agent contract with Stanley to work on his behalf for overseas, and we incorporated that into the agreement. The agreement would last as long as any player contract signed by Stanley was in effect or until December 31, whichever was later.

Andy began to work and fielded some offers for Stanley, and by December 1998, we had offers pending. However, we were following the lockout and monitoring progress toward resolving the labor dispute. By January, Stan was feeling some heat from lack of a paycheck and we had an offer on the table from Aris Basketball Club of Greece, a team located in Thessaloniki, Greece. Greece was one of the bigger markets at that time, and the team was offering substantial money. Arias was putting pressure on us to sign before any decision was made by the players on the lockout. If the lockout was resolved, then Stanley could hopefully get on another NBA team, but at that point an NBA job was not a sure thing, and we would have to negotiate the NBA salary. The Greek offer was a sure thing with a substantial signing bonus. If Stanley signed, I would be flown over to finish the negotiations along with his then-girlfriend.

When news of the player vote spread, Arias told us that Stanley must sign before the vote or the offer would be withdrawn. Stanley and I discussed whether he should take the deal in Greece, or wait for the vote and see if the players accepted the newly negotiated CBA. We figured that the players would vote to take the deal and then play a shortened NBA season; however, even if that occurred, we were still stuck with the uncertainty of getting an NBA deal done and what the terms of that deal would be. With Stanley's injuries and off the court problems, his signing an NBA contract was a non-certainty, particularly with terms more lucrative than the current Greek offer. The ultimate decision was his, but I did point out the advantages and risks to him, and he decided to sign the Greek deal on January 5, 1999, just before the vote.

After the players voted to accept the new deal, the Greek contract was sent to the team for signature, and arrangements were made for our flights to Europe. On January 7, 1999, I received from Andy a fax copy of the contract, signed by the team president, along with a handwritten letter from Andy. He said we needed to obtain a letter of clearance from USA Basketball stating that Stanley was not under contract to any other team, and this should be done as soon as possible. USA Basketball is the governing body of basketball in the United States and represents the United States in FIBA, which is the International Organization governing basketball. I drafted correspondence to USA Basketball with an application for a Letter of Clearance, and wired the application fee of $120, which was to be reimbursed by the team. I faxed the USA Basketball response to FIBA on January 8, 1999, requesting that FIBA contact the NBA to confirm that Stanley was not under contract.

The team arranged the flights for me, Stanley, and his girlfriend who would come from Columbia, South Carolina, and meet me in Atlanta on January 9, 1999. Then we would fly to New York, on to Athens, and then to Thessaloniki, where we would meet with officials to fine-tune the contract. Of course, the trip would be business class, which is always a great way to travel. Though this was a last minute trip, just like Spain in 1990, I was excited to be on another grand adventure with Stanley. I was eager to visit Thessaloniki, engage in some further negotiations, and absorb some Greek culture, which would include some good food and interesting sights. It would also be interesting to compare the basketball in Greece with what I had experienced in Spain. Stanley was an easy person to travel with, and wherever he went he created a spectacle due to his size and personality. Now with his attractive girlfriend on his arm and me by his side, we had a small but colorful entourage and we attracted stares from passersby wherever we went.

When we arrived in Thessaloniki, photographers were there, and several photographs appeared in the Greek newspaper the next day. There was not nearly as much press coverage as when we had arrived in Spain in 1990, but still plenty. Andy met us in Athens, and he did a good job of acting as our guide. After our arrival, we were taken to the hotel where the team would put us up for several days while we finished the negotiations and helped Stanley settle in. I was taken out to dinner by team officials and discussed Stanley and a few aspects of the contract.

The next day, Stanley and I arrived at the team offices where we were to finalize the contract. There were more newspaper reporters and photographers present to cover the contract-signing. The team was worried about Stanley's numerous physical injuries, and wanted him to stay for a few weeks, and then exercise the option to terminate the contract. Stanley and I were not that opposed to the idea since the NBA was gearing up for the shortened season, and he would prefer to play at home if possible. It was agreed that the team would have an option to terminate the agreement up to February 1, 1999; however, Stanley could keep his first month's pay under any circumstances and would receive a platinum Rolex watch made to order by February 2, 1999, if he remained on the team. Stanley and I based this demand on the watch I had received at Real Madrid. There was an agreement added that Stanley had to pass the drug test of the Greek Federation or the contract was null and void. Stanley passed the test.

Another issue addressed at the office meeting was the agent fees for Andy and myself. I had been thinking about this since we had signed the contract, and I told Andy I wanted my fee in American cash. I had learned my lesson on accepting foreign checks for agent fees after my Italian experience. I was determined to make a decent fee on this trip since it was taking a week of my time, and so much of my time had gone uncompensated when I was working as an agent. The team agreed to my demand and

I was given $10,000 in American cash for my portion of the fee, which I would take back to the United States with me. I was to receive an additional payment for fees in the event the team did not use its option to terminate the contract before February 1, 1999. I did take the fee back and it was no problem. I just declared it on my return statement to the United States and deposited the money in my bank. I was a little nervous traveling with that sum of money, but it was worth making sure I ended up in the "black" from this trip. Overall, things worked out well, as the team paid for my airline ticket and my hotel, so I only had a few miscellaneous bills.

The day after our office meeting and final contract negotiations, there were several photographs of Stanley and me in the paper signing the contract. Since it was January and winter, there was not a lot going on outside, but we did visit the local outdoor market and some nice restaurants. While Stanley was busy with his girlfriend, I spent some time at the bar talking to a few of the locals. The day after the signing, Stanley and I went to the basketball facilities and ran into ex-NBA player, Gary Grant, who had signed with Aris earlier. I knew he was on the team, but seeing him and Stanley both in this foreign setting was really strange. I thought it would be helpful to Stanley to have another player on the team with whom he was familiar. The team was aware of Stanley's back problems and had him stretch out in his workout gear. The team promised that Stanley would be allowed to get back in shape with a low-impact workout because of his back.

Since my business was concluded, I arranged to fly back, and the team secured tickets for January 16, 1999. Stan's girlfriend was to return on the same flight to Columbia, South Carolina. The team delivered our business class tickets on January 15, 1999, to my hotel and made arrangements for me and Stan's girlfriend to be picked up by taxi at the hotel at 5:30 a.m. with the flight leaving at 7:00 a.m. By January 14, 1999, Stanley was working with the team trainers, and I was getting pretty bored hanging out by myself. I found the Greek people very friendly and by now had gotten to know the bartenders pretty well. One of them arranged for a local guide to take me out for some night life. There was a fairly well known singer performing at a big auditorium with table seating. The performance was all in Greek and ended with some of the traditional Greek Zorba folk-dancing with everyone clapping and joining arms. Some of the audience went up on the stage and I thought, "Why not? No one knows me." So I went up as part of the dance myself.

The return trip was routine, and I really can't recall much other than declaring the $10,000. I returned to Baton Rouge thinking that I had a great Greek cultural experience, and had done some good business for myself and my client. I kept in touch with Big Stan and he told me that the team was trying to work him out on an outdoor track. Sure enough, his back started giving him problems again, and he started having difficulties playing. By January 28, the team exercised its option to terminate the contract. Stan was given a letter of clearance and an airplane ticket to head home. He had gotten paid for January, so that was a plus, and now we were looking for an NBA job for the lockout shortened season. It was not long before we had a team interested in Stan, despite him having an aggravated back problem.

Stan and the Rockets

The Houston Rockets contacted us and were interested in signing Stanley for the season with the idea that he would get in shape, and then he would be ready for the playoffs. He would be a backup center to help Hakeem Olajuwon, hopefully during the season and particularly in the playoffs. Stanley was in Florida getting ready to go on a cruise when we received the call from the Rockets. He signed with the team officially on February 4, 1999, and was flown from Florida to Los Angeles to catch up with the team, which had its first game with the Lakers the next day. Stanley began a conditioning program to get in shape for the playoffs, which consisted of working out a great deal on the exercise bike. The Rockets were very familiar with Stanley, particularly because Keith Jones, who had been the athletic trainer with the Clippers, was now at Houston.

Naturally, I was happy to have Big Stan only a four-hour car ride away and playing on the same team where B.J. was working. I took Little O to Houston for a game and he had an opportunity to visit with Stanley and B.J. We also were able to see Charles Barkley and Scottie Pippen play, since they were on the team at the time. Stanley had bought a Hummer and took Little O for a ride, which was one of his lasting memories of Big Stan. I had just spent a lot of time with Stanley in Greece, but was really glad to get to see him again.

Stanley ended up playing in only six games that year. He hurt his shoulder near the end of the season, and Keith Jones rigged up a brace that allowed him to play in one game of the playoffs. The Rockets lost to the Lakers, who were led by Shaq and Kobe, three games to one. After the playoffs, the Rockets decided not to re-sign Stanley for next season.

Stan and the 76ers

Stanley and I went through the summer hoping he would be able to get on with a team for the upcoming 1999–2000 season. By this point in his career, Stanley had a reputation of being often injured and a hard player to motivate. Stanley already had two ruptured Achilles tendons, back and shoulder surgeries, and surgery for bone spurs. An opportunity arose with the Philadelphia 76ers because of Stanley's past relationship with

Larry Brown, who had coached Big Stan at the Clippers and was now the head coach at Philadelphia. Larry was a coach whom Stanley really liked and considered a friend. He called Stanley and arranged for him to fly up and play on the team. There was really not a negotiation on his contract, as we were just trying to get Stanley a spot on the team so he could get back into basketball shape and continue his career. Coach Brown knew Stanley could still contribute to the team and signed him as a backup center on October 19, 1999, and I signed the required agent certification on October 22, 1999. I knew Stanley had some issues going on and was glad that he was being coached by someone with whom he had a solid relationship, and was hoping he would have a good season. He had hired other people to handle all his finances and business since he had fired me in 1993. I only handled his agent business, so I really did not get to talk him too often at this point in time.

Stan Is Banned and We Head for Turkey

Stanley's first game of the season was on November 2, 1999, with the San Antonio Spurs. He ended up only playing in five games and starting one for fifty-one minutes in the 1999–2000 season, because on November 24, 1999, it was announced that Stanley had failed an NBA drug test, and would be suspended from the NBA for two years. The NBA's announcement of Stanley's suspension caught me completely off guard, coming just before the Thanksgiving holiday. The announcement said that Stanley had tested positive for "an amphetamine-based designer drug." Stanley was the first player banned under a new drug policy that called for two-year expulsion on the first positive test. The players could only be tested during the preseason and for the first time were tested for drugs other than cocaine and heroin. This was the drug policy placed in the new CBA.

I was not informed when Stanley had initially tested positive. Stanley had several conversations with the NBPA, and they were going to handle the situation for him. He asked for a retest and was told that there was no right of appeal, but the player's association would come up with a "strategy" to handle the situation. There had been very few NBA players actually banned for violation of the NBA drug policy. I read over the account of Roy Tarpley, who came to mind, and was not encouraged about a return to the NBA, but Roy had played in Europe after his NBA ban.

I left the issue of Stanley's test and ban in the hands of the NBPA, because soon after he was banned, I had agents telephoning regarding the possibility of Stanley coming back to Europe, which was governed by FIBA and not the NBA. I teamed up with an agent, Nur Gencer, who had contacts with a very well-known club in Turkey, which was at the time named after Efes Pilsen, a brand of Turkish beer. The team was eager to sign Stanley, and since it looked like he would not play in the NBA in the foreseeable future, I went ahead and negotiated a very nice contract (in the amount of $500,000 (U.S.) (net) plus additional benefits and bonuses). By December 7, 1999, the NBA confirmed by letter to FIBA that Stanley was not subject to or bound by any NBA contract. Stanley and I had a first-class flight scheduled into Istanbul leaving on December 8, 1999, to finish the contract. We met in New York and then boarded the flight to Istanbul. Here I was again in the middle of another Stanley adventure.

I was glad that the team was in a country I had not previously visited, because I had always wanted to see Turkey. I again made a provision for the agent's fees, which would be the usual ten percent or $50,000. I would split the fee with Nur Gencer equally. Another agent wanted in on the deal, but decided to withdraw after Stan and I arrived. The team put us up in a hotel and we ironed out the final details of the contract.

The attitude of the negotiations was slightly different from Greece since Stanley had to play in Turkey; there was no option back home in the United States. Stanley passed the team physical and drug test, and by December 10, 1999, all we needed was the letter of acceptance from FIBA that Stanley was cleared to play for the team so that we could execute the contract. However, to everyone's great surprise, on December 10, 1999, FIBA informed the Turkish Basketball Association, by way of a letter, of a worldwide ban by FIBA prohibiting Stanley from playing for any FIBA-sanctioned team for two years. When Stanley found out, he was on his way to get a Turkish driver's license so he could open a bank account.

We stayed in Istanbul and tried to make some sense of the FIBA ruling from various sources. FIBA had passed a new rule on doping or drugs in 1996 after Roy Tarpley came to Europe having been banned by the NBA. Stanley's worldwide ban was based on the following 1996 FIBA regulation:

> In the event that a basketball player is found guilty of doping during doping control tests conducted under the control of organizations outside FIBA and its affiliated federations (e.g. state bodies, the IOC or other international sports federations), FIBA, after consultation with the President of the Medical Council, shall decide whether and to what extent a sanction shall be imposed on the player for the purposes of FIBA competitions. If such a sanction is imposed, FIBA shall inform the national federations of the sanction thus imposed for the purposes of their national competitions. Whatever the circumstances, a suspended player may not use his license (national or FIBA) for the duration of the sanction. (FIBA Internal Regulations - 6.6.3.5)

The provision had never been enforced against an NBA

player, and FIBA had never made the NBA aware of the change in their policy. I felt it certainly lacked due process in that FIBA was just relying on a newspaper report on the NBA's actions to place a worldwide ban on Stanley. Once we saw that FIBA would not budge, the team lost interest in proceeding with the deal and we had them make arrangements for us to head home. I was back in the office by December 14, 1999, making calls and working on trying to get Stanley back on the basketball court. By now, Stanley was low on funds and could not pay me or any attorney for his time in coming to his defense. I knew that I might not be compensated and certainly wouldn't be reimbursed for my trip to Turkey since the contract never went into effect, but I really wanted to help Stanley and at least get him eligible to play in Europe.

I had some discussions with and drafted correspondence to the NBPA trying to enlist its aid for Stanley to fight this non-negotiated worldwide ban, which now apparently had resulted from an NBA positive drug test. I pointed out that when Stanley won his arbitration against the Clippers, the NBPA took credit for the victory even though I did almost all the work. There was an attorney from the NBPA at the hearing and he examined one witness, but I had done everything else including all the pleadings and all the witnesses at the arbitration except one. Stanley had paid me by the hour for arbitration, and I asked the Player's Association now to come to his defense when he could not afford to mount a defense to a worldwide ban that could be applied to its membership in the event of a positive drug test. It was not lost on me that Stanley obviously had made a mistake, but this was an issue that could affect other players in the future.

I did get some response, and the NBPA allowed one of their attorneys, Ron Klempner, to work with me on helping Stanley appeal the FIBA sanction according to FIBA's internal rules. Ron suggested that we obtain an outside counsel to help us with the FIBA appeal and gave me a name. I went ahead and drafted a grievance against Philadelphia to cover the requirements for an NBA appeal under Article XXXI, Section 2(d) of the CBA. However, as of this time, I still had never seen the drug test or received any notice from either the NBA or the NBPA that Stanley had failed a drug test. I was not happy about how the Player's Association, and Stanley for that matter, had not informed me when he initially tested positive so we could have additional time to plan and prepare our response to the suspension; however, I went ahead and did all I could do to help Stanley. I suggested that the Player's Union refund Stanley's recently paid fees to help fund his defense. The Union agreed, which gave us some initial money to pay some expenses and engage a German attorney, Martin Schimke, whom Ron had suggested. I agreed not to be paid any compensation until Stanley was able to pay me.

I involved my agent friend from Italy, Luciano "Lucky" Capicchioni, to see if he would be willing to go to Munich to help with Stanley's FIBA appeal, he was very familiar with FIBA and had contacts with the organization. "Lucky" was a big time European agent, and his agency located, in San Marino, Italy, was the one that Arturo Ortego had worked for when he helped me with Stanley at Real Madrid back in 1990–1991. "Lucky" agreed to help us. San Marino is located in the Umbria region of Italy. I visited Lucky's office in San Marino in 1996, when I went to visit my Italian friend Steffano Lotto, who lives in nearby Rimini, which is on the Adriatic Sea and is a real Italian beach vacation spot during the summer.

Roberts' Litigation Begins

By December 17, 1999, I had reviewed the FIBA rules and drafted a Statement of Appeal and a Motion to Suspend FIBA's ruling along with the Grievance to file against the 76ers pursuant to the NBA Collective Bargaining Agreement. I drafted and faxed a letter to Dr. Dirk-Reiner Martens, the head of FIBA, informing him of our intent to appeal and asking for a completer copy of all of FIBA's rules on drugging. On December 17, 1999, I received a copy of a letter from Richard W. Buchanan, Deputy General Counsel of the NBA, written to the attorneys for FIBA stating that the NBA had intended its Anti-Drug Agreement to apply only to the NBA and not FIBA. The letter said that the NBA did not support FIBA's actions to rely on the NBA's actions in suspending Stanley. The letter addressed to Dr. Martens at FIBA read as follows:

> We were disappointed to learn that FIBA has barred Stanley Roberts from playing for a FIBA team for the next two years and that it has based this prohibition on the NBA's recent expulsion of Mr. Roberts for failing a drug test conducted pursuant to the NBA/NBPA Anti-Drug Agreement. The penalties contained in the NBA/NBPA Anti-Drug Agreement were intended to apply only with respect to the NBA. As you know, we do not support FIBA's decision to rely on the NBA actions, rather than FIBA's own independent evaluation of the player, in deciding to ban Mr. Roberts.
>
> Sincerely,
>
> Richard Buchanan, Deputy General Counsel
>
> With cc: G. William Huner, NBPA

I thought the letter was a good piece of evidence and showed that FIBA really violated due process in relying on a newspaper story to suspend a player.

The FIBA rules stated that a hearing for an appeal of a suspension had to take place within four weeks of the filing of the appeal, which I filed on December 21, 1999. Accordingly, we were on a tight deadline to plan our defense strategy and file any supporting memorandum in support of our position on appeal. It was about this time that I discovered from FIBA that another agent had contacted FIBA at some point after Stanley's NBA suspension about whether he would be eligible in Europe after being suspended by the NBA. This really aggravated me, because I had no knowledge of this, and I could not tell whether this contact could have influenced FIBA's decision to ban Stanley after we had come to terms with the team in Turkey. Stanley told me he had never heard of the agent. I fired off a short but blunt letter to the agent asking what he had done and by whose authority he had contacted FIBA on Stanley's behalf. I also included a statement that he had contractually interfered with my relationship with Stanley and misrepresented himself to FIBA claiming to be Stanley's agent. The agent called my office three days later and spoke to my assistant Tiffanie. She sent me a memo of the conversation stating that the agent told her that someone on the Philadelphia 76ers coaching staff had asked him to find a job for Stanley since he did not think that I could find him a job. He then admitted that he had both spoken to and written to FIBA about how it would treat Stanley as a player banned by the NBA. He claimed he never told FIBA he was Stanley's agent and he apologized for not calling me, but said I would have been the first person that he called if he had gotten a job for Stanley? I did not follow up on this any further but have always wondered if this unauthorized agent had not focused FIBA's attention on this issue before we completed a contract, would there have been a different decision by FIBA to initially ban Stanley. I contemplated a lawsuit, but proving the effect of this interference would have been extremely difficult in a court of law.

The rest of December 1999, I was in contact with Ron Klempner and Martin Schimke preparing our memorandum for the FIBA appeal. I could not reach Martin initially, but after I spoke with him, he seemed well-qualified to help us with the appeal and we retained him to help us. I filed a Motion to Enroll him as additional counsel toward the end of December 1999. Martin contacted FIBA and helped us obtain a hearing date for January 11, 2000, at FIBA headquarters in Munich, Germany. I also asked "Lucky" Capicchioni to call any contacts at FIBA to give us some feedback on why it was not willing to give some flexibility on Stanley's ban. My hope was that since this rule had not been promulgated to the NBA that perhaps FIBA would let Stanley go ahead and play now and consider his case as notice to NBA players that if they were banned in the NBA they would face a similar ban by FIBA. I filed the NBA Grievance Appeal against Philadelphia and continued to work on the FIBA appeal. I received some faxed documents from Martin sometime between December 22 and December 27, 1999, to aid in preparation of our appeal memorandum. About this time, Martin brought in another German attorney named George Engelbrecht to work with us on the case. George was a real workhorse and a welcome addition to the team.

I made airline reservations to fly out of the United States on January 9, 2000, and arrive in Munich a couple of days ahead of the hearing to meet George and Martin. Ron Klempner was also to fly in from New York to meet with us and prepare for the hearing. I was naturally pumped to have an opportunity to fly to Munich and be involved in a real international sports case. I felt like this was another once-in-a-lifetime opportunity for some great travel and legal work, which I once again owed to Big Stan. Thus far I had been to Spain (three times), Greece, and Turkey with Stanley, and though he was not going to Munich himself, he was the reason for the trip. I had been to Munich on a European trip with my ex-wife when we visited her brother in Italy in 1989, and had loved the history involved with the city, its food, and of course the famous Hofbrauhaus, which served its own brand of tasty German beer.

*Our legal team in Munich
for Stanley's FIBA Hearing.
From left to right me, Ron
Klempner (NBPA), unknown,
Martin Schimke, and George
Engelbrecht (a German legal
bulldog).*

George, Martin, Ron, and I had lunch togther the day before Stanley's hearing and discussed our strategy for the next day, January 11, 2000. We made a compelling argument, I thought, based on notice and due process. FIBA contended that its article was enacted specifically to apply to NBA players, because Roy Tarpley was allowed to play in Europe after his NBA ban. Their argument seemed unreasonable to me because the NBA is not mentioned anywhere in the article. Furthermore, FIBA never gave notice to the NBA or NBA Players Association of such an intent. During the oral argument, FIBA's attorney argued that the reason the NBA is not mentioned is because FIBA did not want to "offend" the NBA. This made no sense to me. How could you offend an organization like the NBA? Moreover, we placed into evidence the December 16, 1999, letter from Richard Buchanan's counsel for the NBA stating that the NBA did not support FIBA's position and never intended for its drug ban to be applied by FIBA. The Chairman of the panel was Professor Doctor Ulrich Haas.

After the hearing, I felt like we presented a sound argument and that we had a chance at winning the in-house appeal of FIBA's initial decision. Of course, by this time the Turkish team had already signed another player, so even if we won, we would have to find a new team and then face other possible appeals. I spent a few more days in Munich and did a little sightseeing with Ron Klempner. Ron and I have remained friendly over the ensuing years, and he is still currently working with the NBPA. I found him to be a crackerjack attorney with a sharp mind and wit.

I returned to the United States on January 15, 2000. Unfortunately, in short order, the FIBA Panel denied and dismissed our in-house FIBA appeal. After the FIBA ruling against Stanley, George suggested we file a case in civil court in Germany asking for an injunction prohibiting FIBA from enforcing the ban against Stanley based on German law since FIBA was headquartered in Munich. An injunction is a judicial order which restrains a person from beginning or continuing an action. I was informed by George that German law very heavily favors individual rights and due process as a result of the abuses to individual rights that took place under Hitler's Germany prior to and during World War II. This sounded like a good idea to me and we obtained Stanley's permission to proceed. I really did not want to begin a long legal proceeding, as Stanley did not have the resources to mount a long legal fight and there was no more help from the NBPA forthcoming. The German attorneys had been paid an initial retainer, but there were no funds immediately available to continue paying them. I was not getting paid but did not mind since Stanley was like part of my family and I had made fees from my work for him throughout the years.

George was willing to move ahead in hopes that Stanley could pay him in the future. He was a dogged and determined fighter. On January 28, 2000, I drafted and faxed to Dr. Martens at FIBA a letter informing him of our receipt of the appeals ruling and informing him of our intent to file a case in German court. In hopes of resolving the matter, I asked if FIBA would be willing to settle the case by suspending Stanley for a shorter time or by just putting him on probation; however, FIBA refused to budge and continued its ban despite the threat of litigation filed in German court to obtain an injunction against FIBA's ban.

George moved forward with the lawsuit for an injunction

against FIBA in German court. What resulted was two years of litigation on two tracks, one in German court and the other on an appeal of FIBA's in-house decision through the World Sports Court in Lausanne, Switzerland. I was mostly an observer and never returned to Europe to work with George, who became the mover. Our resources were limited since Stanley never was able to return to playing any significant basketball after this point in time. I did draft affidavits for George when requested and kept Stanley up to date on what was transpiring. I also kept corresponding with the NBPA with hopes of some financial or other support that never came. An initial turning point came in the injunction lawsuit after a hearing on February 29, 2000, when German Judge Mr. Rabi granted the injunction against FIBA. George was doing a great job and this was a big blow to FIBA, as Stanley could play basketball until this order could be appealed. This also meant that if Stanley could work, he could pay his attorneys and court costs.

There were several teams interested in signing Stanley, but a Spanish team, Taugres, seemed like the best opportunity. A tryout was arranged for Stanley with Taugres in Houston, Texas, for March 7, 2000. A team scout for Taugres came to the workout and Stanley sustained another injury, this time to his back, so he could not play despite the FIBA basketball ban being enjoined. This was another big blow and really the one that sent Stanley down on a further downward spiral. He was now not only banned but hurt.

I was disappointed in the NBPA's response to my pleas for help, but really disappointed when FIBA made a frontal attack on American soil in New York City. In October 2000, Stanley's injunction case was on appeal in German court when FIBA filed an application in United States federal court in New York pursuant to 28 U.S.C. sec. 1782 for a subpoena to compel the NBA to produce Stanley's original drug test. I had always thought that a real weakness in FIBA's case was basing its ban on a drug test of which it did not have a copy and was only reported in a newspaper article. Now FIBA was trying to shore up its case by obtaining a copy of the drug test and admitting it into evidence while on appeal. From what I learned from George, German court allows parties to supplement the record with new evidence while on appeal. This is not allowed in the United States and I felt like this was a really unfair advantage that FIBA was seeking to exploit. I did not have the expertise or resources to become involved in the action in New York and was in a jury trial at the time. I sent a copy of FIBA's seven page memorandum to the NBPA and called on it for help in stopping the production of this test, which I felt was clearly privileged under the CBA and should not be allowed to be produced as a matter of protecting a member of the Player's Union. The NBPA's office was in New York, and I presumed that at least one of their attorneys was a member of the Bar there and it would be the duty of the Union to stop this infringement on a player's rights. However, no help came and FIBA was allowed to obtain the report from the NBA and put it into evidence. Eventually FIBA won the case on appeal. I thought that the NBPA allowing FIBA to obtain Stanley's drug testing was a breach ofits duty to Stanley and set a dangerous precedent for other players in the future.

Damon Jones

Damon at Boston.

Going into the 1999–2000 season, Boston did not make Damon a qualifying offer for the upcoming season, and he became a free agent. He was able to go to summer camp and play for Sacramento in Utah during the summer League. Afterwards he signed with Golden State in November of 1999 and played in thirteen games. I thought he played well for Golden State and was the leading scorer in a Monday night game, but he was released by the team. Shortly afterwards, Damon signed with Dallas in December 1999, and remained with Dallas the rest of the season.

I arranged to go to Dallas for a game against Milwaukee after Damon signed. I wanted to spend some time with Damon, watch Ervin play, and get a visit in with him too. Looking back at the schedule, it must have been the February 15, 2000, game that Milwaukee won 112-90. Both Sam Cassell and Darvin were on Milwaukee's team, which made the game even more interesting, because I knew Sam and had been following him for several years, and Darvin was a former client. Ervin was doing well and played some substantial minutes. Damon only got in the game for about a minute, but he was on the team and improving as a player.

After the game Ervin wanted to crash in his room but I wanted to take Damon out for dinner. Damon was good friends with Sam Cassell as the two had worked out in Houston together. Damon invited Sam and Glenn Robinson to meet us for dinner. I rode with Damon to the dinner and Sam and Glenn came in another car that Glenn had hired with a driver. We had a good dinner which was not surprising. I can't remember where we went, only that we had a very entertaining meal, and everyone enjoyed each other's company. After we ate, Sam and Damon wanted to go out, and Glen and I wanted to head back to the hotel so I ended up in the back seat of Glen's car with him in the front passenger seat. My meal with the players once again reminded me that most NBA players and even the stars are normal guys who just happen to be very talented in playing basketball. Seeing these guys interact made me miss my old high school football days, being on a team and having the kind of camaraderie that can only be built through being teammates. Hanging out with these guys really made me feel I was part of the action and not so old as to not enjoy a night out with the guys.

After the time I spent with Damon, I really felt pretty close to him; I felt like I had helped him when he needed a break to get on a team in the NBA. I was surprised and disappointed when I received a letter from Damon terminating our agency agreement on June 6, 2000. I liked Damon personally and actually felt closer to him than some of my other clients who had fired me. I always believed that, given a little more time and hard work, he would land a substantial NBA deal. He ended up starting out the 2000 season playing in the USBL for the Gulf Coast Sun Dogs and then playing seventy-one games with the Grizzlies with his new representation. He played with three different NBA teams between 2001 and 2003, but proved me right and signed a nice deal with Miami for 2004. He landed a $16.1 million four-year deal with Cleveland in 2005, where he played with his friend LeBron James. He and LeBron worked well together, as Damon's specialty was to be a spot-up three point shooter. After his NBA career, Damon got into coaching and was hired as an assistant coach in Cleveland, where LeBron was playing. He drew some news attention in March 2018 when player J.R. Smith threw a bowl of soup at him. I followed his career and was always glad for his success. I've seen him recently acting as a basketball analyst on the TV show *Get Up.*

My clients seemed to be easy prey for other agents to poach, since I was not in the business full time, and this was a pitch that was used often by agents against me. I wrote Damon and wished him luck, telling him I would follow his career. It seemed that the guys that I took on as free agents who worked their way into the League were under constant pressure from other agents to fire me as a further step to move their careers. Signing free agents and then getting them a shot in the League only to be fired later after you took all the risk and time to help them was not a good business model. This is why all the full-time agents will many times do whatever is necessary to sign first round basketball players and early round football players. Again, I came to realize that landing two first-round NBA picks, Stanley and Ervin, in a short time, given my means, was a real blessing and that it was not going to happen again in the foreseeable future.

I now became content to just continue to represent Stanley and Ervin and enjoy going to some NBA games each year to see Ervin play. It's not like I did not have anything to do. I had a busy law practice where I could make more money than being an agent and could compete on more level ground than sports representation. I did make one more bad decision to sign a player in the D League who took my help and subsequently let me go. I again lost money. This was the last new basketball player I signed. However, I did have a great time going to NBA games watching Ervin play over the next six years and not having to worry about if he was going to fire me.

In 2000, I met Ervin in Miami for one of my more

memorable trips while he was playing for the Bucs. Darvin was on the team, so I was able to see and catch up with him. My cousin, Fred Woltz, who had an apartment in Fort Lauderdale, met me and we went to the game together. "Lucky" had bought a condominium in South Beach, so I was able to meet him and his wife for a visit during the same trip. By this time, I was primarily focused on my law practice, so the trip came as a good break from the day-to-day practice of law.

TWENTY-ONE
The End: 2001-2006
My Law Practice

After leaving my firm, my sports practice continued to decline, but my legal load increased, and I was able to focus more of my energy on becoming a first-class trial attorney. I had prepared and tried numerous cases before, but usually had the help of one of my partners at trial. When trying a complex lawsuit, it really helps at trial to have another attorney who can assist with some of the work, such as taking few witnesses or preparing the opening and closing. Additionally, as the old saying goes, "two heads are better than one," particularly if the other head has more experience. Now that I was alone, I was the lead trial counsel and had to handle the whole of the case myself, which included preparing the case, voir dire (picking the jury), opening statement, examination of our witnesses and cross-examination of the other side's witnesses, jury charge conference with the judge and other attorneys, and closing arguments.

Actually, most of the hard work in trying a case is the preparation, which can be extensive. My cases were mostly medical malpractice, which are usually complex, take at least a week to try, and are very expensive. This is very different than a simple automobile case where you are discussing a driver who is hit from behind and the extent of his damages. Jury trials are extremely difficult because you can do everything right, but a jury of ordinary citizens still may not feel that a physician or nurse breached the standard of care and caused the patient damage. Even after the jury agrees, that the defendant did something wrong, then you have to prove that the wrong caused damages. Finally, after the jury determines or concludes there was a breach of care that caused damages, then the jury has to translate the damages into dollars and cents, which is hard to do for many people. The main issue in most of my cases is whether there was a breach of the standard of care, because I rarely take cases unless the patient has sustained serious damages such as death, paralysis, or brain damage.Due to the difficulty of the cases, the time involved, and expense, it only makes sense to take serious cases with serious damages.

I was able to interview and work with my clients, undertake discovery in the cases, prepare my cases for trial, and try the cases that did not settle, with the help of my secretary, assistant, and my hardworking and patient paralegal, Tiffanie. In 2000 and 2001, we were successful in a couple of million-dollar jury verdicts, which really gave me the confidence I needed. After those victories, my confidence and reputation were set and I never looked back. Since I do not advertise, I rely on old clients and my reputation to attract new cases. For example, I know that after one of the verdicts in a small town in north Louisiana, an attorney heard about the verdict and gave me a call. He was one of my ex-classmates and has a busy practice, but did not want to do medical malpractice. Since that time, we have worked on numerous cases together, and it has been a positive to my business, and we have been become very good friends.

By 1999, I had decided that it would be good for business and might be fun to teach at the LSU Law School. I sensed that teaching at the law school would help enhance my reputation it would also create some contacts with younger attorneys who might need an experienced lawyer to handle medical malpractice cases that they might encounter in their law practice. I could have offered to teach a class on medical malpractice or procedure, but decided that I would have a better shot at teaching sports law since few, if any, attorneys had my experience in that field. Moreover, there was already a medical malpractice course of sorts offered at the law school. I offered my services to teach a class in Sports Law, but was initially rebuffed. I started out co-teaching with Professor John Church, who was an expert in Labor and Antitrust Law.

Roberts Litigation Continues, Ends, and Stanley's Career Ends

The legal cases spawned by the FIBA ban continued well into 2002 until George Engelbrecht had exhausted all the time and resources he could on Stanley without being compensated. I continued to monitor the cases until the end. I have no proof, but was told and came to believe, that FIBA moved its headquarters back to Switzerland from Munich in 2002, at least partly due to the application of German law to Stanley's case. At one point, I drafted a damages lawsuit, which I filed, but did not serve in the United States, and George drafted a damages lawsuit for German court that produced no results.

I really thought that FIBA had gone out of its way to punish Stanley, which not only cost him dearly, but also cost me personally a great deal of time and money. I decided to attempt to collect some damages against FIBA by filing a lawsuit on my own behalf in the United States, acting as my own attorney.

I filed the lawsuit on behalf of my law firm and sports management firm in state court in Baton Rouge. I knew that it would be a real challenge to successfully file a case against a foreign entity with no office in Louisiana. However, I decided it would be an interesting challenge and that you don't know unless you try.

The first issue I faced would be to attempt to serve FIBA with the pleadings in the proper manner. I did some research and decided that the proper method under international law would be to serve it through treaties that had been agreed to among various foreign nations called the Hague Convention. I filed the Petition for Damages (the initial pleading in the case) by a letter dated December 7, 2000. By February 2001, I was still trying to obtain service of the Petition, and applied for additional time to serve the defendant. In July 2001, I filed an affidavit stating that service had been made on FIBA in accord with the law on service. FIBA filed an answer in court but, as expected, contested whether the Louisiana court had jurisdiction or the power to litigate a case against it. A hearing was set to argue whether the Louisiana court had jurisdiction over FIBA. When briefing the trial court before the hearing, I emphasized the contacts between FIBA and Louisiana, which were summarized previously in Chapter 20 regarding my activities in signing Stanley in Turkey. The trial judge ruled in my favor that the Louisiana court did have jurisdiction. FIBA appealed the trial court's decision, and I had to argue the case again in the Louisiana Court of Appeal First Circuit. I won at the Court of Appeal and, finally, in 2003 FIBA and I resolved the case by settlement without going to trial.

Stanley took a run at playing some basketball at the end of December 2000, by signing a contract with the fledging ABA League and its San Diego Wildfire team. The contract was intended to last through August 31, 2001; however, Stanley played a few games and developed knee problems. During the litigation, Stanley signed another NBA player-agent agreement with me in September 2001, and I helped him obtain the forms for reinstatement at the end of 2001. His reinstatement was held up because of an arrest in November 2000. In looking back in my file, it appears that Stanley fired me again in May of 2002, but rehired me again in April, 2003. The May letter was faxed from the NBPA headquarters in New York. I still haven't figured that one out, and had forgotten about it until I started the research for this book! Stanley was reinstated by the NBA in January of 2003. He gave the NBA one last shot when he signed with the Toronto Raptors in 2003, but was waived before the season. Stanley signed a deal in Puerto Rico and blew out his knee in 2004. While in Houston, Stanley went through drug rehabilitation, and with God's help gave up many of his bad lifestyle choices. He found peace with himself and God, and got on a new track of life.

Stanley lived in Houston, and then in 2007, moved back to Baton Rouge to return to college. He was greatly encouraged to complete his degree by all who knew him, but Coach Dale Brown, to his credit, really supported him in this endeavor. Stanley worked hard and, free from the distractions that had held him back in the NBA, he kept plugging away at his degree over a period of time. In December 2012, at forty-two, Stanley received his college degree from LSU. This was a great moment and an answer to all those who criticized him for not living up to his talent in the NBA. Unlike some, Stanley acknowledges his mistakes and encourages younger players to avoid the errors he made in his youth. He lives and works in Baton Rouge where he keeps up with his four children and his friends. I see him every couple of months, and he attended my second wedding in June, 2017. He has been instrumental in my writing this book, both from a subjective point of view and in helping me with the facts I could not remember.

Many times, sports fans say to me when talking about Stanley, "if I had his talent, I would have been an All Star." I just laugh and point out that many attorneys who could be at the top are not, and the same is true of any profession or job. Stan could have performed better, but he was able to play competitively for eight years in the best League in the world, and overcame double Achilles tendon injuries to return and play in the League. Stan was, and still is, a person with a big heart whom God blessed with tremendous physical talent. Unfortunately, at times his heart did not nurture his talent. He always took care of others but at times ignored himself. He had his own plan and at the end has become an All Star of life, taking care of his family, friends, and himself. We remain close, and I am proud to have helped him along the way to the best of my ability. As I grow older, I realize more and more that there are few people you meet that really change your life. Stan changed mine and established me for a good run in the agent business, for which I will always be grateful.

Ervin Johnson: The Beat Goes On and On and His End Is My End

After 2000, my attention was more and more focused on my law practice, but I continued to represent Ervin. By this point, I had been to the pinnacle of my sports-agent practice, the top of the mountain, so to speak, and was on the slow descent down. Ervin was the one client who kept me in the game with his loyalty and his dedication to himself, his family, and the game. It was great to be able to work with him and share his career. He always made me proud and was a credit to any team he played on. I literally traveled all over the country to watch him play.

Milwaukee, coached by George Karl and led by Glen Robinson, Ray Allen, and Sam Cassell, had a great season during 2000–2001, but lost to the Philadelphia 76ers in the Conference Finals. Due to my new focus on law and needing personal time with my kids, I was unable to attend the Conference Finals. Ervin always understood that I had a busy legal career and many family obligations. He supported me as

I attended games that I could fit in my schedule.

In October 2001, Ervin signed a two-year extension with Milwaukee to his seven-year deal that he had signed with Denver in July 1996, worth close to ten million dollars. He negotiated this deal pretty much on his own with the team owner. Wisely, he did have me review the figures, clarify the guarantees, and finalize the contract with my agent certification. This deal would keep him playing through 2005, when he would be thirty-eight years old.

Milwaukee had another great season under Coach Karl in 2001–2002, and again made it into the Eastern Conference Finals with Philadelphia. I was really frustrated again when I could not shake free to attend any of the Conference Finals. I wanted to attend at least a few games in the series, but had legal commitments already set during the games. In the legal profession, trial dates are usually set for a minimum of six months and at times over a year in advance; thus it is very difficult to free up a calendar for a playoff schedule that may or may not be set only a few weeks in advance. In game seven, Milwaukee entered the fourth period ahead by eight points, and I remember traveling through an airport, seeing the game, and thinking that Milwaukee was going to the NBA finals, and I could make that series. However, after the flight, I was disappointed to learn that Philadelphia had prevailed in the contest and was going to the finals instead of Milwaukee.

On June 27, 2003, following the 2003 draft, Ervin and teammate Sam Cassell were traded by Milwaukee to the Minnesota Timberwolves. The trade was prompted by Milwaukee drafting T.J. Ford from the University of Texas, eighth overall in the draft. I was excited about the move because Minnesota was a playoff contender, and had almost upset the Los Angeles Lakers in the first round of the 2003 playoffs before losing four games to two. As a big Kevin Garnett fan, I was looking forward to watching him play more during the year. The fact that Ervin was accompanied by one of my favorites, Sam Cassell, made the deal perfect. I believed that Sam would be the key ingredient that the team needed to move past the first-round of the playoffs. The general manager of the team was still my old buddy Kevin McHale. I was happy about that fact, as I ultimately always have enjoyed knowing Kevin and considered him a friend and business associate. I knew with Ervin playing I would not have to get into any adversarial situations with him or the team. The team had added the talented Latrell Sprewell to the roster on a trade from New York, which put them in even better position to make a playoff run.

Minnesota ended up having a great season and finished on top of the western division with a record of fifty-eight wins and twenty-seven loses. Ervin played in sixty-six games and started in forty-seven, averaging 14.6 minutes a game. Minnesota defeated the Denver Nuggets and the Sacramento Kings in the first two rounds of the playoffs. After a victory in game seven against the Sacramento Kings, Kevin Garnett jumped on the scorers table. It looked like Minnesota was headed to the NBA Finals, but the Timberwolves had to play the Lakers in the conference finals. Unfortunately, Sam Cassell was injured for the conference championship series and entered the event with an injured hip or back. In a 2014 *Yahoo Sports* article by Kelly Dwyer published November 4, 2014, Coach Flip Saunders intimated that Sam Cassell injured his hip performing his "onions" dance, in which he rotated his hips. According to the article, Saunders said Cassell suffered an avulsion fracture, and if he'd been healthy, the team could have beaten the Lakers and then the Detroit Pistons, the eventual champions.

I was really psyched about Ervin being in another conference finals and made plans to attend at least two games in Los Angeles. After not being able to attend his 1992 conference finals with Milwaukee, I wanted to make sure that I was not going to miss out on watching at least a few games in this series. I chose to go to L.A. so I could see some old friends and business contacts at the same time. I made plans to attend and was able to work it out so my oldest daughter, Katie, could accompany me on the trip. Katie was now twenty years old and attending college at LSU. She started at Ole Miss, but had just transferred back to Baton Rouge and LSU. She had never been to Los Angeles, and I thought this would be a good opportunity for us to spend some time together, and I could show her some parts of L.A. that I had become familiar with over the past decade.

My favorite place to stay in Los Angeles was a boutique hotel near the Beverly Center off La Cienega Boulevard. I stayed there primarily when I came for depositions at Cedars-Sinai and to visit my brother. However, I made arrangements to stay with the team at the Ritz Carlton, Marina Del Rey, I often stayed there when I went to Los Angeles to watch games and take depositions. I was familiar with the area also because Stanley had stayed in Marina Del Rey when he was with the Clippers.

The first two games of the conference finals were held in Minnesota, and the Lakers took the first game on May 21, 2004, 97 to 88. The second game was played on May 23, and Minnesota won 89 to 71, despite Sam Cassell's absence. Katie and I headed to Los Angeles with the series tied, but it was obvious to me that Minnesota without Sam Cassell was not the same team that had won the Eastern Conference. At this point, I was still hopeful that Minnesota could pull it out against Los Angeles; however, I was having my doubts that the Timberwolves could win the series without Sam. Naturally, you always hope for a victory, but it's even more hoped for when you are staying with the team, as the atmosphere is much lighter when the team gets a win as opposed to a loss.

The first game at Los Angeles was on Tuesday May 25, 2004. Katie and I went to the game and she enjoyed all the fanfare, but was not so much into the basketball. The Lakers won 100 to 89, with Shaq having a great game: twenty-two points and seventeen rebounds. The Wolves made it a game in the fourth quarter by pulling within eight points of the Lakers, but could not get any closer. I had hopes to say hello to Shaq after the game, but the security around him was too tight, even though Katie and I had passes to see Ervin after the game.

While in L.A. for the game, I took Katie to Cedars-Sinai and we had lunch with my old friend, Dr. Ron Wender. Another friend that I looked up in Los Angeles was David Lancaster, a Los Angeles producer. I met David and his wife, Karen, in the 1990s, when visiting my brother, John. John worked for David a couple of years while he was in Los Angeles. At the time, he had his office in his back yard, so I went to see where John worked and I met David's wife, Karen. She was really nice and a real people person. Karen had worked in film production, where she met David. He was one year older than me and was rather intense and a "go, go, go" person. Although I did not know much about the film industry, I figured that in order to make it in Hollywood as a producer, you had to have a lot of drive and intensity, so his personality fit his job. David and I ended up going to several NBA games together over the years when I was in Los Angeles, and had become pretty good friends. He specialized in lower budget films that were always successful, and around 2000 he ended up moving his office out of his back yard to a location in Hollywood.

In 2003, Louisiana was one of the top places to film movies outside of Hollywood and David ended up filming a movie in New Orleans called *A Love Song for Bobby Long*. The filming took place during the hot Louisiana summer, and David had rented a two-bedroom condominium in the French Quarter. We had been in contact and I had planned to go see him. As it turned out, this time period was a tough one for me, as I was separated from my wife. Getting out of town was really an escape, and David said I could come down anytime I wanted, as he had an extra bedroom in the condo. I took him up on the offer and ended up going to New Orleans for most of the weekends, and some other days while the film was shooting. I spent a lot of time with David and learned just how hard film people work. David always stayed in shape and would get up early around 6 a.m. to exercise and begin his day. He was continuously on the go throughout the day, which included reviewing the "dailys," (the scenes shot the day prior), going out to the set, checking scene locations, and taking care of all the things necessary to support the production moving. From my experience, the producer is the most powerful man involved with the production and is afforded a lot of respect around the set. When I appeared on the set, I usually stuck pretty close to him, but got to know a lot of the people working there. I met the co-producer, the director who had written the script, and various others including the doubles, the head of wardrobe, and the script checker. I was allowed to sit near the director when filming and look at the screen showing what was being filmed.

The primary stars of *Love Song* were John Travolta, Scarlett Johansson, Gabriel Macht, and Deborah Unger. Scarlett Johansson was only nineteen, and from my perspective really broke out as a star with her part in *Lost in Translation* with Bill Murray. I believe David had signed her for *Love Song* before *Lost in Translation* had been such a hit. He really has a gift for recognizing rising talent and signing them to his films. I met all the actors and actresses and watched them work. I have to say, all were very professional and seemed easy to work with. This included John Travolta, who was in my view the biggest star. Travolta was friendly to everyone and as I recall even sprung for a round of coffee for the crew. I did notice that whenever he or

Scarlett was on the set, there naturally seemed to be more excitement in the air and a little more tension. Even I could see at that point that Scarlett had great talent and was headed for big things. It was hard for me to believe that Scarlett was the same age as my oldest daughter, Katie, and was already working the way she did.

I did become accustomed to the fact that there is a lot of time spent in preparation of a scene when the actual actors and actresses are not necessarily present. The crew works long hours trying to get as much shot as possible to cut down on costs. However, overtime is an option to be avoided by the producer who is watching the costs. Frankly, after a couple of hours on the set, I was ready to leave, as there is a lot of down time. David's work style resonated with me, because he was constantly moving from one project to the next; that usually included being on the set for the filming but not a lot of down time. I attended the wrap party for a brief time when the filming was concluded. Overall, I felt like I had learned a great deal about how a movie is made during the filming of *Love Song*, and David I had become close friends after the summer of 2003.

Katie and I went over to David and Karen's house after the first game loss and had a good time visiting with them. David expressed an interest in seeing the second game. Katie and Karen had fun together, and Katie decided that she would rather stay at home with Karen than go to the second playoff game. Part of the inducement was that they would be having dinner with Cheri Oteri from *Saturday Night Live*, who lived next door. David and I went to game four, which was closer, but the Lakers won again, 92 to 85, thanks to a 31-pointeffort by Kobe Bryant. Both games were very entertaining, but I was naturally disappointed that Ervin's team had not won, and it looked like the Lakers would win the series. Katie and I did have a great time and it was an all-star father-daughter trip.

David and I would remain friends and he would shoot another film in Louisiana, this time in Baton Rouge. The name of the film was *Middle of Nowhere*, and I became semi-involved with the filming of this movie at times. In fact, David invited me to the Toronto film festival for its premiere and I even received a thank-you at the end of the film. David, Karen, and his son Jack met my son and me in Pamplona, Spain, in 2009 for the Running of the Bulls. David hit a home run with his film *Whiplash* in 2014, which had a budget of $3.3 million and grossed $49 million. *Whiplash* was filmed in nineteen days and won three Oscars, including Best Supporting Actor for J.K. Simmons. I have to give my friend credit for his work, and I am so glad to see him successful. I really thought *Whiplash* should have won Best Picture for 2014 though *Birdman* was an interesting film.

The Wolves won game five in Minnesota, 98 to 96, but the Lakers finished off the series at home with a 96 to 90 victory. In the playoffs, Ervin took part in all eighteen games and started sixteen, averaging 19.8 minutes and 4.7 rebounds and 2.7 points a game. Kevin Garnett had a great season and received the MVP Award and First Team All-NBA. For the season, Sam Cassell was named to the All-NBA Second Team and finished 10th in the MVP voting.

I was really glad I had gone to the conference finals in 2004, because the next year Minnesota did not make the playoffs. The team ended up struggling, and after going 25-26, Coach Flip Saunders was fired and replaced by "my" Kevin McHale for the rest of the season. The team played better under Kevin but finished with a 44-38 record and missed the playoffs. Ervin did not play as much but played in forty-six games and started twenty-three. He was in the last year of his contract and would be thirty-eight at the end of the season. Sam Cassell was traded at the end of the season to the Los Angeles Clippers. Kevin McHale did not return as head coach, but we would meet again to say hello when he was head coach of the Houston Rockets when I was in Houston visiting B.J. sometime after 2011.

By this time, Ervin was the only client that I kept up with, but my focus was more on personal issues and my legal practice. Ervin had always been mature and anchored, and by now he was a grown man who not only knew what to do but was a true leader for others. Ervin was constantly going the extra mile in keeping himself in shape both mentally and physically, and he wanted to play one more year. It was because of this that he was wanted back at Milwaukee as a team leader at the age of thirty-eight. In September 2005, he signed a one-year deal for the veteran minimum and played one more year in the League, playing in eighteen games. The team finished 40-42 with Terry Stotts, George Karl's longtime assistant as head coach. I had gotten to know Terry over the years, and he was far more friendly and approachable than his mentor. One highlight for me was meeting the team in Charlotte in January, 2006, where I spent some time with Ervin and was able to attend the game with my nephew, nieces, and cousins.

Ervin had now been in the League for thirteen years and was ready to retire. Although he never made All Pro, he had been a tremendous success in the NBA. Though not as talented, perhaps, as many who had been blessed with a "shot" in the NBA, he had taken the skills he was endowed with, and had stayed an active participant in the most difficult basketball league for thirteen years. He was sustained by hard work and belief in himself and God. In the process, he had honored himself, his family, and his beliefs and provided himself and his family with a foundation upon which to build for the remainder of his life. In addition, he had always shown the greatest loyalty and friendship to me during the entire time. True to his nature, Ervin had a plan for retirement. He made a permanent home in Denver and vowed to stay there and raise his two girls until they reached college age. Though he could have had the fame and glory of a coaching job in the NBA, Ervin was true to his goal, and he and his wife raised their daughters in Denver with the youngest leaving to attend Arizona in 2018. At the same time, he has acted as an envoy for the Denver Nuggets, and has been a speaker on hundreds of occasions to young people telling his inspirational story. He founded an AAU Girls' League where he acted as a coach for his daughters and hundreds of other young women. I am proud of his accomplishments both on and off the court.

I have kept up with Ervin on a regular basis, and on June 29, 2013, I was honored that he asked me to attend his induction into the Louisiana Sports Hall of Fame in Natchitoches. I drove up and met with him and his family, which was very special. It just so happened that Shaq (LSU), Tom Hodson (LSU), and Kevin Mawae (LSU) were being inducted at the same time, so I knew several of the inductees personally and was able to wave at them. Each inductee gave a speech at a seated banquet and I was honored that Ervin mentioned me in his speech as follows:

To Oscar Shoenfelt, my agent for 13 years:

And Oscar, I'm pretty sure that I told you this, I'm not a hundred percent sure, but you know when I was picking an agent, a lot of people told me to pick different people, but I listened to God and He told me to pick you. And I'm so grateful for you. I never had to change agents in thirteen years. I knew I could trust you. And I know we went through a few bouts and you were telling me some of the things I should be doing, and I probably didn't want to listen, but I'm glad you had my back and stood beside me no matter what!

I knew that some of the players I had represented did not really appreciate what I had tried to do or had done for them. Some left without a thank-you or a kind word. Those players always made me feel a little disappointed, like I had wasted my time becoming an agent. However, as I listened to Ervin's words with, I admit, a little tear in my eye, it reminded me that there were many players who appreciated my work, and I had been a positive influence in their lives. I had formed lifelong bonds of friendship with many of my players, made many lifelong friends, met an incredible menagerie of characters, and had a cascade of experiences that I will never forget. So, even though I had to carry a few rocks up the mountain and back down, it was a journey well worth taking.